Cognitive Poetics in Practic

'*Cognitive Poetics in Practice* is an impressive book, which combines the best of cognitive science with the best of literary analysis ... a must for anyone with a serious interest in the "literary mind" of the twenty-first century.'

Zoltán Kövecses, Eötvös Loránd University, Hungary

Cognitive poetics is a new way of thinking about literature, involving the application of cognitive linguistics and psychology to literary texts. This student-friendly book provides a set of case studies to help students understand the theory and master the practice of cognitive poetic analysis.

Written by a range of well-known scholars from a variety of disciplines and countries, *Cognitive Poetics in Practice* offers students a unique insight into this exciting subject. In each chapter, contributors present a practical application of the methods and techniques of cognitive poetics to a range of texts, from Wilfred Owen to Roald Dahl. The editors' general introduction provides an overview of the field, and each chapter begins with an editors' introduction to set the chapter in context. Specially designed sections suggesting further activities for students are also provided at the end of each case study.

Cognitive Poetics in Practice can be used on its own or as a companion volume to Peter Stockwell's *Cognitive Poetics: An Introduction*.

This book is critical reading for students on courses in cognitive poetics, stylistics and literary linguistics, and will be of interest to all those involved in literary studies, critical theory and linguistics.

Joanna Gavins is Lecturer in English Language and Literature at the University of Sheffield, UK. **Gerard Steen** is Assistant Professor in English Language and Linguistics at the Free University of Amsterdam, The Netherlands.

Cognitive Poetics in Practice

Edited by Joanna Gavins
and Gerard Steen

Routledge
Taylor & Francis Group

LONDON AND NEW YORK

First published 2003
by Routledge
2 Park Square, Milton Park, Abingdon, Oxon, OX14 4RN

Routledge is an imprint of the Taylor & Francis Group

Transferred to Digital Printing 2006

Typeset in Sabon by
Bookcraft Ltd, Stroud, Gloucestershire

British Library Cataloguing in Publication Data
A catalogue record for this book is available from the British Library

Library of Congress Cataloging in Publication Data
A catalog record for this book has been requested

ISBN 0–415–27798–1 (hbk)
ISBN 0–415–27799–X (pbk)

Contents

Acknowledgements

Reuven Tsur's chapter 'Deixis and abstractions: adventures in space and time' is based on research partly supported by grant No. 717.99–2 of the Israel Science Foundation.

The research for Catherine Emmott's chapter 'Reading for pleasure: a cognitive poetic analysis of "twists in the tale" and other plot reversals in narrative texts' was conducted with funding from The Royal Society of Edinburgh and The Caledonian Research Foundation. The author is grateful to both of these organisations for their support.

Elena Semino would like to thank Kyoko Hendri, Simona Moti and Mick Short for their valuable input in the preparation of her chapter.

Every effort has been made to trace the copyright holders of the literary extracts reproduced in this text. The editors and publishers would like to thank the following for permission to reproduce copyright material: The translation of André Breton's poem 'They tell me that over there' in Chapter 2 is reproduced with the permission of Mary Ann Caws, from *Surrealist Love Poems*, © 2001 Mary Ann Caws; the poem 'Penal Law' by Austin Clarke is reproduced in Chapter 6 with the permission of R. Dardis Clarke, 21 Pleasants Street, Dublin 8, Republic of Ireland; the poems, 'Symptoms of love' and 'She tells her love … ', by Robert Graves are reproduced in Chapter 6 with the permission of The Estate of Robert Graves from *Robert Graves: The Complete Poems in One Volume* (edited by Beryl Graves and Dunstan Ward), Carcanet Press Limited, 2000; 'A very short story' by Ernest Hemingway is reproduced in Chapter 7 with the permission of Scribner, a division of Simon and Schuster Inc., from *The Short Stories of Ernest Hemingway*, © 1925, 1930 by Charles Scribner's Sons, copyright renewed 1953, © 1958 Ernest Hemingway; the literary extracts reproduced in Chapter 10 are reprinted with the permission of Scribner, a division of Simon and Schuster Inc., from *Snow White* by Donald Barthelme, © 1967 Donald Barthelme; the extracts from Shakespeare in Chapter 12 are reprinted from William Shakespeare: *Hamlet*, edited by G.R. Hibbard (Oxford World's Classics, 1998) and William Shakespeare: *The Tempest*, edited by Stephen Orgel (Oxford World's Classics, 1998), both by permission of Oxford University Press.

Contributors

Michael Burke is a Lecturer in English Language at Utrecht University. His publications include his co-edited *Contextualised Stylistics* (with P. Stockwell and T. Bex, Rodopi: 2000). His monograph *The Oceanic Mind*, on emotion, cognition, language and literature, is forthcoming (also with Rodopi).

Peter Crisp is a Senior Lecturer in the Department of English at the Chinese University of Hong Kong. He has published widely in the areas of metaphor theory, cognitive and literary stylistics, the philosophy of aesthetics, literature and religion, and on the work of Ezra Pound. He is the 'P' in 'Pragglejaz', an international group of specialist researchers on metaphor <http://www.let.vu.nl/pragglejaz> (accessed 20 August 2002).

Catherine Emmott is a Senior Lecturer in the Department of English Language at the University of Glasgow. She is the author of *Narrative Comprehension: A Discourse Perspective* (Oxford University Press: 1997) and Assistant Editor of the journal *Language and Literature*. She is currently Principal Investigator on the AHRB-funded project 'Literature, Narrative and Cognitive Science: Interdisciplinary Perspectives on the Nature of Reading'.

Joanna Gavins is a Lecturer in the Department of English Language and Linguistics at the University of Sheffield, where she teaches courses in linguistics, stylistics, and cognitive poetics. She has published a number of articles on Text World Theory and is currently preparing *Text World Theory: An Introduction*, a text book aimed at undergraduate students.

Raymond W. Gibbs, Jr is Professor of Psychology at the University of California, Santa Cruz. He is author of *The Poetics of Mind* (Cambridge University Press: 1994) and *Intentions in the Experience of Meaning* (Cambridge University Press: 1999).

Craig Hamilton is a Lecturer in the School of English at the University of Nottingham, where he is also a researcher in the Institute for the Study of

Genetics, Biorisk and Society. He has published widely in the area of cognitive poetics and is currently completing a monograph *Opaque Enigmas: Mind, Body, and Metaphor in W.H. Auden's Poetry*. He is also editing a collection of stylistics articles for the UK English Studies Subject Centre.

Keith Oatley is Professor of Cognitive Psychology in the Department of Human Development and Applied Psychology, University of Toronto. He teaches courses on cognitive science, and on the psychology of fictional literature. He is the author of five books of psychology, including *Best-Laid Schemes* (Cambridge University Press: 1992), and two novels, the first of which, *The Case of Emily V* (Secker and Warburg: 1993), won the Commonwealth Writers Prize for Best First Novel.

Elena Semino is a Lecturer in the Department of Linguistics and Modern English Language at Lancaster University and has published many articles in the area of stylistics. She is the author of *Language and World Creation in Poems and Other Texts* (Longman: 1997) and co-editor (with Jonathan Culpeper) of *Cognitive Stylistics: Language and Cognition in Text Analysis* (John Benjamins: 2002).

Gerard Steen is Assistant Professor in English at the Free University Amsterdam. He has published widely on cognitive approaches to metaphor and literature, including *Understanding Metaphor in Literature* (Longman: 1994) and *The Psychology and Sociology of Literature* (co-edited with Dick Schram, 2001: John Benjamins).

Peter Stockwell is Senior Lecturer at the University of Nottingham. His most recent book, *Cognitive Poetics*, is the companion volume to *Cognitive Poetics in Practice*. Other publications include *Sociolinguistics* (Routledge: 2002), *The Poetics of Science Fiction* (Longman: 2000), *An Introduction to the Nature and Functions of Language* (with Howard Jackson, Stanley Thornes: 1996), and co-edited volumes in *Impossibility Fiction* (Rodopi: 1996) and *Contextualised Stylistics* (Rodopi: 2000).

Reuven Tsur is Professor Emeritus of Hebrew Literature at Tel Aviv University. He has developed a theory of Cognitive Poetics, and applied it to rhyme, sound symbolism, poetic rhythm, metaphor, poetry and altered states of consciousness, period style, genre, archetypal patterns, and critical activities. His books in English include *Poetic Rhythm: Structure and Performance – An Empirical Study in Cognitive Poetics* (Peter Lang: 1998), *Toward a Theory of Cognitive Poetics* (North Holland: 1992), *What Makes Sound Patterns Expressive: The Poetic Mode of Speech-Perception* (Duke University Press: 1992), *On Metaphoring* (Israel Science Publishers: 1987), and *The Road to 'Kubla Khan': A Cognitive Approach* (Israel Science Publishers: 1987).

1 Contextualising cognitive poetics

Gerard Steen and Joanna Gavins

Introduction

The study of literature has become much less elitist over the past couple of decades. The most obvious manifestation of this development is the rise of cultural studies, which approaches literature as just one element of all culture, including music, film, television, the printed press, and so on. A somewhat more recent manifestation is cognitive poetics, presented to a broad public by Peter Stockwell's *Cognitive Poetics: An Introduction* (Stockwell 2002a). Cognitive poetics, too, sees literature not just as a matter for the happy few, but as a specific form of everyday human experience and especially cognition that is grounded in our general cognitive capacities for making sense of the world.

The present collection of chapters is intended as a companion volume to Stockwell's introduction and aims to demonstrate at a more advanced level what cognitive poetics may look like in actual academic practice. In particular, we are presenting a series of case studies in the general areas delineated by each of Stockwell's chapters, which contain further thoughts for discussion and possibilities for application in class. Some of the cases are more theoretical and others more empirical, and we hope that this combination of approaches offers a balanced incentive for pursuing further work in cognitive poetics. For that purpose, we have also included carefully designed sections for 'further activities' which can be found at the end of each chapter.

In positioning cognitive poetics in this way, we are adopting a historical perspective on the development of the study of literature. Both the position and value of literature itself, as well as of the academic study of literature, have shifted considerably in recent years. The appeal of literature has been challenged by new art forms directed at new groups of audiences through new media, and it has become inevitable to consider the resemblance and difference between these art forms and literature in terms of their psychological and social effects. This is precisely what cognitive poetics promises to bring into view, by relating the structures of the work of art, including the literary text, to their presumed or observed psychological effects on the recipient, including the reader.

Moreover, the standard academic practice of producing yet another interpretation of a text from the canon, or, in more recent years, from outside the canon, has been challenged by the taxpayer, who wants better justification for the spending of their money than an academic's sheer individual interest in a particular text. And this justification, too, is what cognitive poetics promises to offer. It suggests that readings may be explained with reference to general human principles of linguistic and cognitive processing, which ties the study of literature in with linguistics, psychology, and cognitive science in general. Indeed, one of the most exciting results of the rise of cognitive poetics is an increased awareness in the social sciences of the special and specific nature of literature as a form of cognition and communication. What is noted at the same time, however, is that this special position of literature is grounded in some of the most fundamental and general structures and processes of human cognition and experience, enabling us to interact in these special artistic ways in the first place.

So these developments may be partly accounted for by pointing to historical changes in media forms and their audiences as well as in academic practices of interpretation and their societal valuation, as we have just done. However, cognitive poetics could not have emerged without another remarkable development over the past few decades, the rise of cognitive science. New approaches in cognitive anthropology, psychology, linguistics, and artificial intelligence have led to a completely new set of concepts, theories, and insights which are now all available to the student of literature who is interested in describing and explaining the effects of literary texts on the mind of the reader. And the scope of cognitive science is so wide that it is not restricted to purely cognitive phenomena, such as the processing of words or the activation of knowledge schemas from memory. Also part of this undertaking are associations, images, feelings, emotions, and social attitudes, and researchers continue to find and explore new connections between them. For instance, it has now become a genuine possibility that we may be able to give a psychological account of the whole problem of aesthetic and artistic experience, or, another hot issue, literary invention. There are, then, several reasons why cognitive poetics has recently arrived on the academic scene.

Different kinds of cognitive poetics?

The approach to literature through human cognition is not just characteristic of cognitive poetics in Peter Stockwell's specific sense, which is connected to the rise of cognitive linguistics in the study of language. Cognitive linguistics offers an approach to all language, not just literary language, through an examination of its cognitive underpinnings, and is based on the results of cognitive science regarding our cognitive abilities for mental representation and processing (for a good overview, see Ungerer and Schmid 1996). It has been part and parcel of cognitive linguistics to pay attention to features of literary language, such as the role of metaphor and metonymy, from the beginning. In addition, cognitive linguists have proposed many independently interesting ideas that may be fruitfully applied to the study of literature, as has been demonstrated by Stockwell (2002a). Margaret Freeman (in press) offers a more recent and theoretical survey of cognitive poetics in the cognitive-linguistic vein.

However, there are other variants of a cognitive approach to literature. For instance, one of the contributors to this book is Reuven Tsur, who has run a cognitive poetics project since the early 1970s, long before the first publications in cognitive linguistics. He based his work on the early findings of the new cognitive science and applied those insights to the study of the relation between literary structure and effect. In doing so, he expressly continued the work of Russian Formalists and Czech and French structuralists, extending such study in an explicitly cognitive direction. The chapter he has offered for the present volume (Chapter 4) is a fine example of this approach, presenting a somewhat contrapuntal development of the treatment of deixis by cognitive linguists as discussed in the textbook by Stockwell. His case study concerns the treatment of time and place in a number of famous excerpts from such poets as Shakespeare, Marvell, Wordsworth, and Keats. It is best appreciated if it is studied as one of the last chapters in a course, for its topic and treatment are pitched at rather an advanced level of discussion.

Tsur's cognitive poetics is of a more general kind than the one developed in relation to cognitive linguistics, as may be gleaned from his seminal overview *Toward a Theory of Cognitive Poetics* (Tsur 1992). However, it should also be acknowledged that cognitive poetics in the more specific sense presented by Stockwell is still in development. What is more, it does not have a precisely demarcated borderline which would stamp other variants of cognitive poetics, including Tsur's, as non-canonical. Indeed, one of the most interesting things about cognitive poetics today is that it is in such a state of excitement and unscripted development in a multitude of directions.

Similarly, the work of two other contributors to this book, psychologists Raymond W. Gibbs, Jr (Chapter 3) and Keith Oatley (Chapter 12), does not derive from cognitive linguistics either but is firmly based in the social sciences, in particular in experimental cognitive and social psychology. Although Gibbs is closely associated with cognitive linguistics through his work on metaphor (Gibbs 1994), he cannot be regarded as a cognitive linguist or poetician. His main expertise lies in psycholinguistics and cognitive psychology, and his theories, methods, as well as many of his empirical studies are based in those areas. However, Gibbs is also representative of the increasing interest in the social sciences for the special position of literature as a specific form of cognition and communication, which is suggested as well by the title of his successful book on figurative language, *The Poetics of Mind*. We are very happy that he has offered a chapter in a more theoretical and psychological vein, formulating a new, groundbreaking view of the use of cognitive prototypes during online reading. In particular, his chapter goes against the frequently-held view that prototypical concepts are retrieved wholesale from memory every time they are needed for the interpretation of a particular passage. The alternative Gibbs offers should be read as a counterpoint rather than a development of the corresponding chapter in Stockwell's introduction. His chapter is an excellent example of what we mean by the fundamental relation between literary reading and general cognition, written by a psychologist instead of someone trained in language or literature. (It may be usefully connected to Chapter 8 by Crisp on metaphor and Chapter 6 by Steen on scenarios.)

Keith Oatley is well-known for his work on human emotions, in particular through his volume *Best-Laid Schemes: The Psychology of Emotions* (Oatley 1992). Like Gibbs, he approaches cognitive poetics from the standpoint of the psychologist, not the cognitive linguist, or the cognitive poetician inspired by cognitive linguistics. Oatley has also written a theoretical and psychological chapter, in which we have asked him to pull together some of the threads of this volume and consider some potential avenues for future work. He has focused on a reinterpretation of the traditional notion of mimesis as well as on a discussion of the role of emotions in literary reading. He also raises the question of the function of literature from a cognitive perspective. This, then, is another example of a cognitive poetics that is conceived in a slightly more general as well as a psychological fashion. Oatley has moreover the additional interest of being a published and successful writer of two novels, which adds an intriguing twist to his consideration of the cognitive processes of literary reading.

Tsur, Gibbs and Oatley are the three most conspicuous examples in this volume of a more general approach to cognitive poetics. A canonical example of the more specific, cognitive-linguistically inspired approach to cognitive poetics has been put forward in the books by Mark Turner (1987, 1991, 1996; Lakoff and Turner 1989), and we have represented his work in this volume by means of Chapter 9 on parable, by Michael Burke. Burke sets out the main ideas of Turner's theory in order to apply them to a close reading of Shakespeare's Sonnet 2.

Turner's work began as the application to literature of the cognitive-linguistic theory of conceptual metaphor, advanced by Lakoff and Johnson (1980) in their famous *Metaphors We Live By*. Turner first focused on the use of conventional conceptual metaphors in literature in his *Death Is the Mother of Beauty* (1987) and then went on to write 'a field guide to poetic metaphor' with George Lakoff (Lakoff and Turner 1989). We have addressed this particular aspect of Turner's work in Chapter 8 by Peter Crisp on metaphor. Crisp's is a demonstration of the main results and possibilities for application of cognitive-linguistic metaphor research in cognitive poetics. He not only includes work by Turner, but also goes back to Turner's original sources in cognitive linguistics, in particular the work by Lakoff (1987; Lakoff and Johnson 1980). His case study concentrates on a reading of a poem by D.H. Lawrence, 'Song of a man who has come through'.

Turner's major publication is probably his book on 'the study of English in the age of cognitive science', the subtitle of Turner (1991). In that book he lays out the programme for what he called a 'cognitive rhetoric', which has since developed into cognitive poetics. The title of his next book, *The Literary Mind*, bears testimony to this development (Turner 1996). It focuses on the use of stories in literature and in everyday life, and makes the radical claim that both thought and language are ultimately derived from literary story-telling. It is an interesting question whether more generally- and psychologically-oriented cognitive poeticians such as Tsur, Gibbs, and Oatley would agree with this kind of cognitive poetics. As noted above, further explorations of these issues may be found in the chapter by Burke, which also exhibits connections with Chapter 8 on metaphor.

There are, then, two kinds of cognitive poetics. One is more tightly related to the rise of cognitive linguistics, and is in part represented by the chapters by Burke and Crisp. There are two further chapters in our collection which also take this cognitive-linguistic inspiration for their starting point, those by Hamilton (Chapter 5) and Stockwell (Chapter 2), but we will return to these in a moment. The other kind of cognitive poetics is more generally oriented towards cognitive science. It includes work by psychologists such as Oatley and Gibbs as well as by poeticians who have been attuned to cognitive science for a long time, such as Tsur. One of the most exciting aspects of the cognitive poetics of the future may be seeing how these two brands of cognitive poetics finally lead to convergence.

Cognitive poetics and other kinds of poetics

As already hinted above, cognitive poetics does not come out of the blue. However, it is also not just an offshoot of cognitive science, but is first and foremost a new brand of poetics. How does it relate to some of its predecessors, and what exactly is this discipline, poetics? These are the questions that we also need to address.

The last successful form of poetics arguably was structuralism, mentioned above in connection with Reuven Tsur. Structuralism was explicitly launched as a 'structuralist poetics' in the English-speaking world by Jonathan Culler in 1975. His book of that title was a sensation in that it managed to challenge the long-prevailing practice of formal or moral practical criticism. The following rather lengthy quotation from the preface is especially interesting because it not only shows Culler's intention, but also exhibits intimate connections with the aims of cognitive poetics.

> The type of literary study which structuralism helps one to envisage would not be primarily interpretive; it would not offer a method which, when applied to literary works, produced new and hitherto unexpected meanings. Rather than a criticism which discovers or assigns meanings, it would be a poetics which strives to define the conditions of meaning. Granting new attention to the activity of reading, it would attempt to

specify how we go about making sense of texts, which are the interpretive operations on which literature itself, as an institution, is based. Just as the speaker of a language has assimilated a complex grammar which enables him to read a series of sounds or letters as a sentence with a meaning, so the reader of literature has acquired, through his encounters with literary works, implicit mastery of various semiotic conventions which enable him to read series of sentences as poems or novels endowed with shape and meaning. The study of literature, as opposed to the perusal and discussion of individual works, would become an attempt to understand the conventions which make literature possible.

(Culler 1975: viii)

Mark Turner has rejected structuralism as a form of academic imperialism that is incompatible with cognitive poetics (1991: 22), but, as we shall demonstrate in a moment, his own description of his programme is completely identical with the aims of Culler (see Turner 1991: 19).

The first element to be noted in Culler's quotation is the contrast between criticism and poetics. It is clear that by 'poetics' Culler means an encompassing and systematic *theory* of literature, which may or may not be applied in practical criticism as the scholarly interpretation ('perusal and discussion') of individual texts. This is precisely what lies at the basis of Turner's intervention in literary studies as well: 'I offer explorations in this book that do not consist of "giving" and "arguing for" "readings"' (1991: 19).

Structuralist poetics of the French kind, which Culler is introducing above, aligns itself with its main predecessors in literary theory: Czech Structuralism and, before that, Russian Formalism. Culler also refers to the more encompassing discipline of semiotics, which was developing at the same time and led to such different variants as the work by Umberto Eco (1976, 1990) as well as Yuri Lotman (1977). What is more, despite Turner's rejection of structuralism as imperialist, these theories of literature have indirectly had a great effect on some of the work in cognitive poetics, rhetoric and stylistics that is being presented in the present volume and elsewhere (e.g. Semino and Culpeper 2002). Theories of narrative structure and foregrounded language, for instance, are at the centre of attention of various studies in present-day cognitive poetics, but they invariably go back to high-quality theoretical work done in the heyday of structuralism.

Thus the chapters by Emmott (Chapter 11), Semino (Chapter 7), and Gavins (Chapter 10) all depart from narratological as well as cognitive theory to explore different ways in which narrative structure may be held to induce specific cognitive effects in the reader. Emmott concentrates on the study of plot and specifically examines how unexpected plot reversals such as twists in the tale may be accounted for from a cognitive perspective. Narratological analysis is combined here with the basic cognitive insight that readers build, monitor and maintain contextual frames when they read stories from one episode to another. In order to describe how plot reversals work, Emmott's approach makes use of cognitive-psychological findings about default frame assumptions and the inferences readers make, both within and between the contextual frames they construct for a story. Her materials include two stories by Roald Dahl, and her analyses in effect present predictions for what readers do when they read these stories, predictions which could be tested in actual informant work.

This may be connected to the second element noted in Culler's quotation, the emphasis on 'conditions of meaning'. Culler mentions reading, making sense, and interpretive operations as the true object of literary research, and this is precisely what Turner does as well: 'In my view, our profession takes as given exactly what we should be trying to explain. We take for granted our capacities to invent and interpret, and devote ourselves to exercising those capacities and publishing the results' (1991: 19). Modern poetics has incorporated this distinction as one between the eventually incompatible aims of interpretation versus explanation (Fokkema and Ibsch 2000).

Again, the chapters by Emmott, Semino, and Gavins, as well as the chapter by Steen, provide good illustrations of this emphasis on conditions of meaning to be used for explanatory purposes in cognitive poetics. Semino and Gavins explore the cognitive operations required for building a mental representation of the narrative. With reference to Hemingway's 'A very short story', Semino compares two alternative theoretical approaches which lead to the construction of 'possible worlds' and 'mental spaces'. Gavins discusses aspects of Barthelme's *Snow White* to consider the role of 'text worlds'. These notions may be usefully compared with the concept of 'contextual frames' proposed by Emmott.

The chapters by Emmott, Semino, and Gavins deal with the question of which cognitive procedures or processes are a condition for the reader to be able to construct a mental representation for a story. By contrast, Steen's chapter discusses a structural prerequisite for the same goal, in that it addresses the content of a cognitive scenario for the understanding of any love poem. It may be usefully related to the discussion by Gibbs of the role of all concepts during the online reading process, which demonstrates the thin line between structural prerequisites and processing prerequisites. But in general, all of these are attempts to model aspects of cognition that are frequently presupposed by the interpretative critic. More importantly, these aspects demand our close attention if we wish to maintain that professional readings of literary texts also bear a substantial relation with what non-professional readers do when engaging with literature.

To return to Culler, he advocates a similar turn away from the text itself to the interaction between the text and the reader. This is another typical feature of the dramatic change in literary studies since the end of the 1960s. Formal and moral criticism of the text gradually gives way to a theory of reception, which in turn leads to reader-response criticism as a new form of critical practice (e.g. Holub 1984). More important, however, is the evident need to include theories of the reader and the reading process within the scope of the new structuralist poetics. The title of Turner's book *Reading Minds* only needs to be recalled here to see that cognitive poetics as presented in this volume is also explained by this general movement away from the text to the reader and the reading process. This may lead to work in cognitive poetics (as in the case of Emmott, Semino, Gavins, and Steen) as well as in cognitive poetic criticism (as in the case of Tsur, Burke, and Crisp).

Cognitive poetic reception *research*, focusing on real readers other than the literary analyst, is what has eventually come out of reception *theory*, in the form of the empirical study of literature. This approach deliberately aligns itself with the social sciences as practised by for instance Gibbs and Oatley. In particular, the empirical study of literature addresses the psychology and sociology of literature, to which cognitive poetics displays an interesting relation that deserves more attention than we can devote to it here. For an overview of this social-scientific variant of cognitive poetics, see Schram and Steen (2001).

The third element to be noted in Culler's quotation is the distinction but also link between language processing and text processing. Generative linguistics had great success in the 1960s in modelling human language as a rule-governed system that may be put into action in performance. This led to the extrapolation of this approach in structuralism and semiotics to symbolic systems other than language, including literature. Consequently literature was regarded as a symbolic, semiotic system that was governed by conventions of signification, just as language is determined by grammatical and pragmatic rules of meaning and use. How these conventions actually operated during literary reading was still largely a mystery and a matter for intense speculation and theory formation in the 1970s. However, today this has become much clearer through the results in cognitive psychology, discourse psychology, and psycholinguistics. It is precisely these findings about the reading process in general and the literary reading process in particular that were significantly lacking in the 1970s. They are currently being exploited in cognitive linguistics and cognitive poetics to give another turn to the wheel of poetics.

We have noted that some of the correspondences between structuralism and cognitive poetics indicate that the latter continues a familiar line of investigation which may be traced back to the beginning of the twentieth century. There are interesting differences between structuralist poetics and cognitive poetics as well, but this takes us into the next section. For we still have to consider how cognitive poetics is related to cognitive linguistics, and how this has affected its nature as a brand of poetics.

Cognitive poetics and cognitive linguistics

One of the basic tenets of cognitive linguistics is the assumption of an intimate relationship between meaning and knowledge. When we understand language, we do so on the basis of our knowledge of the world, which has arisen out of our embodied interaction with that world. This also applies to our understanding of the language of literature, and is hence also one of the basic tenets of cognitive poetics (e.g. Turner 1991: 20).

It is interesting to consider the historical position of this fundamental assumption. Cognitive linguistics partly arose as a result of a rejection of generative grammar. Generative grammarians made a distinction between lexical and encyclopaedic knowledge, or knowledge of language as opposed to knowledge of the world. As noted above, in making this distinction, they were a major source of inspiration for the structuralist and semiotic endeavours to model the linguistic and conceptual systems as two separate but interacting systems. However, generative grammarians themselves were not interested in this interaction, which they relegated to the realm of performance and later pragmatics. Thus, even though the distinction between meaning and knowledge was recognised from the early days of generative grammar on, it was the difference between the two systems which was emphasised by the first generations of Chomskyans. This led to an artificial separation between meaning and knowledge in linguistics, which was soon rejected by linguists like Lakoff and others, who, through a programme called generative semantics, soon found themselves in an entirely new domain of linguistics altogether – cognitive linguistics. Instead of underlining the distinction between meaning and knowledge, they started exploring those aspects where meaning and knowledge became hard to distinguish, and thus laid the foundations of the new cognitive linguistics (again, for a good introduction, see Ungerer and Schmid 1996).

The most telling example of the overlap between meaning versus knowledge is metaphor, discussed in this volume by Peter Crisp. Cognitive linguists have shown that metaphor is not just special or deviant language used by people such as poets or politicians. Instead, it is entrenched in the language system and may be a reflection of conventional and systematic metaphor in our thought. But cognitive linguists have gone further than that. They have also claimed that thought, including metaphorical thought, in turn is a reflection of many of our ways of dealing with the world. Experience explains conceptual structure, and conceptual structure explains linguistic structure. For instance, our use of expressions for happy or sad moods like 'I feel *high*', 'I feel *depressed*' or '*low*' are not accidental. They are explained by a conceptual metaphor, or metaphorical concept, HAPPY IS UP. And this conceptual metaphor, in its turn, is conventional because it is taken to reflect our basic attitudes when we are happy or sad: 'Physical basis: Drooping posture typically goes along with sadness and depression, erect posture with a positive emotional state' (Lakoff and Johnson 1980: 15).

Cognitive linguists assume a close connection between experience, cognition, and language. Language and expression are not regarded as arbitrary, which was one of the major assumptions of structuralism, both linguistic and poetic. Language and expression are regarded as motivated, by cognition and by its basis in our interaction with reality. This has given rise to exciting new work on aspects of language such as the perception of foreground and background in grammar and text, and their explanation with reference to general principles of perception. The linguist Ronald Langacker, one of the founding scholars of the cognitive linguistic movement, is the main source of inspiration in this connection (Langacker 1987, 1991).

We have two chapters on this aspect of cognitive poetics, one by Craig Hamilton (Chapter 5) and one by Peter Stockwell (Chapter 2). Hamilton discusses 'Hospital Barge' by war poet Wilfred Owen and traces how the reader's perception of a scene is guided by the grammar of the poetic lines. Grammatical constructions highlight (or 'profile') aspects of situations and shift the reader's attention from one aspect to another in sometimes unexpected ways, and Hamilton exploits Langacker's theory to analyse how these shifts of attention are accomplished and what effects they may have on the interpretation process. Peter Stockwell does something similar, but at a more global, textual level of reading, where he traces the processes of establishing and maintaining coherence in texts of a surrealist nature. This is an especially daunting task, as surrealism subverts the usual processes of perception and cognition. But it is precisely the strength of the cognitive poetic approach that it can indicate those moments where default expectations are thwarted, in order to identify significant moments for meaning making in the literary text.

Metaphor and profiling are among the most interesting applications of cognitive linguistics to literature. Another theory that has come out of cognitive linguistics is the theory of conceptual integration networks, or blending (e.g. Fauconnier and Turner 1996, 1999; see also Grady *et al.* 1999). This is a general theory of how words come to be integrated within encompassing conceptual structures (or 'blends') by the reader, and it plays a prominent role in the chapters by Crisp and Burke. For further applications of cognitive linguistics to literature that we have not mentioned in this introduction, the reader is referred to the paper by Freeman (in press).

Conclusion and future prospects

We have emphasised that cognitive poetics may be considered from a number of perspectives. We ended with what may be the most natural perspective for many of our readers, particularly those who come to this volume through Stockwell's introductory volume, that is, the connection between cognitive poetics and cognitive linguistics. However, it has been our express aim to provide more context to cognitive poetics than just through cognitive linguistics. Important as this connection may be, we have shown that there are other influences on cognitive poetics that should not be ignored.

In particular, cognitive poetics should also be understood as a new chapter in the theory of literature, one that has its roots in a long and venerable tradition, tracing back through reception theory and structuralism to formalism at the beginning of the previous century. Moreover, cognitive poetics does not just receive its cognitive input through cognitive linguistics, but more generally through all of cognitive science, including in particular psycholinguistics, discourse psychology, cognitive psychology, and social psychology. In that respect there is an interesting relationship between cognitive poetics and the empirical study of literature which invites further exploration. It is especially interesting to see how both approaches deal with the distinction between theory, research, and application (including criticism). This becomes increasingly important in the present day and age, in which literary studies have to give a better account of their function in society than used to be the case. A cognitive poetics which aligns itself with cognitive science stands a good chance of doing so, for instance through its potential for application in education. In the post-elitism days of literary study, it will be useful for teachers to have access to an approach that can present literature and literary analysis as based in general cognitive experience, including general processes of understanding language. This will be even more so if it also enables them to exploit connections with other art forms and media. It seems to be the most interesting promise of cognitive poetics for the near future.

The potential of the new approach may be underlined by reconsidering the nature of the literary texts included in this volume. They range from canonical poetry such as anthologised love poetry, D.H. Lawrence's 'Song of a man who has come through' or Wilfred Owen's 'Hospital Barge', through notoriously difficult poetry like Shakespeare's Sonnet 2, to completely experimental poetry such as the work by the Surrealists. When it comes to prose, we have a similar range, from fiction for entertainment such as the work by Roald Dahl, through a canonical short story by Hemingway, to a consideration of excerpts of an experimental novel by Barthelme. The third obvious kind of literary text to be considered in this context, drama, is conspicuously lacking from our volume. However, there is no reason to think it could not be handled by a cognitive poetic approach and this has been shown to some extent already in the work by Don Freeman on the language of Shakespeare's *Macbeth*, *King Lear*, and other plays (Freeman 1993, 1995). In general, if the language of drama bears any connection with the language of ordinary conversation, the cognitive linguistic basis of a lot of cognitive poetic work should give rise to a wide range of issues for application. We hope that this volume may inspire future students of cognitive poetics to explore these relatively uncharted waters.

The future of cognitive poetics is heavily dependent on such new explorations. The discipline is still in an early stage of development, and it may evolve in any number of different directions. What we have presented in this volume is not an end-state, presenting a final overview of hard-won facts. On the contrary, we have aimed to show that these are just the beginnings of many new and exciting possibilities for the study of literature. One way of taking this project forward would be to critically engage with the very chapters in this book. We hope that we have offered sufficient background knowledge and incentive for the interested student of literature to take on this challenge.

Further activities

1   Reflect on the distinction between theory, criticism and research. Can you think of a concrete example in the study of literary fiction or poetry in which theory leads to research, and research, in turn, to application in criticism? In your reflections, also include how you would like to make a distinction between reading, giving a reading, interpretation, and criticism or reviewing. What is the nature of these activities? And what is their function?
2   Cognitive poetics rests on assuming a distinction but also a relation between the text and the reader. Consider how the meaning of the words on the page is both independent of the reader, as well as dependent on the reader. Discuss how this relationship may be controlled when you do text analysis. In your considerations, include the role of the author and the context (of production as well as of reception, as well as of analysis).
3   Cognitive poetics has a rather contemporary bias: it is rather difficult to speculate about the minds of people in the past. How can such a challenge be met when you want to do historical research of a cognitive poetic kind? Make a list of difficulties and possible solutions for discussion in class.

2 Surreal figures

Peter Stockwell

Editors' preface

Peter Stockwell opens the main body of this collection with his chapter on figure and ground. These notions are important as fundamental psychological patterns and form the basis of a great deal of work in cognitive science. Stockwell develops the cognitive understanding of figure and ground in order to examine stylistic foregrounding and how a literary work takes a reader's attention. Using some challenging examples of surrealist poetic writing, he demonstrates the connections between stylistic patterns in texts and certain reader-centred effects of appreciation and interpretation. The chapter goes on to explore how the dynamic movement through a reading can be understood as a process of 'figuring' and 'grounding', producing striking images and persistent resonances in the mind of a reader. Stockwell closes by suggesting that literary texture, connotations and associations are built up in this dynamic process. Like all the other chapters in this book, the main topics of Stockwell's analysis are linked with those in the corresponding chapter of Stockwell (2002a), our companion volume. You may also find it useful to read this particular chapter alongside Craig Hamilton's cognitive-linguistic analysis of Wilfred Owen's poetry, which follows later in Chapter 5.

Setting the scene

Picture this woodland scene: a woman in a pale blue coat is riding a chestnut mare amongst the trees. Some of the tree-trunks block your view of the horse and rider, and in turn these figures block the view of trees further away in the wood. But there is something strange here: the trees which seem to be furthest away obscure your foregrounded view, and the trees which seem to be nearest to you appear transparent, so that you can see the woman and horse through them. Foreground and background are confused. This impossible picture is the scene painted in René Magritte's *Le Blanc-Seing* (usually translated as *The Blank Signature*, but perhaps more poetically rendered as

Free-Hand or *Free Rein*). It plays, in typically surrealist fashion, with the viewer's sense of figure and ground in visual perspective.

Surrealism was an artistic movement that swept Europe and America between the two world wars. Perhaps most famous for its dazzling and disturbing paintings and sculptures, surrealism began as a revolution in linguistic expression. The surrealists, emerging from the short-lived dada movement and under the leadership of André Breton, sought to undermine the bourgeois values of rationalism, sanity, decency and order which had generated the horrors of the war in the trenches. This revolution was firstly to be brought about through radical poetic experimentalism. Authorial rationalism and intentionality were undermined by 'automatic writing', in which the poet would empty all thoughts and write as fast and closely to the unconscious mind as possible. 'Chainpoems', in which each line was written blindly by different contributors, subverted the sense of authorial organisation. The rantings of lunatics, accounts of dreams and hallucinations, accidental coincidences of puns and misreadings in street signs, graffiti and the language of children were all valued by the surrealists as being closer to the over-arching 'sur-reality' behind the patina of bourgeois thought.

Contemporaneous with the Russian formalist notion of *defamiliarisation* (*ostraneniye*) as the primary quality of literariness, the radical estrangement that the surrealists sought aimed at destroying the surface aesthetic in order to access the world of the unconscious. Magritte's reversal of the visual figure from its perspectival ground described above is a good example of this. The pattern is a favourite strategy in surrealist writing:

> It doesn't look like a finger it looks like a feather of broken glass
> [...]
> It doesn't look like a finger it looks like a feather with broken teeth
> The spaces between the stones are made of stone
> It doesn't look like a revolver it looks like a convolvulus
> [...]
>
> (Hugh Sykes Davies)

Throughout this poem, Davies (1978) manipulates the reader's attempts to resolve and recognise what 'it' looks like by constantly shifting between parallel binaries at various levels: notice the phonological patterning of 'finger'/'feather', 'revolver'/'convolvulus'; or the semantic shifts from positive to negative polarity, and moving from simile to metaphor (see Stockwell 2000 for a detailed discussion). The poem plays around with the very notion of categorisation: the assertion that the 'spaces between the stones are made of stone' is the linguistic equivalent of the Magritte painting. It is this equivalence that is the focus of this chapter, where foreground and background are reversed and made interchangeable to the point at which the cognitive distinction between the two becomes difficult to maintain.

Making figures out

The distinction between *figure* and *ground* is of central importance in cognitive science. The human cognitive mechanism for distinguishing figure from ground involves understanding how attention works, how categorisation and boundaries work, and how our cognitive capacities for visual and spatial negotiation are extended into the linguistic field. Determining the outline of a potential predator or potential food against the environmental background has obvious evolutionary advantages, and our cognitive faculties for this have reached a very high level of discernment.

Perceiving a figure and ground in a visual field involves *selection for attention*. According to classical gestalt psychology, good shapes that are likely to be recognised as figures tend to have the following criterial properties:

- elements positioned close to each other will be treated as having a unified relationship
- elements that appear similar will be assumed to be related
- figures with a perceived closed boundary will be seen as unified
- elements with few interruptions between them will be seen as connected
- elements which seem to share a function are treated together.

(See Wertheimer 1958; Tversky 1990; and for an overview, Aitchison 1994; and Ungerer and Schmid 1996: 31–7). In other words, the figure will be regarded as a self-contained object or feature in its own right, with well-defined edges separating it from the ground. Extending these properties from the visual field into the textual field, more recent attention theory has added the following determining features:

- the figure will be more detailed, better focused, brighter, or more attractive than the rest of the field
- it will be on top of, or in front of, or above, or larger than the rest of the field that is then the ground
- it will be moving in relation to the static ground
- it will precede the ground in time or space
- it will be a part of the ground that has broken away, or emerges to become the figure.

(See Stockwell 2002a: ch. 2; and Posner 1989; Baddeley and Weiskrantz 1993; Smyth *et al.* 1994; and Styles 1997 for details).

Prominence is conferred on a figure when features such as these are perceived. Notice that the first few features involve drawing the conceptual boundary of the figure on the basis of internal structural characteristics, while the last three points above depend on perceived motion or a process in delineating the figure conceptually. Understanding these in terms of language, we can describe any stylistic feature that draws our attention as an *attractor*. Attractors function to *distract* our attention, while by contrast the rest of the ground is characterised by cognitive *neglect* (see Stockwell 2002b on these terms; also van Peer 1986 and 1992; Fludernik 1993: 338–49; and Short 1996: 36–79 on this effect of foregrounding).

Attractors can be formed by stylistic features in the text that display linguistic *deviance*. Notice that this is not simply a structural matter but is both structural and perceptual. Short (1996: 34) provides a checklist of the levels for investigating stylistic deviance: phonetic, graphological and metrical levels; morphological, lexical and semantic levels; syntactic, pragmatic and discoursal levels. Stylistic deviance is a prominent feature in surrealist writing, used to foreground jarring images or ideas, and create surrealistic figures. For example, surrealist poetry readings in Paris in the 1920s would often take place with many poems all read aloud at the same time, with simultaneous loud music or bells being rung. Surrealism blends phonetic, graphological and morphological deviance: Duchamps' moustachioed Mona Lisa was entitled *LHOOQ* (or, read aloud, '*Elle a chaud au cul* – she has a hot arse'); Roger Vitrac graffittoed 'no smoking' signs to read *Défense de fumer les fusées des femmes* ('do not smoke/light the rockets/ groupings/musical scales of women'). Straight lexical semantic deviance is evident in the collagist Kurt Schwitters' poetic line, 'Blue is the colour of thy yellow hair', or in Bravig Imbs' 'Slowly the ponderous doors of lead imponderous'. Other poems are set out like telephone directories with the identical numbers of unlikely characters; archaic literary terms are blended with colloquial conversation; registers from wildly different domains are collaged together.

Taking together the list of the determining features of figures and the possible stylistic descriptions above, it is possible to sketch out how a text manipulates elements that are likely to distract the attention of a reader. For illustration, here is a surrealist poem by Pablo Picasso:

> in secret
> be quiet say nothing
> except the street be full of stars
> and the prisoners eat doves
> and the doves eat cheese
> and the cheese eats words
> and the words eat bridges
> and the bridges eat looks
> and the looks eat cups full of kisses in the *orchata*
> that hides all with its wings
> the butterfly the night
> in a café last summer
> in Barcelona
>
>   (Pablo Picasso (1978), translated by David Gascoyne)

This poem exercises a series of figure and ground reversals at a variety of levels. It begins by setting out the ground ('in secret') with an implied figure: the conspiratorial speaker who is not to speak. This figure is soon neglected as the next line presents a startling example of a surreal image: 'except the street be full of stars'. Surreal images involve a literalisation of metaphor and were to be taken seriously as a window onto the unconscious. The archaic, portentous grammar here offers a discourse deviant distraction to accompany the fullness and brightness of the attractor. The replacement (or *occlusion*) of the initial figure is effected by the word 'except', which moves the star-filled street to emerge from the background setting.

That bright attractor is almost instantly replaced by a different attractor, this time motivated by action: 'and the prisoners eat doves'. This line is distracting in several dimensions. It features a material action predicate, which contrasts with the stative predicate 'be' chosen in the previous line. The new figure is introduced with 'and', placing it at the same conceptual level as the starry street, which it thus occludes in cognitive terms. The new line features animate humans, who are more likely to be perceived as agentive figures than the inanimate street or stars; and 'the prisoners' is both definite and specific while 'the street' and 'stars' are either non-specific or non-definite (animation, definiteness and specificity all make good figures, according to Langacker 1991: 305–29).

The middle section of the poem effects figure/ground reversals by cohesive chaining. The figured prisoners eat the doves in their environmental ground, but then these doves become the active figures in the next line, and the cheese in that ground becomes the active figure in the next line, and so on. Prisoners eating doves is schematically unusual but not particularly exceptional, and doves eating cheese is schematically similar; however, cheese eating words is conceptually more bizarre. Though of course we can idiomatically eat our own words, cheese cannot usually do so. And the next line with words eating bridges is straightforwardly odd at a conceptual level. At least bridges are tangible, though, whereas 'looks' in the next line are neither edible nor tangible in our cognitive reality. In spite of all the additive conjunctions, neglect sets in cumulatively as the figuration moves on, with the chained figures and ground giving a cosmetic sense of cohesion.

This pattern creates a double effect: the addition of lines and new images and new attractors seems to provide new figures emerging from the ground of each previous line; but the verb 'eat' serves to enclose each figure in the neglected image of the previous line. What seems to be an accumulation and growth is in fact the reverse: smaller and smaller specification (the looks are inside the bridges which are inside the cheese which is inside the doves inside the prisoners who are in the street). All of this apparent accumulation builds up to the longest line, which is also the most domestic and intimate: 'and the looks eat cups full of kisses in the *orchata*' (a sweet milky rice drink). From this point onwards, the addition of lines matches the sense of enclosure. The co-referent of 'that' and 'its' could simply locally be the *orchata*, but the steady figure/ground chaining, the additive conjunctions, the use of 'all', and the mention of 'wings' that return attention to the neglected doves, all serve to encourage a reading that sweeps together all the images into one image of a butterfly with wings. (Note, too, that *papillons* ('butterflies') is the name that the surrealists gave to their flyer leaflets posted around Paris to advertise surrealist activity.) This figure then encompasses all the previous images, standing in its location which is grounded very specifically: 'in a café last summer in Barcelona'.

The poem enacts several surrealist techniques. It draws the reader into the surreal landscape by accumulating images that are increasingly cognitively challenging, so that early images fade by neglect and come to be accepted as a natural background. It sets out lexical items that are semantically related, but places them syntactically in a way that disrupts our usual recognition of the sense relations. It provides much repetition, parallelism and cosmetic cohesion at the textual level while working to create incoherence at the conceptual level. It enacts the process of estrangement by reversing figure and ground.

Such stylistic variation gives surrealism as a genre of writing a highly deviant texture, and it is important to point out that these features can be analysed as attractors for their cognitive impact in a particular reading as well as simply being described on a stylistic level. However, although features like these often contribute on a micro-level to the general impact, the real power of surrealism lies in its conceptual deviance. There is much surrealist writing that is not stylistically deviant at all, but which presents scenes that are unexpected and disturbing, sometimes very minimally:

Seance

The stranger walks into the dark room where the two men sit at the table and talk of travel. The stranger joins in the conversation, saying: 'I have also traveled' and the two men look up and seem surprised at his sudden appearance. In the corners of the ceiling there is a sound as of very swift wings, a muttering of motors, and a chattering of thin voices. The stranger disappears. His voice is heard first in this corner, then in that, until it fades away somewhere near the open window. Where the stranger stood the two men find a railway ticket to an unknown destination.

(Eduard Roditi)

Narratologically, and at any of the levels of discoursal or linguistic patterning, this poem by Roditi (1978) hardly seems deviant at all. It outlines a chronologically consistent narrative in sentences that are grammatically fully actualised. Perhaps the only marked stylistic feature is the use of definite articles in the first sentence, which seems to indicate a narrative already in progress when the text joins it. Rather, readers' common sense of unease in this text seems to be a feature of the cognitive level, where schematised expectations are deviated from, odd things happen and disappear, and the scene is described without much explanation or evaluation. This sense is largely a product of the manipulation of perspective (or point of view) in the story, and this cognitive dimension can also be understood in terms of figural attractors.

For example, the marked definite article, subject theme position, agency, wilfulness and animation of 'The stranger walks' all serve to set up the stranger as the primary figure initially. The definite article makes this a figure in relation to the ground of the 'dark room' (notice the dimming of the background that further throws the figure into relief), but the perspective of this initial attractor is the narrator's and reader's; the two men would surely have begun, 'A stranger walks … '. From this point on, although the narrative remains in the third person, the perspective shifts to the cognitive viewpoint of the two men. In this perspective, the definite articles that follow are normative.

The rest of the story presents conceptual figuration from the perspective of the two men's distracted attention. The primary attraction of the stranger is maintained after he walks in (motion) by him speaking (action) and his appearance being described as 'sudden' (rapidity). All of these features create focused figuration on the stranger. However, the third sentence of the story presents a strong distraction that creates a different prominent focus of attention, so that the neglected stranger is thrown into the background: 'In the corners of the ceiling (spatial shift of perspective to a point above the ground) there is a sound (distracting perception) as of very swift wings (a fast-moving attractor), a muttering of motors (further perceptually marked and specific distraction), and a chattering of thin voices (more perceptual distraction, and a shift from object to human)'. This reconfiguration is so distracting that the neglected stranger 'disappears' even out of the ground in the next sentence, though there is then a suggestion that the distracting sound was in fact connected to his voice, 'heard first in this corner, then in that, until it fades away somewhere near the open window'. Notice, though, how the deictic elements ('this', 'that', 'away') distract the reader's attention around the room in parallel with the perspective of the two men.

The story has cleverly blended what are potentially double figures. The third person narration but strong focalisation on the perspective of the two men serves to make 'the stranger' strange to both the men and the narratee/reader. This perspectival trick distracts the reader's attention at just the central moment in the story between the stranger's 'appearance' and the point at which he 'disappears'. The stranger, neglected out of attention by this middle sentence, is nevertheless maintained by co-reference ('*The stranger* disappears. *His* voice … , *it* fades … '). He has become by this point neither figure nor ground but a sort of empty, stranger-shaped figural hole in the ground. This impression is captured in the final sentence by the figural focus being grounded 'where the stranger stood', but the reader's attention is immediately distracted away and out of the ground of the room and indeed out of the story by the occluding 'railway ticket to an unknown destination'. The ghostly figuration apparent in this story is of course reinforced by the interpretative line that is suggested by the title, 'Seance', which also perhaps explains why the figure that the two men invoked was actually expected and can take that initial definite article. It seems, in retrospect, that even this first phrase was from the two men's perspective after all, and the reader has been drawn into the real experience of the super-natural (or 'sur-real') along with them.

Drawing attention: the edges of figures

So far I have been treating figure and ground fairly simply, as binary dimensions in a field. Towards the end of the previous analysis, I began to suggest that it might be fruitful to think in terms of a more graded texture of attention. Figures which fade into the background by neglect can still be remembered, either unilaterally by the reader or with the active assistance of certain textual features. As described above, this can lead to some bizarre effects of 'felt absence', where an absence is tangible and paradoxically perceived as significantly present.

When we think of a figure emerging out of a background, the figure is largely defined by being the unified element that distracts our attention and causes us to neglect the ground. As illustrated above, distraction and the recognition of attractors are dependent on various gestalt principles, plus various other determinants of prominence such as motion, animacy, functional intentionality, brightness, and size (see Scarry 2001). When a figure is perceived as being separate from the ground, it is interesting to consider what is happening at the edges and behind the figure.

One of the characteristics of figuration is the sense of *depth*, such that the figure/ground field is imagined three-dimensionally. That means, of course, that we must think in terms of the continuity of the ground, which means in turn that we assume the continued existence of the ground behind the figure even when the figure obscures that part of the ground. This conceptual integrity of the ground even under occlusion is noticeably absent in very small babies and non-primate mammals (dogs, for example, are very bad at working out where biscuits have gone if they are hidden out of sight).

Furthermore, when we think of a figure that is moving against the ground, we must keep track of the constantly changing patch of ground which is being occluded as the figure moves obstructively across it. We must also consider what is happening cognitively at the edges of the figure, where there is a shifting point of transition from ground to figure at the advancing boundary, and then from figure to ground as the attractor passes on at the opposite edge.

Before we explore the cognitive linguistics of these issues, it might be useful at this point to return to what the surrealists thought they were doing with language and perception. In many ways, the surrealist view of language was holistically cognitive, though expressed in the psychoanalytical and political terminology of the time. The *surrealist image* – such as those in the texts discussed above – was the principal element in the movement's estrangement of the world. This image was to be taken as a literal presentation of reality, and could be manifest in a displayed 'found' or made object, a painted or cinematic image, in disrupted grammar or a cognitive disjunction through language. Much of Magritte's work, for example, involves the exploration of the boundaries between images, the objects in the world with which they correlate, and the names that designate those objects and images.

In a series of paintings, Magritte would draw an image of an object, such as an apple, a pipe, the sky, or a keyhole, with words in the painting designating a different thing. For example, in *La Trahison des Images (The Treachery of Images*, 1928–9) a picture of a pipe appears above the words 'This is not a pipe'. Of course, the meaning of the words here is true: Magritte was drawing attention to the fact that what was being shown was not the object but the image, and of course the words could not have a truth value since in being part of the painting they too were images. In a 1929 essay, 'La poésie est une pipe', Magritte (1979: 59) set out a series of statements with pictorial illustrations of the relationships between objects, images and words. Among these are statements such as:

> An image can take the place of a word in a proposition.
> An object makes one suppose that there are other objects behind it ...
> In a painting, words have the same substance as images.
> One sees images and words differently in a painting ...
> An object never fills the same space as its name or its image.
> At first, the visible edges of objects, in reality, touch as if they
>   form a mosaic.
> Vague images have a meaning as necessary and perfect as precise images.
>   (Magritte 1979: 59, my translation)

Some of Magritte's thinking in relation to naming and reference is Wittgensteinian, and his ideas also later directly influenced Michel Foucault (see Foucault and Magritte 1983). However, it is Magritte's thoughts on objects, images and space that are interesting here.

The penultimate assertion in the list above is accompanied by a line drawing in which the profiles of a face, a tree and a wall seem to occlude different clouds. The boundaries where the cloud meets the foregrounded object share the same single pencil line. Magritte seems careful to point out that this flat mosaic dimension is a surface appearance only ('At first ... visible ... in reality ... as if'), since earlier he draws a brick wall and points out that 'an object makes one suppose that there are other objects behind it'. There are key points here: the common edges of figures and grounds seem to belong to the figure (it has a closed boundary), while the ground is rendered formless by the figuration (see Haber and Hershenson 1980); the ground is assumed to be continuous behind the figure; and there is a gradation of depth from profile, to cloud, to the blank background.

However, Magritte's formulations are largely static. We must consider what happens when the eye is drawn around a painting, or tracks real or cinematic motion, or spins up worlds by reading through a text. This is *kinetic occlusion* (Scarry 2001), which we can understand further by returning to some cognitive linguistics, and then a cognitive poetic analysis of surrealist writing.

The notion of graded depth, rather than a binary figure/ground distinction, can be understood in cognitive linguistic terms by thinking about how the process of using and understanding language gives dynamism to figuration. Langacker (1991) and Lakoff (1987) analyse the operation of prepositions in single clauses using the notion of figure and ground. In prepositions such as 'into', 'through', 'out' and 'over', the figure is seen as a moving *trajector* that describes a staged *path* in relation to the grounded *landmark*. Diagrammatically, Lakoff (1987: 419ff.) shows the path (as a series of time-lagged positions) that represents the trajector's movement. In 'The city clouded over', for example, the trajector clouds are imagined gradually moving stage by stage over time to completely occlude the landmark city beneath. The stages represent points on the path. Different moments along the path represent different degrees of prominence in the movement of the figure, giving us not simply figure and ground, but a textured relief in figuration.

This analysis is restricted to single clauses. However, we can use the cognitive linguistic view of 'over' to explore the process of figural occlusion across poetic sentences and lines.

> They tell me that over there the beaches are black
> From the lava running to the sea
> Stretched out at the foot of a great peak smoking with snow
> Under a second sun of wild canaries
> So what is this far-off land
> Seeming to take its light from your life
> It trembles very real at the tip of your lashes
> Sweet to your carnation like an intangible linen
> Freshly pulled from the half-open trunk of the ages
> Behind you
> Casting its last sombre fires between your legs
> The earth of the lost paradise
> Glass of shadows mirror of love
> And lower towards your arms opening
> On the proof by springtime
> OF AFTERWARDS
> Of evil's not existing
> All the flowering appletree of the sea
> (André Breton, translated by Mary Ann Caws)

This complete poem by Breton (2001) presents a series of encompassing manoeuvres, in some ways similar to the Picasso poem discussed above, and in common with several other pieces of surrealist writing. It does this by drawing the reader's attention with attractors that are elaborated startling noun phrases, or convey motion and speed, or brightness and attractiveness, or wilfulness, marked size and orientation, and emergence – most of the features of good attractors, in fact.

The poem begins with the first of only two full main verbs ('They tell me'), a report of speech that focuses speaker and hearer in the foreground, only to be immediately followed by an explicit occluding shift in figuration: 'over there'. This shift creates a new spatial ground where 'the beaches are black', an anomaly that is an effective attractor. The anomalous figure is elaborated and explained as being caused by 'lava running to the sea' from a mountain 'smoking with snow'. Attention is taken down to sea-level and then swept up to the sky by the combination of motion ('running') and lightness ('snow'). The distracting brightness is racked up over these first few lines, culminating in the doubled light of 'a second sun' which is made even more distracting as a surreal image 'of wild canaries'. (The original French reinforces this attractor with alliteration: '*Sous un second soleil de serins sauvages*'.)

This brightness is then encompassed by an emerging figure that occludes (we might say eclipses) the sun by rendering its light partially sourced from 'your life'. 'It' – that is, both the previous scene and the accumulated light – 'trembles very real at the tip of your lashes'. There is a further specification of the figural occlusion here, effected by the second of only two main verbs in the poem. All the opening scene has been swept up and overwhelmed in the lover's life, then the perspective has been drawn back so that all is compressed into a point of light on the delicate edge of her eyes. This sense of delicacy is captured by the following image: 'Sweet to your carnation like an intangible linen / Freshly pulled from the half-open trunk of the ages / Behind you'. This is the most startling compression of noun-phrases so far, a surrealist image that gathers together resonant delicate objects that are drawn from the past. 'Behind you', a temporal orientation at the centre-point of the poem, manages to look both backwards and forwards. Connected to the previous line the way I have just quoted it, 'the ages' are 'behind you' and the perspective looks to the past. In this reading, the volcanic formations and bright upheaval of the beginning of the poem (which we are reminded of soon by the 'last sombre fires') are in the dimming distant past, and 'far-off' must be re-interpreted as being temporal rather than spatial.

Alternatively, 'Behind you' could be read as the beginning of a new clause, 'Casting its last sombre fires between your legs / The earth of the lost paradise … '. In this reading, the perspective turns away from the past towards the future that is the moodless, timeless second half of the poem. Here, relations between attractors are held together not by main or even subordinate verbs but by a series of prepositional reorientations: 'behind', 'between', 'of', 'towards', 'on', 'by' and 'afterwards'. Where the first half of the poem worked by occlusions of ever more attractive figures, the second half of the poem works by elaborating different dimensions by which the same complex surreal image occludes the landmark background entirely. The rich wealth of orientating prepositions only serves to focus the figure freshly and in more complexity.

Across the whole poem, the reader's attention is pulled across space and time, drawn from a landscape view to an intimate view, and taken from geological ages to a single season ('snow' to 'springtime'). As each new figure is swept over by each occluding attractor, some of the properties of the displaced and neglected former figure become part of the boundary properties of the new attracting figure: the black beaches are over-run by lava which is covered by the sea which defines the foot of the mountain, and so on. Furthermore, as previous figures become part of the formless ground by neglect, they lose focus and seem to become vague in relation to the new attractor. What vagueness means here is that former attractors neglected into the ground might lose their cognitive focus but they remain in attention as resonances and associations. 'Vague images have a meaning as necessary and perfect as precise images' (Magritte 1979: 59). The neglected ground does not entirely disappear when attractors occlude parts of it, since we assume the continuity of the past underneath the figural attractor. The second half of the poem works hard to make the attractor as specific as possible, with careful prepositional orientation, but the proper state of the end of the poem is expressible only through surrealist contradictions, where complex figure and vague ground are blended.

There are many such blends in the poem. They are not so much figure and ground reversals here as an emphasis on the delicate transitional point where remembered but vague figures blend their resonant properties in new occluding figures. Binaries such as 'glass' and 'mirror', the past and 'afterwards', fire and ice, blackness and the brightness, the wide 'land' and the precise 'lashes', are all gathered together in the cumulative heaping of descriptive phrases towards the end. The poem attempts to obliterate figural distinctions, coming to rest in an eternal state of potential by presenting verbless phrases. It does not even gesture towards this by promising a redemption, which would acknowledge the reality of a rational and conventional past: it denies the Christian fall from Eden; denies the existence of evil while avoiding even the explicit verbal denial ('of evil's not existing'); denies the 'last sombre fires' of shame and guilt; denies the lost paradise as an illusion ('glass of shadows'); denies vanity ('mirror of love'), and replaces it with the surrealist image of the appletree of knowledge coming into continuous ('flowering') blossom, with 'you' at the poetic centre.

As the poem passes on, each attracting figure is neglected in favour of new attractors, but the occlusion is not complete since the vague and obstructed ground retains its resonances. The Breton poem demonstrates this vividly, and makes a significant expressive theme of it, but I think that the cognitive pattern that surrealist writing exploits is one that is common to a lesser degree in all literary reading. That claim, though, is for another time.

In this chapter, I have tried to use a cognitive poetic analysis to explore some of the felt effects of being drawn into the surrealist landscape. This involved developing a rich notion of foregrounding using patterns from the cognitive scientific understanding of figure and ground. In order to approach the issue of texture in literary reading, it was necessary to explore the edges of dynamic figuration. However, I am under no illusions that my account is either wholly satisfactory or comprehensive. Surrealism is a good place to begin to draw out the limits of figural manipulation, but surreal figures need also to be seen against the background of other literary environments, other forms of writing, and other readers.

Further activities

1   In this chapter, attractors are presented as stylistic-psychological features determined by factors such as: gestalt unity, thematised syntactic position, motion, discourse deviance, brightness, wilfulness and animation, marked prominent size and orientation, temporal and spatial precedence, and emergence from the ground. Taking a short, manageable text (such as a very short story or sonnet, for example), try to track your own distractions through your reading process. Do your decisions on which parts of the text work as attractors match up with other readers? Using your chosen text, can you develop a cline of distraction out of this list of features, from *most distracting* to *least distracting*? Does this cline work when applied to other literary texts?

2   Cognitive poetics as presented in this book confines itself to literary texts and matters of language. However, adaptations of cognitive science should also work in other artforms. How might the notions of *attention*, *attractors*, *distraction*, *neglect*, and *occlusion* work in theatrical performance or cinema, or in non-verbal art such as dance, painting, sculpture, gardening, architecture, and music?

3   This chapter draws together some aspects of figuration that actually span different dimensions of cognitive linguistic theory. Langacker's (1987, 1995) three principles of cognition are touched on here: *prominence*, which is taken to be the cognitive processing of the stylistic surface; *specificity*, which involves schematised expectations and norm-recognition; and *perspective*, or viewing arrangement. (These correspond quite neatly, respectively, with Halliday's (1994) *textual*, *ideational* and *interpersonal* metafunctions.) You could explore these relations further. Taking a longer text, such as a short story or a novel, use the notion of readerly attention as set out in this chapter to consider how stylistic foregrounding (prominence) relates to point of view (perspective); or how schematic disruptions (specificity) are made textually prominent in stylistic terms.

3 Prototypes in dynamic meaning construal

Raymond W. Gibbs, Jr

Editors' preface

This chapter is the first of two in this collection to be written by a cognitive psychologist, rather than by an author whose central interests are based in either cognitive linguistics or cognitive poetics. Here, Raymond W. Gibbs, Jr discusses the role of prototypes in the construction of meaning and presents some significant challenges to accepted thought on readers' use of their existing knowledge during the reading process. Gibbs suggests that, contrary to popular belief, prototypes are not fixed mental representations of generalised experiences but are dynamic and creatively composed structures, fundamentally based on immediate, individual contexts. His argument forms a provocative counterpoint to the summary and application of prototype theory put forward by Stockwell (2002a: ch.3). Read alongside Gerard Steen's analysis of cognitive scenarios in love poetry in Chapter 6 and Peter Crisp's discussion of conceptual metaphor in Chapter 8, this chapter also provides a further fascinating insight into the cognitive psychology of literary reading.

Prototypes in dynamic meaning construal

Reading is a skilled activity that relies on familiar knowledge and flexible, adaptive responses to novel situations. Consider what a reader must know to understand the following two passages from different works of literature. The first comes from Anne Dillard's *Pilgrim at Tinker Creek* (1971) and depicts a narrator undergoing a personal journey that is described in a series of images in nature. As the narrator says early on in the novel, 'I am an explorer, and I am also a stalker, or the instrument of the hunt itself' (Dillard 1971: 13). Later on, the narrator describes one special moment of personal revelation:

> ... one day I was walking along Tinker Creek thinking of nothing at all and I saw the tree with the lights in it. I saw the backyard cedar where the mourning doves roost charged and transfigured, each cell buzzing with

flame. I stood on the grass with the lights in it, grass that was wholly fire, utterly focused and utterly dreamed. It was less like seeing than like being for the first time seen, knocked breathless by a powerful glance. The flood of fire abated, but I'm still spending the power. Gradually the lights went out in the cedar, the colors died, the cells unflamed and disappeared. I was still ringing, I had my whole life as a bell, and never knew it until at that moment I was lifted and struck.

(Dillard 1971: 35)

Dillard's imagery shows how the narrator learned to enjoy the flow of experience, and a feeling of being at one with the world. In a different way, the narrator in Anaïs Nin's *House of Incest* (1958) describes her own personal awakening with an image of a woman dancing wildly and alone, yet also at one with all things in the world:

She looked at her hands tightly closed and opened them slowly, opened them completely like Christ; she opened them in a gesture of abandon and giving; she relinquished and forgave, opening her arms and her hands; permitting all things to flow away and beyond her ... And she danced; she danced with the music and with the rhythm of earth's circles; she turned with the earth turning, like a disk, turning all face to light and to darkness evenly, dancing towards daylight.

(Nin 1958: 70–1)

Similar to the narrator in Dillard's novel, Nin's imagery expresses her sense of personal transformation which is both sensual and ecstatic. Readers of these two passages cannot help but appreciate each person's joy at the poetic understanding of their new place in the world.

Our ability to understand these passages depends on us having various kinds of knowledge. Few readers are likely to have experienced the exact same detailed sensations that are described in these two literary passages. Yet skilled readers are somehow able to construct poetic understandings of these texts, despite not having the same personal experiences. How does this happen?

Scholars frequently assume that readers understand texts through the activation of relevant, abstract knowledge (e.g. Emmott 1997; Kintsch 1998). This knowledge is typically viewed as prototypical mental representations that are abstract, disembodied, symbolic, and explicitly part of our internal cognitive structures. One of the most important of these structures is *prototypes*, which are abstract concepts constructed from typical attributes of the many concrete exemplars for that concept. For example, we presumably use our prototypical knowledge of walks in nature to comprehend the woman's revelation in Dillard's novel, and access our prototypes for dancing in interpreting the meaning of Nin's work. Skilled readers not only employ their prototypes to understand what is familiar in texts, but use prototypes to make sense of novel aspects of situations and experiences.

My aim in this chapter is to suggest that the above view of meaning construal as dependent upon the access of pre-stored prototypes is incorrect. Understanding literary texts, similar to any act of meaning construal, is not a matter of accessing highly structured knowledge, in the form of abstract prototypes, from long-term memory. Instead, text understanding is a dynamic activity that relies on concrete, often embodied information, which people creatively compose in the moment of reading. This view of meaning construction allows for the flexibility needed to interpret novel events and language.

The idea of prototypes

Readers surely apply their knowledge of relevant concepts when interpreting texts. The classic view of concepts claims that each concept is uniquely defined by a set of abstract necessary and sufficient conditions. But empirical work in cognitive psychology showed that a 'family resemblance' principle offered a better account than did the classical model for how people identify an instance as belonging or not to a category, or how typical an instance is of a category. For example, sparrows are closer to the prototypical bird for Americans than are penguins or ostriches and this makes it easier for people to verify a statement such as 'A sparrow is a bird' than 'A penguin is a bird' (Rosch 1975; Rosch and Mervis 1975). Such findings are not simply due to some exemplars being more common than others, because even rare instances of a category may be closer to the prototype than more frequent examples. Thus, people rate rare items of furniture such as 'love seat', 'davenport', and 'cedar chest' as being better exemplars of the category 'furniture' than they do frequently-encountered objects such as 'refrigerator' (Rosch 1975). These prototype effects observed for concrete objects have also been found with a variety of other kinds of domains including action-based concepts, artistic style, emotion terms, medical diagnosis, and person perception, to name just a few (see Gibbs 1994). These effects are also observed in the study of linguistic phenomena in phonology, syntax, and semantics (Taylor 1989).

Prototype theories mostly assume that concepts are context-independent. For instance, the concept of 'fire' is presumably an abstract representation that arises from all concrete instances of how fires are understood in specific contexts. Yet typicality judgements often vary as a function of context (Roth and Shoben 1983). 'Tea' is judged to be a more typical beverage than 'milk' in the context of secretaries taking a break, but the opposite is true for the context of truck drivers taking a break. 'Birds' that are typical from an American point of view, such as robins and eagles, are atypical from the point of view of an average Chinese citizen (Barsalou and Medin 1986). These findings suggest that prototypes are closely tied to individual contexts and are not necessarily abstract representations that emerge from specific instances of any concept.

Basic-level categories

A related set of findings on prototypes from cognitive psychology concerns the organisation of concepts into categories. Concepts and categories are not defined by their relations to objects in the external world. A traditional view of the concept 'chair', for instance, sees it as existing in the middle of a hierarchy of concepts, each defined by a list of objective properties. The fact that 'chair' falls into the middle level of the hierarchy is regarded as being simply a result of the objective fact that chairs are types of furniture, and that more specific kinds of chairs (e.g. rocking chairs) have additional properties not shared by all chairs. These 'facts' are seen as directly reflecting the nature of things in the world.

But cognitive science research shows this traditional view to be quite wrong (Rosch 1975; Lakoff 1987; Taylor 1989). Certain cognitive categories in the middle of taxonomic hierarchies have special properties that can only be explained in terms of human embodiment. Thus, chairs are distinguished from higher-level concepts, such as furniture (i.e. a superordinate category), and from lower-level instances such as rocking chairs (i.e. a subordinate category), by virtue of our brains, bodies, and minds. This is due to a variety of reasons (Lakoff 1987):

1   the highest level at which category members have similarly perceived overall shapes. For example, you can recognise a chair by its overall shape. But there is no overall shape that you can assign to a generalised piece of furniture so that you could recognise the category from the shape.
2   the highest level at which a single mental image can represent the entire category. You can form a mental image of a chair. You can get mental images of opposing categories at this level, such as tables and beds. But you cannot get a mental image of a general piece of furniture that is not some particular of furniture, such as a table or bed.
3   the highest level at which a person uses similar motor actions for interacting with category members. People have motor programmes for interacting with objects at the basic level – interacting with chairs, tables, and beds. There are no motor programmes for interacting with generalised pieces of furniture.
4   the level at which most of our knowledge is organised. Think of all that you know about cars versus what you know about vehicles. You know a handful of things about vehicles, but a huge number of things about cars. It is at the basic level that most of our useful information and knowledge is organised.

This evidence explains why the basic level has priority over the superordinate and subordinate levels. Many scholars assume that basic level categories reflect prototypical knowledge. But most importantly, the basic level is the level at which people interact optimally with their environment, given the kinds of bodies and brains that they have and the environments they inhabit. These facts can only be explained in terms of human embodiment, and suggest another reason to question whether prototypes are abstract, pre-existing conceptual representations.

Problems with prototype theory

Despite the great appeal of prototypes in theories of categorisation, there are several problems with the traditional view of prototypes. For instance, proto-type theory assumes that category membership is determined by whether some candidate is sufficiently similar to the prototype or a set of already represented examples where similarity is based on matches and mismatches of inde-pendent, equally abstract features. Yet similarity does not explain many kinds of prototype effects. Thus, goal-derived categories, such as 'foods to eat while on a diet' and 'things to take on a camping trip', reveal the same typicality effects as do other categories (Barsalou 1983, 1985, 1989 and 1991). But the basis for these effects is not similarity to some prototype, but rather simi-larity to an ideal. For instance, typicality ratings for the category of things to eat while on a diet are determined by how clearly each example conforms to the ideal of zero calories. Thus, real world knowledge is used to reason about or explain properties, not simply to match them to some pre-existing, abstract prototype. Even though categories such as 'things to take on a camping trip' have prototypic structure, such a structure does not exist in advance because the category is *ad hoc* and not conventional.

One reason cognitive scientists mostly assume that both concepts and word meanings are pre-existing mental structures is because they commit the 'effects = structures' fallacy (Lakoff 1987; Gibbs and Matlock 1999). This fallacy reflects the belief that the goodness-of-example ratings, for example, obtained in psychological experiments are a direct reflection of degree of cat-egory membership. Categories are assumed to be explicitly represented in the mind in terms of prototypes and that degree of category membership is deter-mined by degree of similarity to the prototype. But the 'effects = structures' interpretation cannot account for many of the types of data reviewed above, especially the problems of complex categorisation (Gibbs 1994). In fact, many kinds of prototype effects can be explained by other principles that do not assume that the effects obtained in experiments reflect the structure of pre-existing knowledge.

Much research points to the flexibility of concepts. One set of studies asked people to provide definitions for categories, such as *bachelor*, *bird*, and *chair* (Barsalou 1993). An analysis of the overlap in the features participants pro-vided for a given category revealed that only 47 per cent of the features in one person's definitions for a category existed in another individual's definition. A great deal of flexibility also exists within individuals when asked to provide definitions for concepts. When participants in the above study returned two weeks later and defined the same categories again, only 66 per cent of the features noted in the first session were produced again in the second session. These results indicate that substantial flexibility exists in how a person conceptualises the same category on different occasions (Barsalou 1993).

The significant flexibility shown by many experiments on defining categories arises not from differences in knowledge, but from differences in the retrieval of this knowledge from long-term memory. On different occasions, different individuals retrieve different subsets of features from their extensive knowledge of a category. In the same way, an individual may retrieve different aspects of his or her knowledge of a category on different occasions. For instance, the statement 'The Christmas bird fed 12 people' makes encyclopaedic information about turkeys and geese most accessible, while seabirds would be most accessible given a statement like 'The bird followed the boat out to sea'. This suggests a view of prototypical concepts as temporary constructions in working memory constructed on the spot from generic and episodic information in long-term memory, rather than as stable structures stored in long-term memory.

The next two sections explore two ideas about prototypical representations (*conceptual metaphors* and *scripts*) often viewed as essential to linguistic and non-linguistic understanding. I argue that both of these theoretical notions are not pre-existing conceptual structures activated during text understanding, but are both created during dynamic meaning construal.

Are conceptual metaphors prototypes?

A significant theory in cognitive poetics is that people make sense of their experience, and understand many aspects of language, through their knowledge of conceptual metaphors (Lakoff 1987; Gibbs 1994). For example, readers may understand parts of the passage from Anne Dillard's novel (see pp.27–8) in terms of a common metaphor LIFE IS A JOURNEY. Under this view, people create conceptual metaphors given their embodied experiences of different kinds of journeys which they use to structure more abstract knowledge domains, such as life. The LIFE IS A JOURNEY metaphor provides a kind of prototypical concept to understand poetic descriptions, such as when the narrator in Dillard's novel talks of her walk along Tinker Creek in terms of being suddenly 'lifted and struck' by the tree she saw with lights and the 'grass that was wholly burning'. The conceptual metaphor provides an abstract framework to interpret this passage as referring not only to a specific walk along a creek, but more importantly, as a significant, transformative moment in the narrator's journey through life.

Conceptual metaphors as prototypical representations are assumed to exist as enduring knowledge structures in long-term memory and are critical to the content of everyday concepts. Yet cognitive psychologists are often sceptical of this claim, primarily because they doubt whether linguistic evidence alone can reveal much about human conceptual systems (Murphy

1996). One instance of this scepticism about metaphors as conceptual proto-types is seen in the problem of multiple metaphors (Murphy 1996; Gibbs 1996). According to cognitive linguistics analyses, the concept of love, for example, can be understood through several different metaphors (e.g. LOVE IS A JOURNEY, LOVE IS INSANITY, LOVE IS AN OPPONENT, LOVE IS A VALUABLE COMMODITY). The entailments of these different metaphors vary in certain respects. Thus, LOVE IS A JOURNEY refers to the structure of a love relation-ship over time, whereas LOVE IS AN OPPONENT personifies love as an oppo-nent against whom we often struggle. These different metaphors appear, at times, to be inconsistent with one another and it is unclear how to resolve such inconsistencies in the mental representation for our concept of love.

This argument preserves a view of concepts as monolithic entities that should be internally consistent. But the so-called problem of multiple meta-phors for concepts can be easily handled if we view these prototypical con-cepts not as fixed, static structures, but as temporary representations that are dynamic and context-dependent. The LOVE IS A JOURNEY metaphor may better reflect a particular conceptualisation of love in certain situations, while LOVE IS AN OPPONENT may arise in forming a concept for love in other situa-tions. These alternative ways of thinking about human concepts allow, even encourage, the use of multiple metaphors to access different aspects of our rich knowledge about love to differentially conceptualise these experiences at vari-ous moments. Each metaphoric construal of a concept in some context results in a concept that is independent as a temporary representation apart from source domain information in long-term memory. My suggestion, then, is that conceptual metaphors may not pre-exist in the sense of continually structuring specific conceptual domains. But conceptual metaphors may be used to access different knowledge on different occasions as people immediately conceptual-ise some abstract target domain given a particular task. Conceptual metaphors may also simply emerge as the product of conceptualising processes, rather than serve as the underlying cause of these processes (Gibbs 1999).

Prototypes as scripts in text understanding

When people read literary texts, like Dillard's and Nin's above, they presum-ably activate their knowledge of the activities normally associated with walking in nature and dancing to fill in the gaps to make the narratives coherent. This type of knowledge, called 'scripts' (Schank and Abelson 1977), consists of well-learned scenarios describing structured situations in everyday life. To comprehend the above narratives, readers must first decide what script is relevant and how it should be modified to fit the situation at hand. Many studies show that readers automatically infer appropriate script-related actions when these are not explicitly stated (Bower *et al.* 1979; Gibbs and Tenney 1980; Graesser *et al.* 1980; Abbott *et al.* 1985). Other experiments reveal that prior activation of script-based knowledge provides readers with a highly available set of causal connections that can facilitate sentence-by-sentence integration (Bower *et al.* 1979; Sanford and Garrod 1981; Garrod and Sanford 1985; Seifert *et al.* 1985; Sharkey and Sharkey 1987).

One difficulty with the idea of script-based narrative understanding is that these categorisations are often too rigid to accommodate variations from what may be typically expected. For example, we do not usually have a 'walking in nature and having a personal revelation' script. A solution to this problem assumes that scripts 'do not exist in memory as precompiled chunks' (Schank 1982: 16). Instead, the different parts of a script may be reconstructed depending on the context.

There are two kinds of high-level processing mechanisms that allow us to create the right script at the right time during text understanding: *memory organisation packets* (MOPs) and *thematic organisation packets* (TOPs) (Schank 1982; Hidalgo Downing 2000). MOPs are processing structures that allow people to relate new information with existing expectations to generate reasonable predictions about future events.

TOPs are related to MOPs, but are specifically abstractions that allow people to establish connections between different events and discover similarities between them. Thus, reading *West Side Story* may remind us of *Romeo and Juliet* because of the similarity between their goals (e.g. mutual goal pursuit), conditions (e.g. outside opposition), and specific features (e.g. young lovers, false report of death). In this way, TOPs are not static memory representations of abstract prototypical categories, but are processing capabilities that allow readers to be creative in their understandings of events, such as those encountered in literary texts.

One analysis of the American novel *Catch-22* (Heller 1961) demonstrates the power of MOPs and TOPs to provide coherence to disparate texts (Hidalgo Downing 2000). *Catch-22* is the story of an American bombardier squadron during World War II on an imaginary island, Pianosa, off the coast of Italy. The novel describes, often quite humorously, the contradictions and absurdities of war and America's military-industrial power in the twentieth century. Consider one excerpt from the novel:

> Sharing a tent with a man who was crazy wasn't easy, but Nately didn't care. He was crazy, too, and had gone every free day to work on the officers' club that Yossarian had not helped build. Actually, there were many officers' clubs that Yossarian had not helped build, but he was proudest of the one on Pianosa. It was a sturdy and complex monument to his powers of determination. Yossarian never went there to help until it was finished – then he went there often, so pleased was he with the large, fine, rambling, shingled building. It was truly a splendid structure, and Yossarian throbbed with a mighty sense of accomplishment each time he gazed at it and reflected that none of the work that had gone into it was his.
>
> (Heller 1961: 28)

This excerpt illustrates an incompatibility between two MOPS: 'help build officer club' and 'refuse to cooperate'. But Nately simultaneously holds both these conflicting beliefs and does so with great pride. This contradiction differs from our usual expectation that people feel pride when they actually do something to achieve a goal. But readers resolve this contradiction by creating a meta-MOP 'Pride' where the prototype and the expectations usually associated with it are not fulfilled. In this way, readers 'soft-assemble' a new concept with its own prototypical structure.

This analysis does not, however, explain why the reader perceives this passage from Heller's novel as funny and informative. But TOPs are useful for this purpose, because they establish connections between apparently unconnected schemas. Thus, readers of the above passage must draw a novel connection between two war situations: one where an officer's club is built, another where cooperation with the enemy takes place. Readers do this by creating an analogy between competing with the enemy and cooperating in the building of an officer's club. Both events are then perceived as thematically related and negative. This analogy between the enemy and the higher officers reflects a parallelism that is recurrent in the novel and is explicitly pointed out by Yossarian when he says 'The enemy is anybody who is going to get you killed, no matter what side he's on'.

The incongruity of this analogy helps account for the humorous nature of Yossarian's predicament. Although cooperating with the enemy is a very serious matter – or to put it in other words, it is something important – building an officers' club, by comparison, is a trivial matter. Understanding this specific theme is representative of a broader theme repeated throughout the novel, where trivial situations reveal a more dramatic background.

This analysis of one portion of the novel *Catch-22* (offered by Hidalgo Downing 2000) demonstrates the adaptive character of many aspects of text understanding. Skilled readers do not comprehend texts by simply activating pre-existing prototypes in the form of scripts. Instead, prototypical understandings arise as the products of dynamic meaning construction processes (in this case through the interaction of MOPs and TOPs).

There are other reasons to doubt whether people activate pre-stored prototypical knowledge, like scripts, when understanding texts. Most prototype event sequences (e.g. the events that occur at a restaurant) are typically part of common knowledge within a given culture. However, routinised sequences of events can also be quite idiosyncratic. For example, my friend John regularly gets up at 5.30 a.m., drinks a glass of tomato juice, puts out the cat, and goes jogging. When he finishes running, John puts on the coffee, shaves, brushes his teeth, and sits down to read seventeenth-century English poetry. Although John engages in this sequence of events each day, the sequence is unlikely to be performed by anyone but him. In fact, John's wife has her own morning script and engages in behaviours quite different from her husband.

Do people form person-specific prototypes that are then used to comprehend new experiences that exemplify them? One may believe that prototypes for the self and well-known others' actions may be the most enduring
scripts, given that they are continually embodied in everyday life. My argument has been, however, that prototypes of any type need not necessarily
be pre-existing mental representations that get activated to facilitate processing of related events. In fact, research shows that when individuals read
descriptions of events that pertain to themselves or to a familiar other (i.e. a
parent or room-mate), they do not activate a prototypical representation of
the behaviour in interpreting these events (Colcombe and Wyer 2001). This
is true regardless of whether the sequence is similar to one that they personally experience or observe on a daily basis, or whether it exemplifies a more
general prototype of the events that occur in a particular type of situation
(e.g. cashing a cheque). Thus, even if a prototype sequence of events (i.e. a
script) exists in memory and is used to comprehend the behaviour of unfamiliar persons, individuals do not apply it when comprehending events that
pertain to themselves or someone with whom they are familiar. These
recent research findings suggest, at the very least, that people do not form
abstract representations for the most familiar event sequences they experience in daily life.

Embodied text understanding

The research described above suggests that people's recurring embodied
experiences, such as that associated with one's morning routine, are not used
as stored representations in text understanding. But several psychologists
contend that readers use their embodied abilities to immediately create
construals of the different perspectives, and shifts of perspective, of the
objects and actions described by language (MacWhinney 1998).

Consider the sentence 'As far as the eye could see, stalks of corn were
bending as waves under the battering force of a surging curtain of rain'
(MacWhinney 1998). How might readers construct a meaningful interpretation of this sentence? One could argue that readers comprehend this sentence
by simply creating a picture of heavy rain pouring down on a large corn field.
But this characterisation underdetermines the embodied richness of what
people normally understand from this sentence. A more embodied view of
understanding claims that readers adopt different perspectives to make sense
of the complex actions described in the sentence. Thus, readers might first
adopt the perspective of 'the eye' and imagine scanning the scene from the
foreground to the horizon. This spatial perspective provides an interpretation of the phrase 'As far as the eye can see'. The spatial perspective required
to imagine 'stalks of corn' necessitates a shift from our point of view as readers to enable us to understand the corn stalks to be a distributed figure
located across the vast ground. Readers next view the stalks as bending,
which arises from the secondary spatial perspective suggested by 'under the

battering force', and then elaborated upon by the shift of perspective to the 'surging curtains of rain'. Each perspective shift, therefore, is guided by specific words, like 'as far as' and 'under'. In general, people's embodied comprehension of this sentence requires a shift across four perspectives: 'eyes', 'stalks of corn', 'battering force', and 'curtains of rain'. Note that the syntactic form of the sentence, emphasising 'corn' as the subject responding to an external force, shapes the dynamic character of sentence processing as a series of embodied perspective shifts.

Consider now a different sentence, this one with a metaphorical content: 'Casting furtive glances at the seamstress, he wormed his way into her heart' (MacWhinney 1998). Readers first adopt the perspective of the implied subject and imagine him casting glances at the seamstress. After this, readers shift to the subject's embodied action of worming (i.e. moving as if a worm), yet soon recognise that the action here is not literal but metaphorical in the sense of the subject trying to place himself inside the seamstress's heart. Even here, readers soon comprehend that by metaphorically inserting himself into the seamstress's heart, he has really placed himself closer to the seamstress's emotions and affections. The embodied action of worming, again, suggests a slow, deliberate process of becoming emotionally closer to the seamstress, which she implicitly accepts, allowing the suitor to enter into her affections. The different spatial perspectives readers adopt as they comprehend the sentence gives rise to a rich, embodied interpretation.

This approach to language understanding argues that people create meaningful construals by simulating how the objects and actions depicted in language relate to embodied possibilities. Thus, people use their embodied experiences to 'soft-assemble' meaning, rather than merely activate pre-existing abstract, prototypical conceptual representations.

Empirical research also indicates that readers use spatial perspective to construct mental models of narrative texts. One study asked participants to first memorise the layout of unnamed rooms in a building, along with objects in the rooms (Morrow *et al.* 1989). Afterwards, participants read a story describing a person's movements throughout the building. At various points when reading the story, participants were asked to judge the location of specific objects. The results showed that people were quicker to make these judgements when the objects were located in rooms visited by the protagonist. Thus, participants constructed a spatial model of the narrative by adopting the embodied perspective of the person in the story, and not by simply creating an objective sketch of the rooms and the objects in them.

There is other work showing that readers construct mental models for narrative by adopting the perspective of the protagonist. Participants in one study read texts describing a protagonist and a target item, such as a jogger and sweatshirt (Glenberg *et al.* 1987). The protagonist and target item in one experimental condition were spatially linked (e.g. the jogger put on the sweatshirt before jogging), while in a different condition the two were dissociated (e.g. the jogger took off the sweatshirt before jogging). After reading the main part of the story, participants judged whether they earlier read the word 'sweatshirt'. The results showed that people were faster to make this judgement in the linked, or associated, condition than when the protagonist and target were dissociated. Thus, readers appear to create mental models for narrative in which spatial information (e.g. the location of the sweatshirt) is tied to the story's characters and their embodied actions.

The claim that embodiment underlies people's understanding of language is more fully developed in the 'indexical hypothesis' (Glenberg 1997 and 1999; Glenberg and Robertson 2000). This view assumes that three major steps occur when language is understood in context. First, words and phrases are indexed to objects in the environment or to perceptual symbols in long-term memory. Second, the affordances structures (i.e. the possible actions that can be done to an object by a person) are derived for each object in the situation. Third, the listener must combine or 'mesh' the affordances according to the constraints on embodied possibilities in the real world. For instance, the affordances of a chair include those of sitting on, or using to hold off a snarling lion, but they cannot ordinarily be meshed with the goal of propelling oneself across a room. This constraint on the meshing of embodied affordances predicts that people will have an easier time understanding a sentence like 'Art used the chair to defend himself against the snarling lion' than to interpret the sentence 'Art used the chair to propel himself across the room'. Some empirical work shows that the indexical hypothesis does an excellent job explaining different aspects of linguistic interpretation (Glenberg 1999; Glenberg and Robertson 2000). These psycholinguistic findings highlight the importance of perceptual, embodied information when people create meaningful construals of narrative texts.

Implications

My claim that prototypes are not abstract, pre-existing conceptual structures, but are better understood as products of meaning construal, has several implications for cognitive poetics. First, the process of linguistic interpretation takes on a different character from what was previously understood. Instead of assuming that language activates fixed prototypical conceptual representations, language serves as an immediate pointer to encyclopaedic knowledge from which conceptual meanings are created 'on the fly', or as an *ad-hoc* comprehension process. This view provides a much reduced role (or even no role) for what is traditionally thought to be 'semantics', as language comprehension immediately makes use of enriched pragmatic knowledge that is readily available for interpreting context-sensitive meaning. Task demands, expectations about genre, and previously understood utterances in context, all function to constrain the process of accessing relevant encyclopaedic information to create meaningful interpretations of what speakers/writers say and implicate.

A related implication of this view is that linguistic interpretation, such as that required for skilled reading, is fundamentally adaptive to the moment-to-moment dynamics that arise in any interpretive situation. Meaning construal exhibits a degree of flexibility not seen in traditional prototype models. Under the traditional view, comprehension is focused around the process of computing the degree of similarity between what is heard or read and pre-existing prototypes. The result of that comparison process is thought to drive people's intuitions of the novel, creative, even poetic, nature of any piece of language. Yet the new view of prototypes advocated here suggests no need to compare linguistic information with prototypical representations, at least as a first step in linguistic interpretation. Judgements of novelty are a product of understanding, and do not serve as input to slower-developing processes of resolving differences between an abstract prototype and some text. Thus, readers may recognise that a particular interpretation of some text, or even its linguistic form, varies from what they typically know about that genre (e.g. a poem, a mystery story, a scientific report). But that judgement rests on a reader being reminded of previous texts, perhaps normally associated with that genre, rather than judging what has just been understood against some abstract prototype for a genre that serves as part of the basis for constructing meaningful interpretations of what was read. Of course, the judgement that a text is unusual or novel within some genre may alter readers' ultimate judgements about what they have read, and may shape their reinterpretations of a text.

Finally, my argument that prototypes are products of understanding also suggests that linguistic interpretation is significantly based on embodied possibilities. For instance, our understanding that some concepts are 'basic' is not dependent on abstract features, but is grounded in the ways people perceptually/kinaesthetically interact with objects and events in the world. Meaning construal does not simply result in an internal representation of some text for archival purposes, but prepares people for situated action (Barsalou 1999). Under this view, meaning construal is not a matter of understanding what words mean, but includes how language evokes the perception of physical objects, physical events, the body, and other people in interaction. The meaningful representation of language includes both a depiction of what has happened and potential perceptions and embodied actions that may take place in the future. Linguistic meaning, therefore, is inherently embodied, not only in the sense of what has happened, but in the sense of what is likely to occur next in a discourse situation. An embodied view of narrative understanding, for example, gives a far better account of why readers experience a visceral 'feeling' for what they have read than does the idea that interpretation depends on activating abstract prototypes. In this way, an embodied view of meaning construal nicely captures at least some of what people see as poetic during their reading experiences.

Further activities

1   You may wish to give some more thought to the claims made in this chapter about the fundamental connection between prototypes and immediate context. Consider novels written within a particular literary genre: detective fiction or romance novels, for instance. How much do you think your reading of such texts depends on the words on the page in front of you and how much on your previous experiences of similar texts?

2   There has been some discussion here of the use of multiple conceptual metaphors for a single domain of human experience, such as love. To explore this phenomenon further, examine a themed collection of poetry. How many different conceptual metaphors can you identify at work in, say, a dozen, love, war or city poems? Why do you think the author of each separate poem has chosen one particular metaphor over another?

3   Examine the opening paragraphs of three or four novels that you consider to be heavily descriptive in some way. Can you identify points at which the perspective you have on the unfolding scene shifts or changes? Is there a particular character who forms the central embodied experience through which your focus is filtered, or is the perspective floating and disembodied? Compare the effects of a text in which the former is the case with one in which the latter perspective is created.

4 Deixis and abstractions
Adventures in space and time

Reuven Tsur

Editors' preface

Reuven Tsur's pivotal role in the development of cognitive poetics was initially secured in the 1970s, when he became one of the first academics to apply the findings of cognitive science to the analysis of literary texts. He has continued to write and research in this area prolifically ever since and here presents an analysis of the deictic texture of poetry by Shakespeare, Marvell and Wordsworth, as well as by the Hebrew poets Nathan Alterman and Abraham Shlonsky. This challenging chapter makes use of cognitive-scientific knowledge about activity in the right and left sides of the brain to throw further light on the initial responses of students to particular literary texts. The latter sections of the chapter then go on to provide a detailed examination of the treatment of time in poetry.

Deixis and abstractions

Adventures in space and time

This article tells the tale of my adventures with a special verbal structure in poetry: deixis combined with abstract nouns. *Deixis* is the pointing or specifying function of some words (as definite articles and demonstrative pronouns), tense and a variety of other grammatical and lexical features whose denotation changes from one discourse to another. When one says *I*, or *here*, or *now*, the denotation of these words depends on who the speaker is, and where or when he or she is speaking. By the same token, *there* and *then*, the antonyms of *here* and *now*, change their denotations too. Deixis instructs the reader to construct from the verbal material a situation in which such denotations are pertinent. My adventures began in the late 1960s with a poem called 'Shepherd', by the Hebrew poet Abraham Shlonsky:

1   This width, that is spreading its nostrils.
     This height that is yearning for you.
     The light flowing with the whiteness of milk.
     And the smell of wool,
     And the smell of bread.

A more sophisticated version I found in a poem by another great Hebrew poet (of the same school), Nathan Alterman:

2   This night.
   The estrangement of these walls.
   A war of silences, breast to breast.
   The cautious life
   Of the tallow candle.

When I read such poetic texts, I have an intense sensation. As a teacher, I had here two problems. First, how can I explain with words the nature of this sensation? Second, how can I make my students *feel* this sensation, not merely repeat my words? To this end, I have developed the following teaching strategy. I tell my students: 'Say about this stanza [or line] anything you feel relevant'. I ask no guiding questions. Since it is sometimes difficult to suppress some response of assent, I add 'Whenever I say "yes", it means that I have understood, not necessarily that I agree'. At some point they begin to produce responses that witness to perceptions similar to mine.

   At first, most students point out that 'there is an intense emotional atmosphere' in both stanzas. 'In excerpt 2 the phrase "A war of silences, breast to breast" suggests the presence of some persons facing each other, who are hostile and don't talk'; 'In this verse line attention is directed away from the persons to the atmosphere'; 'Walls with no decoration may be very unfriendly'; 'The phrase "The estrangement of these walls" shifts attention from the walls to the estranged atmosphere in the room'. Other relevant responses include such suggestions as 'The words evoke [or represent, or can be construed as] some coherent scene'; 'The concrete nouns *Shepherd, wool, bread* in excerpt 1, and *walls, breast to breast,* and *candle* in excerpt 2 give some vague clues for a reconstruction of the physical situation'; 'The deictic devices *this* and *these* have to do with the generation of a coherent scene'; 'The deictic devices suggest that there is some perceiving "I" in the middle of the situation'; 'The line "This height that is yearning for you" reinforces the presence of such a perceiving self'; 'The verb *yearning* charges the abstraction with energy, and turns it into some active, invisible presence'; 'There are many abstract nouns in this stanza'; 'All the sentences of this stanza are elliptic'. Sometimes there is even some suggestion that 'the elliptic sentences have here a deictic function: they point to the percepts of the immediate situation'. '*Width* and *height* are pure geometrical dimensions; but here they are somehow emotionally charged'. When encouraged to provide further responses, you may hear such comments as 'as if the emotional atmosphere were thick'; 'I feel as if I were plunged in this thick atmosphere'. Some of those who report the latter feeling say that they feel some faint tactile sensation all over their skin; some others, on the contrary, that the boundary between their body and this thick texture was suspended.

Two unusual grammatical structures are conspicuous in these two excerpts. The first one concerns the noun that occurs in the referring position (that is, the noun denoting that of which something is predicated). The normal, 'unmarked', syntactic structure of such constructions would be that concrete, 'spatio-temporally continuous particulars' as 'bread', 'wool', 'walls', 'candle' occur in the referring position (Strawson 1967). (By 'spatio-temporally continuous particulars' Strawson means objects that are continuous in space, and if you go away and come back they stay unchanged.) Such more abstract or more general qualities as 'whiteness', 'smell', 'estrangement', should occur as attributes or predicates, e.g. 'the white milk', or 'the milk is white'; 'the smelling wool', or 'the wool has smell', or 'the wool smells'; 'the estranged walls', or 'the walls are estranged'. In these two excerpts, the adjectives are systematically turned into abstract nouns, and the abstract nouns are manipulated into the referring position instead of the spatio-temporally continuous particulars. (I have called such transformations *topicalised attributes*.) Thus, in these two excerpts, not the concrete objects, but their attributes that have no stable characteristic visual shapes are manipulated into the focus of the perceiving consciousness. Such transformations are quite characteristic of poetry that displays some intense, dense emotionally-charged atmosphere. In everyday life and language we do not usually distinguish between physical objects and their attributes (or perceptual qualities). When we perceive (or speak of) the one, we are inclined automatically to identify it with the other. But the two are far from identical. One of the tasks of the 'ABSTRACT of the CONCRETE' genitive phrases ('estrangement of these walls') may be to de-automatise the relationship between the attributes (or perceptual qualities) and the physical object.

The other conspicuous grammatical structure concerns elliptic sentences. Some of my students did discern in them a deictic element. This deictic element may have far-reaching poetic consequences. The function of an indicative predication is to *affect the beliefs* of the addressee, and to connect the utterance to extralinguistic reality (by suggesting 'it occurred'). A noun phrase without predication places some event (or state of affairs) at the disposal of one's *perception,* without affecting the addressee's beliefs or attitudes. If the phrase contains deixis it *may*, as we have seen, connect the utterance to extralinguistic reality, without affecting our beliefs.

Sequential and spatial processing

There is a problem concerning the use of words to convey emotions. Words refer to compact concepts but, apparently, they are capable of conveying diffuse perceptions and emotions. Even such words as 'emotion', or 'ecstasy' communicate only the compact concepts of emotion and ecstasy, not the diffuse mental processes. We have already seen that such verbal constructs as topicalised attributes may loosen the tight relationship between objects and their attributes, or percepts that convey them. That may be one technique for overcoming this problem. But all the foregoing examples suggested that the deixis too, and the immediate space to which it points, may have to do with rendering conceptual language more diffuse. This led me to ask what is it about space perception that may render an utterance diffuse. Eventually it led me to recent brain research (it was recent in the 1960s). Brain scientists claim that the two hemispheres of the human brain have different functions. The right hemisphere controls the left side of the body, while the left hemisphere controls its right side. But they differ in their mode of operation too. The left hemisphere is predominantly involved with analytic, logical thinking, especially in verbal and mathematical functions. Its mode of operation is primarily sequential. The right hemisphere, by contrast,

> seems specialized for holistic mentation. Its language ability is quite limited. This hemisphere is primarily responsible for our orientation in space, artistic endeavour, crafts, body image, recognition of faces. It processes information more diffusely than does the left hemisphere, and its responsibilities demand a ready integration of many inputs at once. If the left hemisphere can be termed analytic and sequential in its operation, then the right hemisphere is more holistic and relational, and more simultaneous in its mode of operation.
>
> (Ornstein 1975: 67–8)

> This mode of information-processing, too, would seem to underlie an 'intuitive' rather than 'intellectual' integration of complex entities.
>
> (Ornstein 1975: 95)

This is a very rough, imprecise characterisation of brain functions. But it may pinpoint the source of our problem. Such experiences as feelings, emotions, intuitions, and orientation are diffuse, global, non-sequential processes, and are related to the right hemisphere, whereas the words that refer to them do so *via* concepts that are compact, analytic, sequential, and are related to the left hemisphere. Telling about diffuse, global, illogical experiences becomes necessarily compact, analytic, logical. It is, however, the nature of the problem that also offers the nature of the poets' solution; and our discussion of excerpts 1 and 2 appears to supply a typical example of this solution. Since such global activities as emotions and spatial orientation both are intimately associated with the right hemisphere, one might surmise that in these excerpts the definite spatial setting may be an instrument for transferring part of the processing of the verbal message to the right hemisphere.

At least two kinds of information about semantic categories are stored in memory: the *names* of the categories and representations of their *properties*. In the course of normal speech we perceive the representations of these properties *categorically:* we do not perceive the semantic features (or meaning-components), but a single compact semantic entity which they constitute. Ornstein brings some convincing experimental evidence that when some memory image concerning spatial orientation is called up, the right hemisphere may be activated, even though one may be engaged in some verbal activity. 'Which direction a person gazes is affected by the question asked. If the question is verbal analytical (such as 'Divide 144 by 6, and multiply the answer by 7' or 'How do you spell "Mississippi"?'), more eye movements are made to the right than if the question involves spatial mentation (such as 'Which way does an Indian face on the nickel?') (Ornstein 1975: 77). When a landscape-description and certain stylistic devices transfer a significant part of the processing of the message to the right hemisphere of the brain, representations of some or many properties of these categories escape the control of categorical perception, and constitute some global, diffuse atmosphere in a concrete landscape. At the extreme of this technique, there may be no stable objects at all in the description, the concrete landscape being compellingly indicated by emphatic deictic devices only. In excerpts 1 and 2, the abstractions 'width', 'height', 'The light flowing with the whiteness of milk', 'smell', 'estrangement', and 'A war of silences' supply the intense, shape-free, fluid, diffuse input that is processed by the orientation mechanism. Hence the feeling of some thick, supersensuous texture engulfing the perceiving self.

There is no evidence in Ornstein's discussion for my conjecture concerning this effect of the orientation mechanism on poetic language. My rescue came from neuropsychological studies of religious experiences. A dominant purport of Ornstein's book is that meditation is related to the right hemisphere of the brain. During the past two years I have been engaged in a study of cognitive processes in religious and mystic poetry. I had recourse to the above conception of the orientation mechanism for the solution of another paradoxical state of affairs: some meditation involves voluntary switching to a state of consciousness in which voluntary control is relinquished. A few weeks ago I encountered some brain research that may support or refute this conception. Newberg, D'Aquili and Rause (2001) conducted a SPECT camera brain-imaging study (the acronym stands for Single Photon Emission Computed Tomography) of Tibetan meditators and Franciscan nuns at prayer. To my pleasant surprise, these researchers claim that what they call the 'orientation association area' (OAA) is 'extremely important in the brain's sense of mystical and religious experiences, which often involve altered perceptions of space and time, self and ego' (Newberg *et al.* 2001: 29). This would massively support my speculations based on the structure of literary texts, introspection, and earlier brain research. The brain scans taken at the peak of their subjects' meditative state, however, show a sharp reduction in the activity levels of the orientation area. These results prove that the orientation mechanism *is* involved; but the changes go opposite to the predicted direction. This was encouraging and dismaying for me, at the same time. But the authors, after gathering all the available information, came to a conclusion that lent, in fact, massive support to my hypothesis.

We know that the orientation area never rests, so what could account for this unusual drop in activity levels in this small section of the brain? As we pondered the question, a fascinating possibility emerged: What if the orientation area was working as hard as ever, but the incoming flow of sensory information had somehow been blocked? That would explain the drop in brain activity in the region.

(Newberg *et al.* 2001: 6)

Such an explanation seems consistent with our foregoing findings concerning a verbal structure that combines deixis with abstract nouns, or nouns denoting entities that have no characteristic visual shape. The deixis activates the orientation mechanism; but, instead of stable objects, it acts upon abstractions, or at least entities and qualities that are deprived of stable characteristic visual shapes. Not all subjects in this research were found to have a specific decrease in activity in the orientation area. One possible reason the researchers suggest is this: 'we were limited in this study by looking only at one time point of the meditation. It is possible that in the early stage of meditation there is actually an increase in activity in the orientation area while the subject begins his focus on a visualised object. Thus, we might capture the orientation area either increased, unchanged, or decreased depending on the stage of meditation the person was actually in' (Newberg *et al.* 2001: 176). Thus, even the conception that the abstractions serve as the rich unstable information processed by the orientation mechanism and may generate some thick, supersensuous texture engulfing the perceiving self is consistent with the findings of this neuropsychological research. We must assume that we are dealing with one of the earlier stages of this kind of information processing.

Time in poetry

Let us briefly explore now one of the most venerable abstractions in poetry, *time* with its subordinate nouns ('hyponyms'), and see whether they bear out, in changing contexts, the foregoing theoretical considerations. To answer this question, we have to make a few distinctions concerning the meaning of *time*, and then relate them to our foregoing cognitive considerations. *Time* may refer (a) to a sequence (a nonspatial continuum that is measured in terms of events which succeed one another from past through present to future), (b) to the principle of that sequence, or (c) to a specific point in that sequence (see Figure 4.1). In sense (a), *time* is a mass noun that refuses the indefinite article, but accepts the quantifier *some* (e.g. 'some time ago'); in sense (c), it is a count noun in accepting the definite and indefinite articles (e.g. 'this time', 'once upon a time'); in sense (b) it is usually considered as a mass noun; but, since it denotes a category that denotes a single generic principle, it resembles a proper name in uniquely referring to one referent only (it is quite frequently capitalised; see excerpts 4 and 8 below).

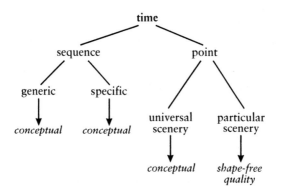

Figure 4.1 Time may refer to a sequence or to a specific point in that sequence. In some conditions the abstract noun tends to be perceived as a concept; in some as a shape-free perceptual quality.

Thus, both in sense (b) and (c) *time* is a singular term but whereas in sense (c) it is frequently individuated in a particular situation, in sense (b) it is necessarily considered as a general object, apart from special circumstances.

Thus, in sense (b) *time* has a somewhat ambiguous status: in some respects it is a mass noun (it could be paraphrased by 'duration'), in some respects it resembles a proper noun (in uniquely referring to one referent only). In several poems by Shakespeare and Marvell, this ambiguity is resolved in the direction of proper nouns, by attributing to *time* some characteristic visual shape and some visible, often violent action. In this way, *time* becomes a superpersonal agent. By 'superpersonal agent' I mean 'of the nature of an individual rational being', and 'of superhuman dimensions and power'. In this capacity, *time* features compact consciousness, definite will, patent purpose and so on. In light of our foregoing cognitive considerations, then, we might expect *time* in these instances to be nearer to the conceptual pole.

Since both sequence (of time) and purposeful actions (of a superpersonal agent) are 'linear, sequential', both time-as-a-sequence and time-as-a-generic-principle will tend to be perceived as compact concepts, intellectual abstractions. When *time* denotes a particular point in a sequence, part of a situation defined here-and-now, the abstraction may be related to spatial orientation, and perceived as a diffuse quality: a mood, an atmosphere. In such instances *time* has a double function: it defines the immediate situation in time, and provides the abstraction that is to be perceived in it as a diffuse entity (see, for instance, excerpt 9 below). Universal scenery (as in excerpt 6 below, for instance, where we do not know where and when it occurs) will reinforce general concepts, a particular immediate scene (located in space and time) will enhance shape-free quality. Conclusive statements, logical arguments, and clausal (verbal) syntactic structure tend to enhance the definable conceptual entity, whereas descriptive utterances, suspensive (non-conclusive) statements, and phrasal (nominal) syntactic structures tend to reinforce some mood or atmosphere, that is, elusive, sensuous *qualities*.

In some of the excerpts discussed below time generates some vague, diffuse atmosphere; and in some a compact concept or an allegorical representation thereof.

3   Those hours that with gentle work did frame
      The lovely gaze where every eye doth dwell,
      Will play the tyrants to the very same
      And that unfair which fairly doth excel:
      For never-resting time leads summer on
      To hideous winter and confounds him there [...]
                            (Shakespeare, Sonnet 5)

4   Devouring Time, blunt thou the lion's paws [...]
                            (Shakespeare, Sonnet 19)

5   Being your slave, what should I do but tend
      Upon the hours and times of your desire?
                            (Shakespeare, Sonnet 57)

6   Since brass, nor stone, nor earth, nor boundless sea,
      But sad mortality o'ersways their power,
      How with this rage shall beauty hold a plea
      Whose action is no stronger than a flower?
      O how shall summer's honey breath hold out
      Against the wreckful siege of battering days,
      When rocks impregnable are not so stout,
      Nor gates of steel so strong but Time decays?
                            (Shakespeare, Sonnet 65)

7   That time of the year thou mayst in me behold
      When yellow leaves, or none, or few do hang
      Upon those boughs which shake against the cold,
      Bare ruined choirs, where late the sweet bird sang; [...]
                            (Shakespeare, Sonnet 73)

8   But at my back I always hear
      Time's wingéd chariot hurrying near.
                            (Marvell, 'To his Coy Mistress')

9   It is a beauteous evening, calm and free:
     The holy time is quiet as a Nun
     Breathless with adoration; the broad sun
     Is sinking down in its tranquillity;
     The gentleness of heaven broods o'er the Sea.
     Listen! the mighty Being is awake,
     And doth with his eternal motion make
     A sound like thunder – everlastingly.
          (Wordsworth, 'Composed upon the Beach near Calais')

10   Soul-soothing Art! whom Morning, Noontide, Even,
     Do serve with all their changeful pageantry [...]
          (Wordsworth, 'Upon the Sight of a Beautiful Picture')

What arguments can be brought in support of our intuition that in a given passage *time* refers to some (allegorised) compact concept, or some elusive, diffuse quality? In the excerpts by Shakespeare and Marvell above, *time* is placed in what Wilson Knight (1964: 57–8) characterises as the 'eternal now'. It should be distinguished from Wordsworth's 'immediate now' in excerpt 9. Whereas Wordsworth implies 'at *this* particular time, at *this* particular place', Shakespeare, in speaking of 'all those beauties whereof now he's king', implies 'at *any* particular moment, at *any* particular place you care to consider', that is, apart from specific circumstances. There *are* instances, as in excerpt 5, when Shakespeare refers to particular points in time. Here, however, the particular 'hours and times of your desire' are in the plural and, again, apart from specific circumstances; so the phrase is turned into a *conceptual summary* of momentary emotional qualities. In Marvell's 'To his Coy Mistress' (excerpt 8), *time* is set in what appears to be a vigorous logical argument that has the psychological atmosphere of patent purpose to persuade his coy mistress to enjoy the present day, trusting as little as possible to the future. The poem plays up, on the one hand, time against timelessness, and on the other hand, sequential time against the eternal now. In excerpt 8 *time* has been associated with a conventional visual image and an intense action, in a definite direction. Excerpt 8 exhibits the 'eternal now' indicated by 'always' and by the stable visual shape of 'chariot' as well as by the other elements discussed in this paragraph, and *time* is perceived as the allegorical presentation of a compact, near-conceptual entity.

In Shakespeare's sonnets, *time* is frequently associated with logical arguments, occasionally introduced by some causal conjunction (such as 'Since' in excerpt 6). The logical argument also prevails in the sonnets persuading the friend to get married, in which *time* occurs several times. Or, consider excerpt 4. Here *time* acts as a superpersonal agent: two violent actions are attributed to it ('Devouring', 'blunt'), the first one being part of a vocative phrase, the other being expressed by an imperative verb. Both these grammatical forms are noted for their psychological atmosphere of definite direction. In addition, there is no definite setting in which the action might take place.

In excerpt 3, *time* acts as a superpersonal agent, constructive and, in due course, destructive, in a temporal sequence, strongly associated with several actions, partly in a universal setting, and partly in no setting at all, with a causal argument beginning in the fifth line. A different effect is produced in excerpt 7. Here there is an atmosphere, evoked by the images; there is a prevailing autumnal quality, hovering, as it were, in the quatrain. *Time*, as could be expected, refers to a particular season of the year, not to sequential time. The season is described in spatial terms, which are descriptive rather than persuasive. The setting described fluctuates, so to speak, between a particular landscape and a *typical* representation of Autumn. There is a very detailed description of the landscape, particularising every subtlety, attempting to achieve maximum accuracy. The four finite verbs (unlike as 'blunt', 'frame', or 'lead' in excerpts 3 and 4) do not denote any conclusive action of time or related objects. 'Behold' denotes an act of perception; 'hang' denotes a state rather than an action: 'sang' denotes a continuous action that 'supplies food to the senses'; 'shake', although denoting physical movement, is anything but a conclusive action; furthermore, in a context of bestowing emotions upon a landscape, it suggests a *state of mind* or a *state* of being cold. In neither case can it be described as having a psychological atmosphere of certainty or patent purpose. The auxiliary verb 'mayst' in excerpt 7 is far less conclusive than 'did' or 'doth' in excerpt 3. Two prominent phrasal constructions draw attention: 'Yellow leaves, or none, or few ... ', and 'Bare ruined choirs', which have no parallel in the former excerpts. The suspensive (non-conclusive) quality of the first phrase is reinforced by the hesitating tone of ' ... or ... or', and, by the same token, by delaying the expected predicate. Thus, the Autumnal mood of decay is abstracted from parallel instances of autumnal decay, subsumed under a coherent landscape, and reinforced by the inconclusive tone of the quatrain.

Now let us return to excerpt 9. Though a nun has, in principle, a visual shape, here she serves as a simile: she is not really in the scene, and therefore cannot be seen. The 'holy time' is invisible, and may show no visible sign of excitement. In the present context of abstract qualities (no visible parts of the nun are mentioned), the excitement is devoid of physical activity, and all its immense energy is fused, to intensify these abstract qualities, with others of *calm*, *holiness*, *tranquillity*, and *solemnity*.

'The holy time' (like 'beauteous evening') is, obviously, an abstraction from certain natural objects *at a given time*. It occurs in a fairly particularised situation. It is not sequential time, but a particular *now* in a particular *here*. The immediate subtlety of the minute is reinforced by the particular 'tiptoe effect' of 'calm excitement', which, as suggested by Cleanth Brooks (1968: 6), is dependent on the particular combination of apparently incompatible elements. The abstractness of *time* is reinforced, as we have seen, by the surrounding abstract nouns, even by the adjective 'holy'. On the other hand, *time* serves here to shift attention away from the perceived objects of the scene to its felt quality. In the physical reality represented, it is not *time* that is quiet, but the natural objects of the landscape seem quiet *at this time*. Thus, 'the holy time' is perceived as a thing-free quality hovering in a concrete landscape. The nun may be 'breathless with adoration', but this meaning does not come into full focus. 'Breathless' may apply to a landscape as well, in the sense of 'there is not the slightest current of air'. This is corroborated, in retrospect, by one of the meanings of *calm* – 'not windy'. Similarly to the invisible presence of 'breathless' air and the 'mighty being' – thing-free qualities such as holiness, adoration, tranquillity, solemnity are intensely present. The nominal style of the quatrain is remarkable. There are only three finite verbs in four lines, only one that denotes spatial motion ('is sinking down'), the verb 'is' twice, once as a copula, and once denoting existence in a deictic phrase. Time is not associated with violent actions (as in so many of Shakespeare's sonnets), but with states and shape-free qualities.

Although the atmosphere of the sonnet has been subsumed under a well-defined scene, this has been indicated only in the title in some editions ('Composed upon the Beach near Calais'), and by two concrete nouns: 'sun', 'sea'. What is important here is not the landscape but the atmosphere, the impressive solemnity hovering over it. Instead of talking about natural objects in the landscape – as usual with Wordsworth – he talks about the spirit that informs them, by turning some attributes and circumstances of the possible landscape into abstract nouns, which have a strong cumulative impact of thing-free qualities, together with some other abstract nouns: 'evening' (with *time* as its synonym), 'the gentleness of heaven', 'adoration', 'tranquillity'. The phrase 'gentleness of heaven' is noteworthy in this respect, especially if one compares it to a possible alternative phrasing: 'the gentle heaven broods o'er the sea'. Wordsworth resorts here to the poetic device which I have called 'topicalised attribute', or 'nominalised predicate', or simply the-ABSTRACT-of-the-CONCRETE metaphor. This, as I said, is a conspicuous device to direct attention *away from* the objects and concepts *to* their felt qualities.

I wish to make three further comments on lines 6–8. First, 'Listen!' shifts the mood of the poem from description to the imperative; this is a vigorous deictic device to place the perceiving consciousness right in the midst of the situation, activating its 'emotional' mechanism of locating itself in its environment with reference to time and space. Second, some important aspects of the object of 'listen' are inaudible. 'The mighty Being' may be an abstract periphrasis for 'God', imperceptible to the senses. 'Is awake' denotes a state, and suggests activity; but the sense-data that might indicate it are not specified at this stage. Thus, again, a more refined sensation of a supersensuous presence is evoked, possibly intimating a pantheistic deity. 'A sound like thunder' is introduced only two lines after 'listen'. Third, the thing-free sound-perception of line 6, then, gets belatedly a 'thingy' (though shape-free) motivation in lines 7–8. It should be noticed, however, that 'And doth with his eternal motion make / A sound like thunder – everlastingly' is to be attributed to the sea more suitably than to an abstraction. One could suggest, therefore, that lines 7–8 as well comprise intense, thing-free sound-perceptions, a supersensuous atmosphere which has, in line 5, nonetheless, a motivation – displaced from 'mighty Being' to 'sea'. This displacement is, of course, 'mitigated' by an animistic pantheistic view, informing this and some other poems by Wordsworth.

This style of accumulating emotionally-loaded abstract nouns is less common in Wordsworth's poetry than in Keats's. Even when Wordsworth writes a sonnet on a typically Keatsean theme, 'Upon the Sight of a Beautiful Picture', his abstract nouns tend to the conceptual pole. Compare the perceived effect of excerpt 10 to Keats's 'On Seeing the Elgin Marbles', for instance. Both sonnets purport to express an emotional response to some work(s) of art. But in 'Mortality / Weighs heavily on me like unwilling sleep' the verb 'Weighs' transfers mass and weight to the abstraction 'Mortality', and the description is perceived as some undifferentiated, diffuse though intense essence, whereas in excerpt 10 all the abstract nouns remain compact, conceptual, anything but diffuse. Hence, the two lines are perceived as 'rhetorical' rather than emotional.

The first thing that strikes the reader is that at this point of the sonnet, the beginning of the sestet, it invokes art *in general,* transferring the discourse to a highly generalised level, with no attempt to create a particular situation defined here-and-now. Second, the hyponyms of Time, 'Morning', 'Noontide', 'Even', constitute a linear sequence, and thus, according to our foregoing assumptions, they assume a compact conceptual character, and even tend to reinforce the conceptual character of any other part of the discourse. Third, the temporal sequence, as in Shakespeare, is associated with a verb of action, but, unlike in Shakespeare, the verb ('do serve') is highly generic and tends to present the abstractions as 'merely conceptual' rather than poetic. Fourth, 'pageantry', too, suggests a succession, and so it has a grain of linearity. It *may* refer to some colourful succession, but it merely summarises it on a highly conceptual level. Fifth, a vocative phrase may have an ingredient of a specific direction (in being directed to its addressee), or may have the potential of a powerful deictic device. Here (as in Shakespeare's 'Devouring Time') the vocative phrase strengthens the linear conclusive tone of the poem, and – in the absence of an immediate situation – it does not act as a deictic device as in excerpt 9.

One notable way in which excerpt 10 attempts to achieve poeticity is the peculiar use of the epithet in 'Soul-soothing Art' and 'changeful pageantry'. These adjectives are non-restrictive (the poem does not distinguish art that soothes the soul from art that does not), and they act here in a way that is similar to stock epithets in classical and neo-classical poetry. As Riffaterre (1978: 28) has pointed out, in such phrases 'the agent of poeticity is a specific relationship between epithet and noun, which designates a quality of the noun's referent [...] as characteristic or basic', where the adjective's meaning 'is represented *a priori* as a permanent feature'; 'in one way or another they must be *exemplary*, strikingly representative' (Riffaterre 1978: 28–9). So, whereas in excerpt 9 we have an elusive quality in an immediate situation, in 10 one may regard the epithets 'Soul-soothing' or 'changeful' as reverse kinds of deictic devices, that 'shift' their respective nouns to an 'eternal now' rather than to an 'immediate now'. The nouns thus qualified become instances of general ideas, apart from specific circumstances, even when they happen to occur in some particular situation; they tend to focus on stable and permanent properties, rather than on fleeting, elusive qualities. In excerpt 10, at any rate, they tend to reinforce the conceptual nature of the whole discourse.

The following comment has been made – by a sympathetic but critical reader – on an earlier version of my discussion of *time* in poetry. 'In the lines of Wordsworth and Marvell, we have not only two different senses of 'time', but two different words, one a mass noun and one a count noun. How much of the poetic difference (concept and mood, etc.) is just a consequence of this grammatical fact?' In the concrete realm, at least, mass nouns tend to designate undifferentiated, diffuse entities, some general extended substance, whereas count nouns tend to designate differentiated entities with stable visual shapes. So we might expect mass nouns to be the source of undifferentiated moods, and count nouns the source of (allegorised) differentiated concepts. In our poetic sample, however, we find that the reverse is the case. *Time* as a count noun helps to define the immediate situation in time and provides, by the same token, the abstraction that is to be perceived in it as a diffuse entity. Time as a sequence, on the other hand, is a mass noun, it designates a general extended entity, but it is extended in one specific direction, from the past (or present) to the future: so it is linear time and tends to be conceptual. *Time* as a general principle is, on the one hand, a mass noun, but, on the other hand – being a general principle – it is a concept. So, it occupies a somewhat ambiguous position between an undifferentiated mass and a differentiated concept. Shakespeare and Marvell disambiguate *time* (in the differentiated direction), by endowing it with a particular identity, a personal will, purposeful actions and characteristic visual shapes. *Time* both as a count noun and a mass noun designates a concept; and both have definite elements (a definite point or a definite direction); the poetic difference arises from the different exploitations of these definite elements. The 'definite' character acts in different ways against a generalised background and in a specific situation. In the former it counts toward a conceptual entity; in the latter it may help to define it in time (and space), so that an abstraction may be perceived in it as a diffuse entity. Thus, the poetic quality of *Time* is determined by its *sequential* or *spatial processing* rather than its being a *mass* or *count noun*.

Further activities

1   Literary critical analysis usually presents the products and conclusions of interpretation. This chapter explicitly describes a process of exploration, research and discovery. Using it as a model, try to trace your own thinking processes in response to a literary text you have read in the past.

2   Take another poem or prose passage that generates an intense emotional effect for you – possibly in the style of a startling turn of phrase, or the aesthetics of sound, or the apparent texture of the words. Use what you know of cognitive poetics to try to make your response explicit and discussable.

3   Much work in cognitive poetics (and in cognitive science) is keen to distinguish the activities of the mind from the neuroanatomical activities of the brain. Tsur occupies a specific position of his own here. What do you think of the particular linkage between brain activity and emotional experience that he makes? How does it relate to the cognitive-linguistic position on embodied experience?

5 A cognitive grammar of 'Hospital Barge' by Wilfred Owen

Craig Hamilton

Editors' preface

Craig Hamilton's analysis of Wilfred Owen's poem 'Hospital Barge' makes use of the cognitive grammar initially devised by Ronald Langacker in the 1980s. Hamilton examines the notion of 'profiling' in relation to Owen's depiction of a vivid wartime scene. 'Hospital Barge' describes the slow progress of a barge laden with wounded soldiers from World War I as it makes its way down the Somme. Hamilton provides a detailed analysis of how readers' attention is directed around this poignant scene by means of the grammatical constructions contained within the poem. The chapter is perhaps most usefully read in conjunction with Peter Stockwell's examination of figure and ground in surrealist poetry in Chapter 2. Together, these analyses provide a practical illustration of some of our most basic cognitive processes at work in our experience of literary texts.

Introduction

The British poet Wilfred Owen is remembered for both his life and his language. Owen is widely considered to have written some of the greatest ever war poetry. His poems are all the more unusual because Owen served in the British Army from 21 October 1915 until his death on 4 November 1918 at the age of 25. Owen was a soldier and an officer, and saw terrible action on the Western Front for six months in 1917 and for three months in 1918. When he was not on the Front, he was recuperating from shell shock in Britain. Not surprisingly, one striking quality of Owen's war poems is their autobiographical inspiration, which gave his poetry 'a new quality of terseness' (Kerr 1992a: 293) that was lacking previously. Additionally, Owen's use of assonance and consonance made for poems 'unique in sound' (Hamilton 2001: 70) while pararhyme was his 'prosodic signature' (Kerr 1992b: 530).

Owen's life forced his language to evolve, since once in the Army he 'was immersed in and set to learn the army's language in what must have seemed the most blatant discursive clash with what he wanted language to be' (Kerr

1992a: 287). This struggle for an ideal language is visible as Owen turns 'from an aloof and cultivated aesthetic of fine language and fine feeling to a committed realism and an impure diction' (Kerr 1992b: 534). Many of Owen's poems are therefore unique in how their content contrasts dramatically with their conventional form, so much so that Owen's readers today often immediately notice his striking language. Yet, while the effects of that language are noticeable because of what Stockwell (2002a: 60) has called our 'readerly intuitions' when encountering texts, what is less noticeable is how that language achieves its effects. In short, our intuitions when reading Owen merit some explanation.

Cognitive grammar is a bold and ambitious research programme in linguistics. Its 'ideal objective', as Langacker (1991: 512) puts it, should be 'the most complete description possible of those aspects of cognitive processing which constitute the mental representation of a linguistic system'. This is a tall order but one that cognitive linguists like Langacker nevertheless strive toward. Perhaps the greatest advance made in cognitive grammar so far has been the direct link shown between the conceptual system and the grammatical system. The best-known example of this connection is *profiling*. Profiling refers to a perceived relationship between two entities. This relationship is most common in visual perception where, as is normally the case, a smaller and more easily recognised *figure* is profiled against a larger *ground* (i.e: background). The very recognition of the figure in contrast to the ground is a result of profiling. In general, this is how we cognitively organise the world. Apart from visual perception, profiled figures and non-profiled grounds are evident elsewhere. For example, at a symphony concert it is possible to focus on one instrument as it is being played, to single it out against the background of the larger orchestra. The same is true as we eat, when it is often possible to taste separately a single spice in a dish containing many. Along with vision, hearing, and taste, we could easily find examples of cognitive profiling in smell and touch too because the phenomenon is so pervasive. For our purposes here, however, as students of literature we should recognise that profiles structure not only perception but conceptualisation and language as well.

Is it fair to posit a link from perception to conceptualisation to language in the manner of cognitive grammar? Consider this short sentence: 'The dog is under the table'. Such a sentence entails at least two things. First, a direct or imagined perception of the dog as a figure and the table as a ground. The figure is profiled against the ground: the dog 'stands out from' the table. Second, the sentence itself prompts us to profile the dog as the *trajector* and the table as the *landmark* against which the trajector is profiled. Whereas figure and ground refer to profiled entities in conceptual structure and perception, trajector and landmark refer to the same profiled entities in semantic and grammatical structure. A trajector is 'the figure within a relational profile' (Langacker 1987: 494) and a landmark is 'a salient substructure other than the trajector of a relational predication or the profile of a nominal predication' (Langacker 1987: 490). We profile figures in relation to grounds while we profile trajectors in relation to landmarks. Grounds and landmarks are not profiled but comprise vital halves of the profiling equation. So in 'The dog is under the table', the figure ('dog') and the ground ('table') in mental structure are analogues to the trajector (*dog*) and the landmark (*table*) in linguistic structure.

The analogous relation between these two structural levels is the product of cognitive profiling. Again, in our kitchen we may see and then say, 'The dog is under the table' to structure and report a conceptual relationship we have construed (a) by profiling the figure and (b) by linguistically marking it as the trajector. The belief that the same process of profiling holds at both the conceptual level and the linguistic level is a central theoretical tenet of cognitive grammar. The belief leads to the conclusion that our linguistic system is the way it is because our conceptual system is the way it is. This has become a major rhetorical commonplace in cognitive grammar and it recognises language's iconic nature. Such iconicity is visible, of course, when placing the word 'dog' before the word 'table' in our example utterance, which reveals how typical (i.e. prototypical) it is for us to profile subjects as agents in clausal semantic roles (Stockwell 2002a: 61). If the first noun phrase in a sentence is often the more important one, then 'The dog is under the table' signifies that we are more concerned with the dog than with the table, more concerned with the trajector than with the landmark, more concerned with the figure than with the ground. Depending on which profile we 'opt for' (Langacker 1997: 62), this is to be expected.

We may not notice profiles in our utterances but this does not mean that they are not there. Our perspectives on the world are subjective by definition and the same is true of our language. For instance, 'The dog is under the table' indicates a 'canonical viewpoint' (Langacker 1991: 123) for such a scene. We would be hard pressed to see the dog as the ground and the table as the figure, and we would be even harder pressed antithetically to say, 'The table is above the dog'. To think and talk everyday like this would land us quickly in a psychiatric ward. Yet, such a strange sentence could be a fine example of poetic diction: it is the kind of expression we often find in poetry. For example, in the Paris metro in autumn 1999 I saw the following short poem: '*N'est-ce pas plutôt le jardin / qui traverse doucement / le chat?*' [Isn't it rather the garden / that quietly crosses / the cat?] The reversal of the trajector and the landmark is an important factor that makes this poem a poem. It provides us with a set of imaginative instructions for revising the figure/ground profile between the garden and the cat. Without that profile reversal, there is no poem. Why? The canonical viewpoint is banal rather than extraordinary. A cat crossing a garden is entirely unremarkable. A garden crossing a cat, however, is poetic and worth contemplating.

Poems like the one I saw in Paris and sentences like 'The table is above the dog' remind us how subjective our conceptual and linguistic systems are.

This is what Langacker means by 'our multifaceted capacity to conceive and portray the same situation in alternate ways' (Langacker 1999: 147). To demonstrate, consider these five examples:

1   Fred broke the window with a rock.
2   The window got broken by Fred with a rock.
3   It was with a rock that Fred broke the window.
4   It was a rock from Fred that broke the window.
5   It was the window that got broken with a rock from Fred.

Some of these sentences, provided by the psychologist Michael Tomasello (1999: 155), reveal subjectivity. They show that we can (and do) take different views of essentially the same scene. As Tomasello (1999: 155) puts it, 'In each case one of the participants is singled out as the "primary focal participant" (subject) and the other potential participants are either included as the "secondary focal participant" (direct object), included as an ancillary participant (marked by a preposition), or excluded altogether'. What does this suggest? We can vary the focus of our utterance by putting different participants in different roles. By changing the way we report the event in language, and altering our choice of subject in grammatical structure, we can decide to focus on Fred, the window, or the rock.

However, we seem cognitively predisposed to profile agents as trajectors in our utterances since the figures that we profile are often agents as well. To profile objects conceptually first as figures and then as trajectors linguistically entails marking some objects as *agents* (e.g. Fred) and others as *patients* (e.g. rock); things that are more active in relation to less active things, or things that act versus things that are acted upon. As Stockwell (2002a: 61) says, 'Taking semantic role first, a subject is prototypically the *agent* in a clause, rather than functioning in the *patient* role. Choosing a patient as the subject (such as in a passive) is a marked expression that requires some special explanatory motivation: defamiliarisation, or evading active responsibility, or encoding secrecy'. This point is clearly visible in the five examples above with Fred and the window. Unlike example 5, example 1 with regard to topic continuity clearly profiles Fred: he is the *figure, trajector, agent,* and *subject* of the utterance. He becomes such by what Goldberg, following Jackendoff, calls 'fusion' (1995: 50) or what Fauconnier and Turner call 'blending' (1999: 407).

Profiles in 'Hospital Barge' by Wilfred Owen

In essence, profiling pervades poetry. It highlights the subjective construal a poet puts on a particular scene. The poet's construal, in turn, prompts us to take a similarly subjective view of a scene in a poem. In Owen's sonnet 'Hospital Barge', for example, we can imagine Owen perceiving the original scene, recording that scene in his poem, and finally inviting readers to share his view of the scene. This would explain how perception gives way to imagination, which certainly appears to be true of 'Hospital Barge':

> Budging the sluggard ripples of the Somme,
> A barge round old Cérisy slowly slewed.
> Softly her engines down the current screwed,
> And chuckled softly with contented hum,
> Till fairy tinklings struck their croonings dumb.
> The waters rumpling at the stern subdued;
> The lock-gate took her bulging amplitude;
> Gently from out the gurgling lock she swum.
>
> One reading by that calm bank shaded eyes
> To watch her lessening westward quietly.
> Then, as she neared the bend, her funnel screamed.
> And that long lamentation made him wise
> How unto Avalon, in agony,
> Kings passed in the dark barge which Merlin dreamed.

The most obvious profile within this 1917 sonnet is that of an object moving against a background that does not move. Initially, then, the hospital barge is the figure and the surroundings form the ground. The barge, which carries wounded soldiers, is conceptually set against the backdrop near the town of Cérisy in northern France. The barge is linguistically the trajector in the poem, moving relative to a landmark that does not move. And yet, although the profiled configuration organises the entire poem, we intuitively sense other profiles too within the sonnet.

As Langacker (1987: 490) suggests with his distinction of 'relational predication' from 'nominal predication', nouns like 'barge' involve profiles just as verbs like 'slewed' involve profiles. For instance, as Adele Goldberg has demonstrated (1995: 46), in verbs like 'rob' and 'steal' there are 'participant roles' in the semantics of the verb: the thief, the victim, and the goods. Despite the same three roles for both verbs, however, what we profile is different. In 'rob', we profile the thief and the victim, whereas in 'steal' we profile the thief and the goods. That is, we choose 'rob' to draw attention to the *thief* and the *victim*, and 'steal' to draw attention to the *thief* and the stolen *goods* (Goldberg 1995: 46–7). In general, verbs may have anywhere from one to three participant roles (Goldberg 1995: 45), and choice of verb can subtly alter the perspective taken towards an event based on which role is profiled. If we turn to Owen's verbs in 'Hospital Barge', we see how verb profiles offer an important key to the experience of reading the sonnet.

Perhaps the easiest way to examine verbal profiles in detail is at the sentence level. Owen's 'Hospital Barge' is a sonnet of six sentences divided into fourteen lines in two stanzas: an octave and a sestet. The first sentence comprises lines 1 and 2 of the sonnet: 'Budging the sluggard ripples of the

Somme, / A barge round old Cérisy slowly slewed'. 'Budging' in its transitive sense means 'to cause to move' and it profiles two participants: the mover ('barge') and the moved (water). 'Slewed' in its intransitive sense means 'pivoted' and it profiles one participant: the pivoter ('barge'). What these profiles tell us is rather interesting. Owen apparently subordinates the main clause in line 2 to a 'dangling participle' (Alexander 1988: 32) in line 1, which does not prototypically profile the subject in grammatical terms even though 'barge' is nevertheless profiled in verb semantic terms (as mover and pivoter). What Owen does, in other words, is present a viewpoint of the scene that is neither prototypical nor canonical. The first sign of this is his diction, which is poetic because it does not follow English's 'canonical sentoid' structure of *noun phrase–verb–noun phrase* (Aitchison 1997: 204). The second sign is his shift from a verb–object construction in line 1 to a subject–verb construction in line 2. And yet, as we will see in many instances here, Owen's syntax seems not to profile the grammatical subject ('barge'), although, given the participant roles inherent to the sonnet's verbs, Owen's verbs cannot escape from semantically profiling the barge.

The second sentence of the sonnet involves some more intriguing verb profiles: 'Softly her engines down the current screwed, / And chuckled softly with contented hum, / Till fairy tinklings struck their croonings dumb'. 'Screwed' in its transitive sense profiles two participants: the agent ('engines') and the patient ('current'). We know 'screwed' is transitive because the verb has an object. The current is a patient for it is the object of the active verb. 'Chuckled' in its intransitive sense profiles the agent ('engines') in its sole participant role. In contrast, 'struck' in its transitive sense and three participant roles profiles the agent ('fairy tinklings'), the patient (the engines' croonings), and the resulting effect ('dumb'). The smooth sound of the engines falls silent when the bells of the lock signal that the lock is opening. The engines are actors until the moment they are apparently acted upon when the tinkling sound of the lock is heard and the engines quiet down. The shift in profile from agent in one participant role to patient in another suggests a *causal* relation between the lock and the barge, or, more specifically, between the lock's bells and the barge's engines. The persona's perception of this causal relation is manifested in Owen's diction.

In the third sentence of the sonnet, the lock rather than the barge becomes a primary focal participant: 'The waters rumpling at the stern subdued; / The lock-gate took her bulging amplitude; / Gently from out the gurgling lock she swum'. 'Rumpling' in its intransitive sense profiles 'waters' in its sole participant role, but 'subdued' functions primarily as an adjective (to modify 'stern') rather than as a verb replete with different participant roles. With 'took', we have the clearest example of agency whereby 'took' in its transitive sense profiles 'lock-gate' and 'barge' from the verb's two participant roles: the taker and the taken. When we process 'swum', the final intransitive, something interesting takes place. The sole participant ('barge') is semantically profiled. However, by beginning the line grammatically with the adverbial phrase 'Gently from out', Owen does not seem to want to profile the agent of the motion (the barge) and the subject of the scene. Rather, he seems to wish to profile the barge's location and manner of motion instead. Even so, the semantics of an active verb like 'swim' attest to the fact the agent (the barge) is nevertheless semantically profiled despite what happens at the grammatical level.

The fourth sentence of the sonnet introduces another person in the scene: 'One reading by that calm bank shaded eyes / To watch her lessening westward quietly'. The persona in this sestet is omniscient because he knows the thoughts of the person he sees on the canal bank. More importantly, this viewpoint reveals a profile where a person (a trajector) is singled out against the bank of the canal (a landmark). This canonical perspective is what we might call the scene's default profile: a smaller or animate object (trajector) set against a larger or immobile object (landmark). As for the verbs – 'shaded' in its transitive sense profiles an agent (shader) protecting a patient (shaded eyes), while the infinitive 'to watch' in its transitive sense profiles an agent (watcher) and a patient (drifting barge). In the final phrase, 'her lessening westward quietly', 'lessening' can be taken intransitively to mean diminishing and its one participant role would be the barge, which carries out the motion under observation.

In typical Italian sonnets, those comprised of octaves and sestets, the turn normally takes place after the octave at the start of the sestet. As in most other types of poems, turns are signalled by words such as 'but', 'now', 'and yet', or 'then', to establish a contrast between that which has come before the turn and that which follows the turn. Here, Owen's turn is novel for it comes in sentence five (line 11) of the sonnet: 'Then, as she neared the bend, her funnel screamed'. The canal scene depicted up to now has been rather quiet as engines 'chuckled softly' and 'fairy tinklings' signalled the opening of the lock. Now, however, the shrill sound of the barge's horn disrupts the quiet of the scene although in the verbs' participant roles the barge remains profiled. 'Neared' in its transitive sense profiles the barge against that which it nears (the bend), making of the figure a trajector and of the ground a landmark. In semantic role terms, we would call the barge an agent and the bend a patient. 'Screamed' in its intransitive sense profiles its sole participant role: the barge (metonymically represented by 'funnel', a smaller part of the whole). This aural profile of the horn's scream against the quiet background is roughly analogous to the relation between a *profile* and a *base* (Langacker 1987: 184). As Langacker argues (1987: 184) with examples such as 'circle' and 'arc', the lexical items involve different profile–base relationships. Whereas the semantic value of 'circle' comes from its being profiled against the base of space in general, the semantic value of 'arc' comes from its being profiled against the base of a circle in particular. With regard to the funnel scream in Owen's poem, the sound of the funnel is likewise profiled against a quiet background but it only has meaning in relation to that against which it is profiled. This is because hearing the noise is to recognise it conceptually as a figure, and mark it linguistically as trajector. When we do this we profile the scream against a base of a quieter background. A scream next to a Boeing 747 jumbo jet on take-off could not be heard because the base would swamp the profile. However, a scream in a quiet setting such as that in 'Hospital Barge' would have a very different effect. Nevertheless, in both scenarios the effects are reached by cognitive profiling.

When we reach the last sentence of the sonnet, the barge seems to disappear from view entirely: 'And that long lamentation made him wise / How unto Avalon, in agony, / Kings passed in the dark barge which Merlin dreamed'. The barge that is imagined now is not the hospital barge in France in 1917 carrying casualties away from the Western Front. Rather, the barge has become one that carries dead kings. The change is brought about by two metaphorical redefinitions. First, the funnel scream is redefined as a 'long lamentation'. Second, the casualties on board the barge are redefined as 'Kings'. The profiles inherent to Owen's verbs in this final sentence also tell us something important about the poem. Unlike the barge's engines, that are struck dumb, here the barge's horn makes the observer wise. 'Made' in Owen's sentence has two participant roles: one for the maker (agent) and one for the made (patient). In its transitive sense here, 'made' profiles the agent (the horn) provoking the emotion of lamentation in the observed person (patient). The effect of this is to make the person 'wise' to great kings of the past who, according to Merlin's dream (and Tennyson's 1869 poem, 'The Passing of Arthur', which is thought to have inspired 'Hospital Barge'), died on vessels somehow similar to these carrying World War I casualties. To continue, in its intransitive sense meaning to die, 'passed' profiles in its sole role the passing agent (the kings), while 'dreamed' in its transitive sense profiles in its two roles the dreamer (agent) having the dream (patient). In short, the linguistic level of the poem reveals what occurs at the conceptual level of the poem: the barge is fading from view, and it is doing so both semantically and grammatically because it is no longer profiled by the sonnet's end. Perception has given way to imagination.

What I am saying here may be hard to appreciate but if language is a window onto the human mind, it is a window because it reflects cognitive structures. Those structures exist in the mind of the writer and the mind of the reader, which is the necessary condition for communication to occur. Likewise, Owen's shift between transitive and intransitive verbs, and his inversion of standard syntax or his use of what Kerr (1992b: 534) calls 'impure diction', make the scene in 'Hospital Barge' interesting rather than ordinary. The barge itself is often a primary focal participant at one level even if it is not always one at another level. Why should Owen do this? Because the barge is no simple barge, it cannot be described in just any old way. If it were, it would cease to be poetic, it would cease to captivate us and might never have captivated Owen in the first place. In rhetorical terms, the poem depicts an extraordinary scene that to some might seem entirely ordinary. In essence, the language of the poem invites us to take an extraordinary perspective on a rather simple scene. One of the ways that perspective is helped along as we read is through Owen's choice of verbs with subtly shifting participant roles and profiles.

My 'interpretation' of Owen's poem is not at all exhaustive. We could say much more about this sonnet if we wanted to. For example, we could talk about its perfect end rhymes, its form, or its metrical patterns. The pentameter lines are essentially regular but contain pyrrhic feet both in trochaic lines (l. 1) and iambic lines (ll. 4 and 9). But, as this less-than-even metre suggests, the calm canal scene may not be so grand. Indeed, it goes from good to bad because the barge is specifically carrying war casualties. The war has left the front to make its way into quiet Cérisy (if we decide to see the barge metaphorically in this manner). Also, the soldiers are uncommon: they remind the person in the poem of noble kings like King Arthur, transforming an everyday hospital barge into a rare and beautiful royal barge. Oddly enough, the wounded on the barge are barely profiled although the barge carrying them is, which is something else we could consider if we wished to elaborate on the poem. Other aspects we could discuss more fully are metaphor, metonymy, irony, voice, versification, sound symbolism, or Owen's biography as it relates to this poem. All this information could be brought to bear on a longer interpretation of this poem and could be poetically correlated with the profiling analysis presented thus far. Of course, many of these points are precisely the ones that critics have made for decades because they seemed important for reading. They are points that have informed critical machinery for quite some time.

However, to approach Owen's poem through the lens of cognitive grammar is to have concerns with the imagination and with language that differ from traditional ways of handling these topics. A great deal of criticism concerns itself with commenting on rhetorical effects, but cognitive poetics concerns itself with the mental *causes* that bring about those effects. Profiling is just one framework to use with a poem like Owen's if we want to attempt to depict how effects are achieved in the mind, by the mind, and for the pleasure of the mind. If cognitive poetics is anything, it is different in some respect from most literary criticism preceding it. Its main difference is its critical grounding of literature in language and language in cognition. However, if cognitive poetics is a 'mere duplication of terms', as Tsur (1998) once argued, then it is hopeless. But since we are not bent on doing what new critics could do better fifty years ago (i.e. *explications de texte*), the saving grace of cognitive poetics is that it is not good old-fashioned hermeneutics at all: it is poetics.

Concluding discussion

If we are readers of a book like *Cognitive Poetics in Practice*, our mastery of language is so complete that we may not see why nuances should matter when we yoke language to thought in cognitive grammar. After all, language is not a problem for most of us. With the exception of severely neglected children or those born with some developmental problem (such as autism), everybody everywhere acquires language and begins using it successfully for communication. And unless we suffer brain damage from an accident or a stroke, most of us will speak and understand speech quite normally all of our lives. Why should this be the case? Simply put, language is cognition. It is cognition for communication. Because we all have brains, cognition and language are facts of daily life. That language should thus be understood as a form of cognitive behaviour is a central tenet in cognitive linguistics. Having said that, language can be problematic at times. For example, it poses a challenge for the critic trying to account for certain phenomena like the use of poetic diction in poetry. The difficulty arises because that which is simple is never simple to describe. It may be easy for us to read and appreciate a poem like 'Hospital Barge', but to explain our processing of its language is often far from simple. However, if we are to take literature seriously as an object of study that tells us something about the human mind, then some attempt at describing language is necessary.

As our experience with literature is essentially an experience with language, to study literature is to study language and to study language is to study the mind. This means that the student of literature is really a student of the human mind. As the critic Mark Turner puts it, 'Literature lives within language and language within everyday life. The study of literature must live within the study of language, and the study of language within the study of the everyday mind' (1991: 4). This may be clear enough but what, we might ask, does it actually mean? For starters, dividing literary language from everyday language, or literary cognition from everyday cognition, simply creates artificial barriers between literature, the world, and our lives. To best understand literature we need to understand it within the context of the life of the mind. Certainly, it is within this context that our appreciation of literature is shaped. Many of us, I would venture, may find ourselves doing the dishes while at the same time thinking about the novel we just put aside. This is because for us the life of the mind *is* literary since our imaginations contemplate at length many of the texts we encounter. As my own language here suggests, we should not ask how do texts do what they do but how we do what we do when reading texts such as poems. My shorthanded use of the verb 'profile' in the previous section should not hide the fact that our minds, not verbs themselves, are the true agents behind profiling. Indeed, to personify texts as the agents responsible for meaning, to evacuate the mind from the scenario as it were, incorrectly removes agency from human beings with human minds in human bodies in a human world. This is precisely what cognitive poetics is not about.

Further activities

1   There are many possibilities for reading poetry through the lens of cognitive grammar. Profiling is certainly applicable to literature in many different ways. Meaning is never static since it is built on combinations we make between words, ideas, and what words and ideas relate to in our minds as we read. Consider these opening stanzas from another poem by Wilfred Owen, 'The Show':

> My soul looked down from a vague height, with Death,
> As unremembering how I rose or why,
> And saw a sad land, weak with sweats of dearth,
> Gray, cratered like the moon with hollow woe,
> And pitted with great pocks and scabs of plagues.
>
> Across its beard, that horror of harsh wire,
> There moved thin caterpillars, slowly uncoiled.
> It seemed they pushed themselves to be as plugs
> Of ditches, where they writhed and shrivelled, killed.

Consider these lines in relation to the discussion of cognitive grammar put forward in this chapter. What does the notion of profiling enable us to do if we try to describe the effects of these two stanzas? Why should mismatches between figure, trajector, and grammatical subject profiles strike us as unusual? Are mismatches of this sort a condition for poetic diction? How do profiles in the nouns and verbs compare and contrast in 'The Show'? Do any intransitive verbs become transitive? When Owen says the soldiers 'writhed and shrivelled, killed', how iconic of the action represented is this verbal sequence? Why should it be so? Consider also what Owen's alternatives might have been.

2   This chapter has focused solely on profiling in poetry. You may now wish to go on to consider the cognitive grammar of prose fiction. Romance novels, in particular, can be very productive texts for an analysis using cognitive grammar. Look in detail at the first descriptions given of the central characters in the fiction of Catherine Cookson, or Barbara Cartland, for example. What relationship do these figures have with the background against which they are depicted? How is the interaction between separate characters presented? Try to track the first encounter between a pair of lovers in terms of trajectors and landmarks. How does the profiling constructed in your chosen passage contribute to your understanding of the unfolding relationship?

6 'Love stories'

Cognitive scenarios in love poetry

Gerard Steen

Editors' preface

This chapter by Gerard Steen explores the nature of the knowledge structures needed by readers during their interpretation of love poetry in its numerous textual forms. Steen examines a range of text types, from canonical verse by poets such as William Shakespeare, Robert Graves and A.E. Housman, to the lyrics of contemporary rock and pop love songs. Some of these examples have a narrative structure, while others can be classified as argumentative or descriptive. In all cases, Steen argues, readers must activate dynamic cognitive structures, known as 'scenarios', in order to make sense of the text at hand. You may find is useful to read this chapter alongside Raymond W. Gibbs, Jr's discussion of prototypes in Chapter 3, and Peter Crisp's analysis of conceptual metaphors in Chapter 8.

'Love stories' and cognitive scenarios

The prototypical 'love story' is probably the Hollywood film, but novels, poems, plays, and pop and rock songs are almost equally good examples. These are artistic representations of the 'love story', but there are also many other genres where you need your knowledge about love to deal with the meaning of the text: celebrity reports in boulevard magazines, for instance, also contain texts that heavily rely on our knowledge of 'love stories'. Self-help books on marital problems are another angle on the same content. And what people say in court cases for obtaining a divorce or what they discuss with their therapist in counselling sessions is similarly informed by our world knowledge about love. So there is a sense of constancy behind all these different messages about love. What we need is a kind of cognitive model in which we may represent these constant features, so that we may apply that model in our examination of the possible cognitive effects of individual textual instantiations of the 'love story'. It is the purpose of this chapter to advance such a model and explore its relations with the analysis of text content and text types of love poetry.

The attention to text type is an important feature of this chapter, and explains the use of the scare quotes around the notion of 'love story'. As may be checked against the above illustrations, not all 'love stories' are stories or narrative texts in the text-typological sense, and this is why we need to distinguish between 'love stories' and stories proper. We shall return to this later on in this chapter.

The nature of knowledge representations in cognitive science has been various, and includes notions like cognitive schemas, scripts, and *scenarios* (e.g. Lakoff 1987). These are all abstract knowledge representations that model the conceptual structure of a particular piece of knowledge. Thus, our concept for 'table' includes the facts that it usually has a surface and four legs, serves to seat a number of people, and is one type of furniture. This is not the meaning of the word *table*, but it is (part of) the content of the concept TABLE. (I distinguish between words and concepts and signal this in the notation here by putting words in italics and concepts in small capitals.)

What is the content of our concept of a 'love story'? Or more generally, what is part of our knowledge about love? Peter Crisp's chapter in this volume mentions the discovery of the many metaphorical expressions about love in Lakoff and Johnson (1980). This led to an extended line of research on the language of love, the conceptual structure of love, and the proposal of a love scenario (Kövecses 1986, 1988, 1990, 2000). The present chapter takes its cue from this work and presents a sympathetic but critical development of it. However, there is no space to go into the reasons and consequences of the differences between my approach and the one by Kövecses (see Ungerer and Schmid 1996 for some discussion).

The number of pop and rock songs containing lines like 'I want you' and 'I need you' may serve as a good way in to the structure of our knowledge about love. LOVE may be approached as just an isolated concept, which includes information about the fact that it is one of the human emotions, and moreover one of the emotions which is relatively lasting, as opposed to anger and happiness, which are of shorter duration. Moreover, LOVE is closely associated with other concepts, such as DESIRE, PASSION, LUST, SEX and HAPPINESS. It is also antonymically related to concepts such as JEALOUSY and HATE. There is hence a rich conceptual structure that may be reconstructed around the concept of love.

However, this conceptual structure is rather static. A more dynamic way of looking at love is to see it as a scenario. Scenarios are complex conceptual structures consisting of sequences of action concepts, which actions are to be performed in recurrent situations with a particular goal. The most famous scenario in the literature is the so-called 'restaurant' scenario, which has characteristically been anglicised into a 'pub' scenario by Stockwell (2002a: 77). Such a scenario provides a complex store of information for people who are about to enter a restaurant or a pub so that they may have all kinds of expectations about the situations they may foresee in the next couple of hours, which facilitates their orientation and interaction in those situations. We have scenarios for all kinds of situations, and one of them has to do with our management of social interactions where love plays an important role. You might think of this scenario as a dating scenario. If the ultimate purpose of the restaurant scenario is to have a meal, the ultimate purpose of the dating scenario is to have and possibly keep another person.

This observation may sound crude in Great Britain and some other countries, but it would be perfectly acceptable in the United States, where dating may be said to constitute a culture of its own. This is an indication of the importance of the cultural variability of the love scenario and scenarios in general. It is unfortunate that there is no space to explore this theme any further in this chapter, but it might be an interesting topic for further class work.

Table 6.1 shows the basic structure of the love scenario as I see it. The love scenario captures the fact that love has to do with three main stages of amorous relationships between people: they either do or do not want each other, then they either do or do not get each other, and finally they either do or do not keep each other. These are the issues that explain almost any love story, and they form a causal chain that is the basis for our interest in any story, as has been recognised by both narratologists and psychologists (e.g. Bremond 1964, 1966; van den Broek 1994). What is more, they are related to our interest in success or failure, or the question of whether people actually reach the goals they set themselves (Bremond 1966).

Table 6.1 A simple love scenario

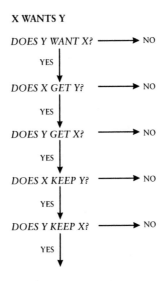

This approach leads to a further development of the love scenario in the direction of motivation and result. People either want, get, or keep each other *because of* particular causes; and when they do want, get, or keep each other, this has a particular *result*. The same holds for the negative variants of these possibilities. All of these possibilities are listed in Table 6.2.

Table 6.2 Causation in love stories: motivation and positive and negative results

> WANT / GET / KEEP BECAUSE OF
>> DESIRE
>> PASSION
>> NEED
>
> WANT / GET / KEEP RESULTS IN
>> HAPPINESS
>> AFFAIR
>> RELATIONSHIP
>
> NOT WANT / GET / KEEP BECAUSE OF
>> INTERNAL LACK
>>> OF DESIRE, PASSION, NEED
>> EXTERNAL IMPEDIMENT
>>> COMPETITOR, SOCIETY
>
> NOT WANT / GET / KEEP RESULTS IN
>> LACK OF HAPPINESS
>>> ANGER > HATE > JEALOUSY
>> LACK OF AFFAIR
>>> DISAPPOINTMENT
>> LACK OF RELATIONSHIP
>>> LONELINESS

The combination of Tables 6.1 and 6.2 provides a basic grid for the analysis of most 'love stories'. I do not offer them as the only model for representing our knowledge about love, but as one sensible starting point for exploring its use in cognitive poetics.

There is one interesting consequence of this approach. Most of the emotion concepts in Table 6.2 have a partially metaphorical structure, as has been shown by Kövecses. For instance, we conventionally think of DESIRE AS HUNGER, or of HAPPINESS AS UP. Thus, it is perfectly natural for us to say things like 'I feel *down*', 'I feel *depressed*', 'You're in *high* spirits today', 'Her presence always *lifts* my spirits', and so on. A lot of attention has been paid to this metaphorical structure of our thought in recent years (see Crisp, Chapter 8), and we can now use these results to further enrich our understanding of the love scenario. Table 6.3 gives an illustrative, incomplete list of the conventional metaphors involved in the concepts in Table 6.2.

Many of these concepts have been investigated by Kövecses and others, but the present scenario places them in a new, interaction-oriented relationship to each other.

Rock lyrics make abundant use of the conceptual metaphors listed above, as may be seen from the following examples. The concept of HUNGER is used

Table 6.3 Metaphorical aspects of love

WANT / GET / KEEP BECAUSE OF
    DESIRE = HUNGER
    PASSION = NATURAL FORCE
    NEED = ADDICTION, ILLNESS

WANT / GET / KEEP RESULTS IN
    HAPPINESS = UP
    AFFAIR = UNION
    RELATIONSHIP = POSSESSION

NOT WANT / GET / KEEP BECAUSE OF
    INTERNAL LACK
        OF DESIRE, PASSION, NEED (see above)
    EXTERNAL IMPEDIMENT
        COMPETITOR, SOCIETY = ENEMY

NOT WANT / GET / KEEP RESULTS IN
    LACK OF HAPPINESS
        ANGER > HATE > JEALOUSY (other metaphors)
    LACK OF AFFAIR
        DISAPPOINTMENT
    LACK OF RELATIONSHIP

in a song by Van Morrison called 'I'm hungry for your love'. Passion as a natural force may be discerned in the hit song 'Light my fire' by the Doors. Another dramatic example would be Neil Young's 'You are like a hurricane / There's foam in your eyes / and I'm getting blown away'. The need for another person as an addiction is expressed by Brian Ferry's 'Love is the drug'. It receives somewhat more extensive treatment in Garbage's song 'Temptation waits' from their second album, 'You come on like a drug / I just can't get enough / I'm like an addict coming at you for a little more [...] / I never needed anybody like this before'.

Turning to the happy results of a love story, here are some examples of HAPPINESS AS UP: 'Take me higher' (U2, 'Even better than the real thing'), 'Lift up my days and light up my ways' (U2, 'Mysterious ways'), 'Is this desire? / Enough enough / To lift us higher?' (P.J. Harvey, 'Is this desire?'). Notice that HIGH also often means that HAPPINESS IS LIGHT, as opposed to dark. When people keep each other, the result is POSSESSION, which is illustrated by Garbage's 'You are a secret / A new possession' ('Temptation waits'). Here it might be noted that possession by somebody else may in turn result in loss of power and self: 'Love is suicide' (The Smashing Pumpkins, 'Bodies'). And one of the most explicit expressions of the basic idea that keeping each other leads to union, which in turn implies a whole, can be found in the U2 hit song 'One'.

It should hence be clear that there is a lot of metaphorical structure to our knowledge of love. However, it is also important to point out that not everything we know about love is metaphorical. The basic structure of the scenario offered above is anything but metaphorical, and there are essential roles for abstract as well as concrete literal conceptualisations. Moreover, it should also be realised that not every emotion concept in the love scenario can be equated with love itself – desire for another person is not love, loneliness as a result of desertion is not love either. The advantage of the present cognitive model is that it facilitates making these distinctions while remaining focused on the encompassing notion of the love scenario.

From love scenarios to text content

Love scenarios are general cognitive models that may be presumed to be possessed in at least some partial form or other by most people in a particular culture. These models would also be employed for interpretation when people read texts about love, including love poetry. It is one task of cognitive poetics to show how such models might work in facilitating the interpretation of a love poem. In order to provide an illustration, consider George Crabbe's 'A marriage ring':

> *A marriage ring*
>
> The ring so worn as you behold,
> So thin, so pale, is yet of gold:
> The passion such it was to prove;
> Worn with life's cares, love yet was love.

This poem cannot be understood without resorting to the love scenario. Although it does not present a complete reflection of the entire scenario, it does have an obvious connection. The scenario is triggered by the word 'marriage' in the title, for marriage is one specific kind of love relationship. The additional concept of the ring is also part of the marriage scenario, and its generally accepted symbolic value for perfect love reinforces the relevance of the love scenario.

What is said about the ring in the first two lines can be easily accommodated in the overall scenario. There is also a comfortable transition to the PASSION concept in line 3 because we all know that the ring is a symbol of the passion of the lovers. One important remark is that the word *passion* in line 3 does not have to be identical with the concept PASSION in our postulated scenario. We have used the concept PASSION as a technical notion, a conceptual label for a particular stage in love affairs. In everyday language, however, people may use the related word in slightly more varying and loose ways. In this case the word *passion* evidently relates to the stage of keeping each other, which we have analysed as a stage of NEED. These are issues not just of terminology but also of theory development, which are worthy of further investigation. Another opportunity for class work might be to consider how far everybody agrees with the labels for the three stages.

Finally, the idea that love may be 'worn with life's cares' is compatible with the view of the last stage of the love scenario as an elongated period of keeping each other. It is part of our knowledge of the world that such long periods do not go by without difficulties. This does not have to be explicitly represented in the scenario for it to be connected to it with relative ease.

What the example of Crabbe's poem shows is that the love scenario may be found in more concrete instantiations of the general 'love story', such as the marriage scenario, which therefore also has additional structure and information (for instance regarding the role of the ring). Moreover, we need to activate general knowledge, for instance about the duration of stages of the love scenario, to account for other concrete details in texts. And finally, what it also shows is that the relation between words and concepts needs to be used with circumspection: labels of concepts in the scenario are tentative and should not be allowed to have a misleading effect on our view of the words used by a particular poet.

It may also have struck you that there is something strange about the Crabbe poem: it is not strictly speaking a story. Even though it makes use of the love scenario, which could provide the basis for a genuine love *story*, its text type is not that of the story, or narrative. The poem is more like a description: it offers a number of properties of the marriage ring in question. This distinction concerns the difference between the content of texts and their type.

The love scenario may help us interpret the content of any love poem as a textual representation of, ultimately, some causally connected sequence of events or actions. However, such a textual representation itself does not have to exhibit the overall form of a causal sequence of events, as is characteristic of narratives. How can we account for this aspect of texts, the relation between content and type? To give an answer to this question is the purpose of the next section.

Text content and text types

Hitherto we have presumed that all messages about love could be called 'love stories'. However, as hinted on the first page of this chapter, this has been a loose description that cannot really serve our purposes. For it is a fact that not all 'love stories', or texts about love, are actual stories. Stories are one text type, narrative, but not all texts about love come to us in the form of narratives. Love can also be the content of an argumentative text, a descriptive text, or an expository text. Narrative, argumentative, descriptive, and expository messages are four basic types of message organisation, and they each have their own characteristics that are used by the language user to construct an overall representation of a particular text.

Thus, if you know that a particular text is in a genre that is conventionally argumentative, you will look for the most important claim and the supporting evidence. But if you know that a message is in a genre that is conventionally narrative, you will look for a plot and a story line and construct your representation according to those basic guidelines. It is hence important to go into the differences between these four basic text types and to see how they are related to the dimension of content.

In general, love stories in poetry (as well as in rock songs, for that matter) can be of all four above-mentioned text types. Let us first examine some narrative poems and contrast them with the descriptive poem by Crabbe, in order to highlight the most important features of these two text types. A fairly telling example is the following poem by Sir Henry Wotton:

Upon the death of Sir Albert Morton's wife

He first deceased; she for a little tried
To live without him, liked it not, and died.

Notice how the use of the word *wife* in the title activates the marriage scenario as a specific variant of the love scenario again.

We can use the love scenario to situate this love story in the last stage: the lovers do not keep each other, because one of them dies. This predictably results in unhappiness on the part of the wife, and this in turn causes her death. The unhappiness is explained by the bottom part of Table 6.2, while the result of the unhappiness is a further possible extension of the overall plot that gives this story its particular twist. Notice, finally, how this dramatic love story is couched in completely literal language: talk about love is not necessarily metaphorical.

The main reason that this text is a narrative text is the fact that it presents a series of events that are causally related to each other. Moreover, the drive behind the causally related events is some goal of one of the participants in the series of events, which leads to a number of actions to achieve the goal, a classic topic in narratology which has also received attention from cognitive psychologists (e.g. Brewer and Lichtenstein 1982; Trabasso and Sperry 1985). The outcome of the attempts to achieve the goal determines whether the story is a success story or not. The overall goal-directed nature of the story also explains that the last clause in the poem, 'and died', has a funny intentional connotation: it is as if Sir Albert Wotton's wife negatively evaluates life without her husband and then decides to die and does so.

These observations also mean that most stories have their beginning in the past and may extend to some more recent past or even into the present situation. They also have a conventional three-part structure: setting of the goal, attempt to achieve the goal, and outcome of the attempts. All of these elements are present in this short poem, and that is what makes it a narrative.

Contrast this with the Crabbe poem. Even though reference is made to what may be a long series of actions, events and processes ('worn with life's cares'), these are not presented *as* actions, events and processes in the text. They are presented in just one nominal phrase, 'life's cares'. Instead of a series of events or actions, Crabbe's poem contains two couplets which each present a state, and their connection is one of (non-literal) comparison. Even though we have had to make use of the conceptual love scenario in order to interpret the rich text world that the poem evokes, this does not make the poem a story in the text-typological sense. As we read from sentence to sentence, we do not see a causally connected sequence of actions unfolding before our eyes. Instead, the poem presents two observations, or descriptions, which are placed in parallel. It is an artistic description of a wedding ring and what it stands for.

More generally speaking, a narrative love poem presents a rather explicit verbal representation of the love scenario, by thematising some of the causal relationships between the scenes that lie at the basis of the love scenario and the causation/motivation table. By contrast, a descriptive love poem makes use of our knowledge of the causal structure inherent in love relationships, but does not present its message in the form of a series of causally connected situations. Instead, it picks out one aspect of the love scenario and describes it without adding a dynamic and causal structure to the series of situations it presents about that aspect. In a description, we are not dealing with the presentation of a series of causally connected events.

In order to see another typical case of a narrative love poem, consider the following flippant example by A.E. Housman:

Oh, when I was in love with you,
Then I was clean and brave,
And miles around the wonder grew
How well did I behave.

And now the fancy passes by,
And nothing will remain,
And miles around they'll say that I
Am quite myself again.

The situation in line 1 causes the situation in line 2, and the situation in line 2 causes the situation in lines 3 and 4. Stanza 2 has exactly the same structure. (Observe the linguistic reflection of this parallel text structuring in terms of phrasing and punctuation.)

What is especially interesting is the link between stanzas 1 and 2: notice how you will look for an explanation of the change of heart between lines 4 and 5. This demonstrates how narrative texts are dependent on the assumption and construction of a continuous causal chain of events. Even though there is no explicit indication of any action, event, or process that has caused the change of heart between the two stanzas in the form of a complete line, there is one subtle but devastating word that gives the reader a clue, the word *fancy* in line 5. This suggests that the initial cause of the first stanza, the cause for the wanting stage, has turned out to be insufficient to achieve the subsequent stages of getting or keeping.

All of these elements can be accounted for by the love scenario and the motivation table, and they are all presented in the form of a narrative. If you contrast this poem to 'A marriage ring', the differences between the overall structure of a narrative and a descriptive message will be manifest.

Another example of a descriptive love poem is the following text by Robert Graves:

> She tells her love while half asleep,
> In the dark hours,
> With half-words whispered low:
> As Earth stirs in her winter sleep
> And puts out grass and flowers
> Despite the snow,
> Despite the falling snow.

Just as with the Housman poem, the relevance of the love scenario is indicated by the use of the word 'love' in the first line.

There are two sets of actions in this poem, the telling by the 'She' and the stirring and subsequent putting out by the Earth. There is no causal connection between the two in terms of the chronology of the events; indeed, they are simultaneous. To the experienced reader of literature, this may suggest a symbolic connection, which in turn may mean that the two events are the result of the same (implicit) cause. But this does not turn the poem into a narrative. It is a description of one moment in the night, which may be understood against the background of the love scenario. To paraphrase a possible application of the scenario, 'they at least have got each other and may keep each other'.

Let us now turn to a comparison between a 'love story' in narrative form and one in argumentative form. They are both poems about jealousy, accounted for in the bottom part of Table 6.2. Here is the narrative poem, by William Blake:

> *My pretty rose tree*
>
> A flower was offered to me,
> Such a flower as May never bore;
> But I said 'I've a Pretty Rose-tree',
> And I passed the sweet flower o'er.

Then I went to my Pretty Rose-tree,
To tend her by day and by night;
But my Rose turned away with jealousy,
And her thorns were my only delight.

It is an interesting question, also eligible for class work, to consider how we know that we need to activate the love scenario and not a gardening one when we read this poem. A useful connection may be made with the chapter by Peter Crisp again. Apart from that, most of the connections between the lines in this poem are causal and there is mention of motivation in lines 3 and 7. There is also a clear beginning, middle, and end. The text type of this poem is evidently narrative.

By contrast, here is an argumentative poem, by William Walsh:

Love and jealousy

How much are they deceived who vainly strive,
By jealous fears, to keep our flames alive?
Love's like a torch, which if secured from blasts,
Will faintlier burn; but then it longer lasts.
Exposed to storms of jealousy and doubt,
The blaze grows greater, but 'tis sooner out.

The reason why this love poem is argumentative is that it presents a claim about the undesirable nature of a particular attitude, to strive, 'by jealous fears, to keep our flames alive'. All argumentative texts either present claims of this kind, regarding the desirable or undesirable nature of something, including actions; or they may assert the good or bad quality of something, or the likely or unlikely chance that something will happen (e.g. McCroskey 1987; van Eemeren *et al.* 1997). Here we have an argument of the first type, based on a lack of desirability. That this takes place by means of a rhetorical question should not deceive the analyst – it is obvious that the effect of the first lines is to assert that you should not strive to keep your flames alive by jealous fears.

The second property of argumentation is that the central claim is presented as controversial and in need of support by further statements that function as evidence. If there is no support, there is no argumentation in the text-typological sense we are developing here (see Azar 1999). Adding support is what happens in lines 3–6. That the evidence takes the form of a non-literal comparison is irrelevant. In fact, argumentation by analogy, be it literal or non-literal, is one of the stock methods of this type of discourse (McCroskey 1987). Apart from that, whatever the form of argumentation that supports the claim, a good test for checking whether you are dealing with argumentation is whether you can insert the conjunction 'for' between the claim and the support. In this case, it does not change the meaning of the poem to insert 'for' at the beginning of line 3.

Note how lines 3–6 also make use of causal structures between events. Indeed, the events depicted in them have to be understood with reference to our scenario again. However, the content of these lines does not present a narrative in the text-typological sense, because it presents a generalised, timeless content. Moreover, it is of an abstract nature, dealing with the concept of love, not with lovers and their actions. In addition, the causal links are couched in terms of general conditions and effects, using the 'if ... then' formula which is characteristic of argumentation. These are some of the typical differences between narrative and argumentative messages.

It may gradually have become clear that an important criterion for the distinction between text types lies in the nature of their typical coherence relations, the meaning connections between subsequent utterances (clauses, sentences, or lines) in the poem. Narrative and argumentative messages typically display causal connections between utterances, but descriptive message types do not. The relations between utterances in description are not causal but simply additive: one utterance is just placed after another. There are other connections between those utterances, of course, such as referential and topical relations, as in the case of 'The marriage ring'. But the coherence relations between the utterances of descriptive messages are additive. The difference between causal and additive coherence relations has been recognised by several theorists, including Halliday and Hasan (1976) and Sanders, Spooren and Noordman (1992).

In narrative and argumentation, utterances are not just added one to the other, but there is a causal relation between them. In narrative one event leads to the other, or is the result of another. And in argumentation, one claim supports another in the form of a logical syllogism. Arguments often tacitly presuppose the validity of some logical premise 'if p then q' and in effect present the resulting argument: 'p, therefore q', or 'q, for p'. For instance, in 'Love and jealousy', the underlying premise is 'if jealousy does not work as a motor for love, then do not use jealousy'. The poem itself presents the argument in the reverse order: 'it is undesirable to use jealousy (ll. 1–2), for it does not work as a motor for love (ll. 3–6). This is a typical structure for an argumentative poem, as may be seen from another example, by Austin Clarke, that you can analyse for yourself:

Penal law

Burn Ovid with the rest. Lovers will find
A hedge-school for themselves and learn by heart
All that the clergy banish from the mind,
When hands are joined and head bows in the dark.

What you have to do here is find the claim and the evidence and reconstruct the underlying premise.

One of the interesting aspects of argumentation analysis is that you may then proceed to examine the validity of the underlying premise itself. If you have doubts about the validity of the 'if p, then q' structure, you have an instrument to criticise the quality of the argument presented by the message.

Thus, even though narration and argumentation are characterised by causal coherence relations, the difference between them may be characterised as follows. In narrative, there is a causal chain of specific events in reality, which is presented by the producer of the message as relatively independent of that producer. In argumentation, there is an assumption of a causal connection between situations or events in a logical premise, and it is understood that this is not an objective connection between two specific events that have already taken place. Instead, the premise is a logical construction on the part of the sender, who wishes to use the premise to argue a particular and relatively controversial claim. Moreover, the elements of the logical premise are not specific but of a more general nature. In brief, the causal relations in narrative are relatively independent of the sender, but the causal relations in argumentation are relatively dependent on the sender. Sanders *et al.* (1992) refer to this distinction as coherence based in the semantics versus the pragmatics of the connections between the sentences.

The distinction between a semantic versus pragmatic source of coherence may also be used in explaining the difference between the use of additive relations in descriptive and expository texts. In description, the additions to the previous utterances in a message are relatively independent of the sender: they are about specific properties of the topic and based in the semantics of the connections between the sentences. In exposition, by contrast, the additions consist of utterances that are more dependent on the sender: they may involve the background knowledge a sender has about that topic which needs to be made explicit for the addressee, so that the addressee can understand previous utterances better. Or they may involve the sender's interpretation of a particular topic, by invoking an additional, sender-dependent frame of reference that was not active in the message before. Utterances of this kind would display additive relations with the previous utterances in the message, but they would be relatively more sender-dependent (pragmatic) than in the case of description.

Typically expository messages are the ones which explain something to the addressee by adopting a posture of expertise or teaching. An interesting example would be the following poem by Robert Graves:

Symptoms of love

Love is a universal migraine,
A bright stain on the vision
Blotting out reason.

Symptoms of true love
Are leanness, jealousy,
Laggard dawns;

Are omens and nightmares—
Listening for a knock,
Waiting for a sign:

For a touch of her fingers
In a darkened room,
For a searching look.

Take courage, lover!
Can you endure such grief
At any hand but hers?

The explanatory attitude of the expert is evoked here by the quasi-medical vocabulary. The first stanza appears to give a definition of the 'disease' under examination (a conventional metaphor for love, but exploited in an original way in this poem). The connection with the next stanza is additive: a disease has symptoms, and this is what the voice of the poem continues with in lines 4–6. Line 7 adds a description of the more severe cases: we are not dealing with symptoms here, but omens and nightmares. This is a typical example of an expert offering an interpretation of a set of phenomena. The phenomena are listed in lines 8–12.

It will be appreciated that it may be difficult to distinguish between description and exposition. The connection between stanza 1 and 2, for instance, might just as easily be seen as descriptive. However, this is where the distinction between a top-down and a bottom-up approach to discourse analysis should play a role. We know that many genres are either typically descriptive or expository and so on. This genre-knowledge should at least partly inform our analysis of the text type of the message. At the same time, we also know that there are many genres that display a typical mixture of different text types. Expository text seldom comes in a pure form, and often contains elements of other types. This is where a bottom-up analysis should at least be used to relativise any strong claims about the pervasive validity of a top-down analysis. Indeed, 'Symptoms of love' provides us with an illustration. The last stanza presents a mini-argument that advocates a positive attitude to the lover-as-patient, despite the preceding list of terrible symptoms. The claim is in line 13 and the support in lines 14–15. The complete last stanza functions as the second major part of the poem, which itself turns out to consist of four expository stanzas and one argumentative one. The relation between the two parts is a familiar rhetorical pattern of 'description' (or rather: exposition) and 'evaluation' (see Winter 1994), which often occurs in consultations between doctors and patients.

The proper perspective from which to look at the text type of a message is the one of genre. Some genres are predominantly narrative, argumentative, descriptive, or expository, and others are less so. Moreover, even though a genre may predominantly be realised as one of the four types, this does not mean that it may not have local stretches of discourse of another type. This may complicate the typological analysis of messages, but it only means that a top-down approach to the type of a specific message in a particular genre always has to be complemented by a bottom-up approach. The first step, however, is to achieve a provisional division of the field by checking whether a text tells a story, presents an argument, offers a description, or an exposition. For this is what would capture the conventional and average expectation of the general language user.

Conclusion

A cognitive linguistic and poetic perspective on texts enables the analyst to look *through* the language or the words on the page, to examine a number of different cognitive dimensions of text. I have distinguished between text content, type and structure, while hinting at a fourth dimension called form. Each of these four dimensions are relatively independent 'levels' of text analysis, even though they display obvious relations with each other.

In this chapter I have fixed the dimension of content, in that I only considered what people commonly call 'love stories'. I have suggested how we have a general notion for 'love stories' in the form of a cognitive scenario and shown how it can accommodate many observations about the language of love produced in cognitive linguistics. Moreover, this scenario facilitates making a distinction between our world knowledge about love in general and the way we apply it in the particular interpretation of the content and type of specific love poems.

I have also suggested that any 'love story' may come in one of four different types: narrative, argumentative, descriptive, and expository. One interesting property of such text types is their tendency for exhibiting a typical structure in their use of different sets of coherence relations:

- narratives exhibit a marked use of semantically causal relations
- arguments exhibit a marked use of pragmatically causal relations
- descriptions exhibit a marked use of semantically additive relations
- expositions exhibit a marked use of pragmatically additive relations.

It should be noted that I do not claim that these tendencies are their sole and defining property, for text type and text structure are relatively independent dimensions of text. That is, text types have other typical features that have nothing to do with local and global coherence structure, and, vice versa, there may be narratives that do not make great play of semantically causal relations in their structure. However, that there is an intimate association between text type and text structure does not seem to be very controversial, and it will be interesting to explore this assumption further. It will be of particular interest to describe the nature of these typical uses of groups of coherence relations in text types: for instance, are we talking about high frequencies, prominent functions at a global level of text organisation, or about other forms of typical use? I hope that this chapter has given enough basis for exploring these issues further in other 'love stories' in poetry, rock music, and elsewhere.

Further activities

1   Take a critical look at the love scenario. Which aspects of love does it either minimise or not include? How could these aspects be accounted for? Could there be more variations of the love scenario than just the 'dating' and the 'marriage' versions referred to in this chapter? What sorts of default assumptions do you have about the implicit elements of the scenario? (Consider, for instance, the difference between a straight and a gay version, and the possibility in The Netherlands for gay people to enter a marriage scenario as well.)

2   Take your favourite love song and bring it to class. Explain which aspects of the song are related to the love scenario in explicit and implicit ways. Decide which aspects of the song are not related to the love scenario. Compare the quality of the use of the scenario in your lyrics with the quality of this use in the poems discussed in this chapter: is there an argument for a distinction between high and popular culture in this connection, in particular with regard to the cognitive effects exerted by both genres on their audiences?

3   Discuss a small sample of the lyrics collected in 2 above, and try to decide which text type each lyric represents. Do you find clear examples of each of the four text types? Are there clear segments in the lyrics which may be classified in one way or another? Can you see the predicted typical use of the various kinds of coherence relations discussed in this chapter? Are there other criteria which make you say that a text is narrative, argumentative, and so on? Are there other text types that have not been accounted for in this chapter? If so, what are they, and how should they be defined?

7 Possible worlds and mental spaces in Hemingway's 'A very short story'

Elena Semino

Editors' preface

Elena Semino's application of possible worlds theory and mental space theory to a Hemingway short story in this chapter sits comfortably alongside Chapter 10 and Chapter 11 of this collection. All three chapters discuss aspects of the mental representations readers create when processing literary texts and, read together, they provide a helpful overview of some of the most interesting research currently being developed in this area of cognitive poetics. In this chapter, Semino examines the relationships between the various worlds constructed during the course of a short narrative. She uses both possible worlds theory and the related cognitive framework of mental space theory, assessing the advantages and disadvantages of both these approaches as a means of deepening our understanding of Hemingway's text.

Introduction

An important aspect of the comprehension of texts generally, and narrative texts in particular, is the cognitive representation of the 'world' of the text – the sets of states of affairs, events and relationships that the text refers to. This does not simply involve the ability to conceive of a sequence of events that 'happen' in the text world, but also the ability to contemplate and make sense of other events that are just imagined, wished for, hypothesised about, and so on. Indeed, part of the appeal of fictional narratives is the setting up of complex relationships between what counts as 'reality' in the story and alternative, unrealised ways in which that reality might have turned out.

In this chapter I analyse Ernest Hemingway's 'A very short story' in terms of two different theoretical approaches to the 'worlds' of texts: possible worlds theory (as proposed in Ryan 1991), and mental space theory (as proposed in Fauconnier 1997).

The text for analysis

'A very short story' by Ernest Hemingway

Before I begin my discussion of 'A very short story', it is best to give readers the chance to (re-)read it in full.

One very hot evening in Padua they carried him up onto the roof and he could look out over the top of the town. There were chimney swifts in the sky. After a while it got dark and the searchlights came out. The others went down and took the bottles with them. He and Luz could hear them below on the balcony. Luz sat on the bed. She was cool and fresh in the hot night.

Luz stayed on night duty for three months. They were glad to let her. When they operated on him she prepared him for the operating table; and they had a joke about friend or enema. He went under the anaesthetic holding tight on to himself so he would not blab about anything during the silly, talky time. After he got on crutches he used to take the temperatures so Luz would not have to get up from the bed. There were only a few patients, and they all knew about it. They all liked Luz. As he walked back along the halls he thought of Luz in his bed.

Before he went back to the front they went into the Duomo and prayed. It was dim and quiet, and there were other people praying. They wanted to get married, but there was not enough time for the banns, and neither of them had birth certificates. They felt as though they were married, but they wanted everyone to know about it, and to make it so they could not lose it.

Luz wrote him many letters that he never got until after the armistice. Fifteen came in a bunch to the front and he sorted them by the dates and read them all straight through. They were all about the hospital, and how much she loved him and how it was impossible to get along without him and how terrible it was missing him at night.

After the armistice they agreed he should go home to get a job so they might be married. Luz would not come home until he had a good job and could come to New York to meet her. It was understood he would not drink, and he did not want to see his friends or anyone in the States. Only to get a job and be married. On the train from Padua to Milan they quarrelled about her not being willing to come home at once. When they had to say good-bye, in the station at Milan, they kissed good-bye, but were not finished with the quarrel. He felt sick about saying good-bye like that.

He went to America on a boat from Genoa. Luz went back to Pordonone to open a hospital. It was lonely and rainy there, and there was a battalion of arditi quartered in the town. Living in the muddy, rainy town in the winter, the major of the battalion made love to Luz, and she had never known Italians before, and finally wrote to the States that theirs had only been a boy and girl affair. She was sorry, and she knew he would probably not be able to understand, but might some day forgive her, and be grateful to her, and she expected, absolutely unexpectedly, to be married in the spring. She loved him as always, but she realized now it was only a boy and girl love. She hoped he would have a great career, and believed in him absolutely. She knew it was for the best.

The major did not marry her in the spring, or any other time. Luz never got an answer to the letter to Chicago about it. A short time after he contracted gonorrhoea from a sales girl in a loop department store while riding in a taxicab through Lincoln Park.

'A very short story' was written in the years following Hemingway's return to the USA after his World War I experiences in Italy, and was first published in 1925. It is generally regarded as a fictionalisation of Hemingway's love story with Agnes von Kurowsky – a nurse in the American Red Cross hospital in Milan where Hemingway was treated in 1918 for shrapnel wounds to his legs (see Baker 1969; Scholes 1990). The story features some of the themes Hemingway is associated with – war, love, and loss – and is written in the kind of lucid and minimalist style that the more mature Hemingway became famous for. Like other works by Hemingway, it presents women in an unfavourable light: the blame for the unhappy ending of the wartime romance is attributed to the female character, while the male character is presented as sincere and loyal. Indeed, it is through his point of view that most of the story is told. The title of the story can be read as referring simultaneously to the text (which is only 634 words long), and the plot (the love 'story' between the protagonists turns out to be short-lived).

The understanding and appreciation of the story involves, amongst other things, keeping track of the sequence of events in the world of the text, and relating those events to alternative sequences of events that are contemplated by the characters but never realised. This is a prerequisite to the reader's ability to (a) draw conclusions about the wider significance of the story (e.g. the futility of human relationships and the effects of war on ordinary people), and (b) relate this story to other stories that deal with similar topics (e.g. fairy tales or romances).

Possible worlds theory and 'A very short story'

Possible worlds theory was originally developed by philosophers and logicians in order to deal with logical problems, such as the truth values of propositions and the ontological status of non-actual entities (Bradley and Swartz 1979). It was subsequently developed by narratologists and semioticians to account for some of the characteristics of fictional texts. In particular, possible worlds theory provides a useful framework for the definition of fiction, the description of the internal structure of fictional worlds, and the differentiation between different genres (e.g. Eco 1990; Pavel 1986; Ryan 1991). I will now demonstrate this in relation to Hemingway's story.

The 'world' of the story, the 'actual' world, and genre

In possible worlds theory, what I have so far called the 'world' of a text is in fact best seen as a 'universe', with a central domain counting as actual, and a range of alternative worlds counting as non-actual. In Hemingway's story, the male character's operation is an event in the actual domain, while the marriage between him and Luz is part of a possible world that is contemplated by the characters for some time but never realised. Ryan (1991) calls the actual domain of a particular textual universe the 'text actual world', and all unrealised worlds 'textual alternative possible worlds'. This provides the basis for a distinction between fictional and non-fictional texts: in non-fiction, the text actual world corresponds to the readers' 'actual' world; in fiction, on the other hand, the text actual world is separate and different from the readers' 'actual' world.

This distinction is relevant to Hemingway's story. In spite of its historical setting and autobiographical inspiration, the fact that the text was produced as part of a fictional genre (the short story) means that readers aware of generic conventions will not conflate the text actual world with their 'actual' world. Indeed, there are many differences between the plot and what is known about the relevant portion of the 'actual' world. The female character is named Luz and not Agnes, the initial setting is Padua rather than Milan, the male character goes back to the front and later contracts gonorrhoea, unlike the historical Hemingway, and so on (see Baker 1969; and Scholes 1990 for more detail). In addition, although the historical Hemingway did return to America hoping to marry Agnes in due course, there is no evidence that he did so under the strict conditions presented in the fifth paragraph of the story.

Whether Hemingway's story is read as autobiographical or historical fiction (Ryan 1991: 31–5), however, readers are likely to assume that the text actual world corresponds in all other respects with their 'actual' world, and will therefore flesh out the fictional world on the basis of their geographical and historical knowledge. This applies to all 'actual' places and historical events mentioned, or implied, by the text, such as Padua and World War I. Ryan introduces what she calls the 'Principle of Minimal Departure' in order to account for the fact that fictional worlds are generally assumed to resemble the actual world in all respects other than those which are textually suggested to be different (see also Teleman's (1989) Principle of Isomorphism and Eco's (1989) notion of 'parasitical' worlds).

The internal structure of the 'world' of the story, the development of the plot, and 'tellability'

A possible-world approach is particularly useful in describing the internal structure of the textual universe, and in accounting for the development of the plot. This results from seeing the textual universe as a dynamic combination of a text actual world on the one hand, and different *types* of alternate possible worlds formulated by characters on the other. Ryan describes these alternate possible worlds as different versions of the text actual world which may correspond to characters' beliefs (*Knowledge worlds*), expectations (*Prospective Extensions of Knowledge worlds*), plans (*Intention worlds*), moral commitments and prohibitions (*Obligation worlds*), wishes and desires (*Wish worlds*), and dreams or fantasies (*Fantasy Universes*) (Ryan 1991: 113ff.; see also Semino 1997: 71–4; and Stockwell 2002a: ch.7).

Overall, 'A very short story' is characterised by the formation and subsequent frustration of successive romantic Wish worlds: neither the protagonists' relationship, nor that between Luz and the Italian major lead to the conclusion that was desired by at least one of the characters at some point in the story. In this respect, 'A very short story' differs from love stories in other genres. In fairy tales and romantic novels, for example, the protagonists' Wish worlds are normally realised in a traditional happy ending. Although most possible-world accounts of plots tend to be made at a similarly high level of generalisation, it is also possible to trace the development of the story's textual universe in more detail.

The first two paragraphs introduce situations and events in the text actual world (from the male character's point of view). In the third paragraph, Luz and the male protagonist form a joint Wish world in which they get married. However, the circumstances of the text actual world make it impossible to realise this Wish world before the male character fulfils his Obligation world of going back to the front. There is therefore a conflict between the joint Wish world on the one hand, and, on the other, the male protagonist's Obligation world and the current state of the actual world (no passports, no time for banns). Ryan argues that a conflict between some of the worlds that make up a textual universe is necessary to get a plot started: if there was no conflict, there would be no need for any action, and therefore no plot (Ryan 1991: 120). In the fourth paragraph, the characters' behaviour in the text actual world is still compatible with a commitment to the Wish world formulated in the third paragraph.

In the fifth paragraph, the characters appear to form a joint Intention world which will ultimately lead to the realisation of the original Wish world. However, there are ample signs that all is not well, such as the reference to a quarrel between the protagonists before they say goodbye. In the sixth paragraph the characters go their separate ways in the text actual world, and Luz starts on a new romance cycle with the Italian major. In her letter to the male protagonist, she presents a new view of their relationship according to her more mature Knowledge world ('theirs had been only a boy and girl affair'), and outlines what she presents as a Prospective Extension of her Knowledge world ('she expected, absolutely unexpectedly, to be married in the spring'). This Prospective Extension of her Knowledge world, which implies a new romantic Wish world, is incompatible with the future realisation of the original joint Wish world.

In the final paragraph, we find out that Luz's new Wish world was also never realised in the text actual world, and we are told about the unfortunate consequences of the male protagonist's anonymous and apparently brief new affair. It is typical of Hemingway's style that no reference to either character's emotional distress is made, although readers are likely to make inferences about this. In particular, the nature of the male character's liaison with the 'sales girl' and the deadpan tone in which it is told (without access to his internal point of view), may suggest that the disillusionment he experienced with Luz led him to look for sex with no emotional involvement. It is ironic that, rather than the marriage of his original Wish world, what he finally ends up with is a venereal disease.

Ryan (1991) suggests that plot development can be explained in terms of changes in the mutual relationships between the worlds contained within a textual universe. This can account for how the central events in the plot of Hemingway's story include not just 'happenings' in the text actual world, but also changes in the mutual relationships between the characters' private worlds. According to Ryan, the study of different types of inter-world conflicts in textual universes can lead to a typology of plots (Ryan 1991: 120). Hemingway's story, for example, is characterised by conflicts between characters' romantic Wish worlds, and by the fact that, at the end of the story, all Wish worlds have been frustrated.

Ryan also makes the important claim that the creation of complex networks of unrealised possibilities is central to the aesthetic potential or 'tellability' of plots. This idea is captured by means of the 'Principle of Diversification': '*seek the diversification of possible worlds in the narrative universe*' (Ryan 1991: 156, italics in original). In other words, the aesthetic value of plots crucially depends 'on the richness and variety of the domain of the virtual' within a narrative universe, i.e. on the way in which the characters' alternate possible worlds form 'private embedded narratives' that enter in complex relationships with each other (Ryan 1991: 156). In 'A very short story', the various non-actual worlds clash with the actual domain and with each other, and form a series of virtual narratives, the most complex of which is outlined in the fifth paragraph. I will return to this below.

Possible worlds theory and cognitive poetics

Possible worlds theory is by no means a cognitive theory. However, in the move from logic to narratology, the nature of the 'worlds' considered by the theory changes considerably. The possible worlds of logic are abstract, complete and consistent sets of states of affairs conceived for the purpose of logical operations. In contrast, the possible worlds of fiction are 'furnished', incomplete, and potentially inconsistent constructs conceived by interpreters in their dynamic interactions with texts (Stockwell 2002a, for example, adopts the term 'discourse worlds' when applying the notion of possible worlds to text analysis) (see also Eco 1989; Semino 1997: 63ff.). Indeed, narratologists who work with possible worlds theory mention the role of interpreters' background knowledge in the mental furnishing of fictional worlds (e.g. Eco 1989; Ryan 1991), and, in a few cases, attempt to address the problem of the construction of fictional worlds from propositions derived from the text (e.g. Ryan 1991: 126).

Overall, however, a possible-world approach to fiction focuses on what we may call the 'product' of comprehension: the structure and characteristics of fictional worlds as the result of complex interpretative processes. The advantage of this kind of approach for cognitive poetics is that it addresses 'live' issues in poetics: the definition of fiction, the internal structure of fictional worlds, the differences between different genres, plot development, the aesthetic potential of plots, and so on. On the other hand, possible-world approaches do not ultimately treat fictional worlds as cognitive constructs, and do not deal with cognitive processing. As a consequence, there is no systematic consideration of how worlds are constructed in the interaction between the reader's mind and linguistic stimuli, and no attention for the role of linguistic choices and patterns in texts. In the case of Hemingway's story, a possible-world approach does not explain how readers conceive the different Wish worlds and virtual narratives, and does not account for some important inferences. The way in which the characters' 'agreement' is presented in the fifth paragraph, for example, may lead readers to suspect that Luz has had a change of heart well before the revelation of her new love story in the sixth paragraph. This may affect the way in which readers conceive what is presented as a joint virtual narrative in the fifth paragraph.

In Semino (1997) I showed how possible worlds theory can be usefully combined with schema theory in text analysis (see also Freeman 2000). In the next section I will show how mental space theory addresses some of the issues that are not dealt with by possible worlds theory.

Mental space theory and 'A very short story'

Like possible worlds theory, mental space theory also considers the way in which texts project complex sets of states of affairs, that can stand in different ontological relations to each other. However, mental space theory is part of cognitive linguistics, and aims to account for the online production and comprehension of language. One of its central claims is that text processing involves the incremental construction of networks of interconnected mental spaces. Mental spaces are defined as short-term cognitive representations of states of affairs, constructed on the basis of the textual input on the one hand, and the comprehender's background knowledge on the other (Fauconnier 1997: 11; Fauconnier and Turner 1996). Mental space theory has been used to account for a range of linguistic phenomena (e.g. counterfactuals, metaphor, etc.), including the incremental understanding of short (and often invented) narrative texts (Fauconnier and Sweetser 1996; Fauconnier 1997).

In order to introduce the mechanics of mental space analysis, I will briefly outline Fauconnier's (1997: 42–3) account of the comprehension of the following sentence:

Maybe Romeo is in love with Juliet.

Fauconnier's diagrammatic representation of the mental space configuration relevant to this sentence is reproduced as Figure 7.1.

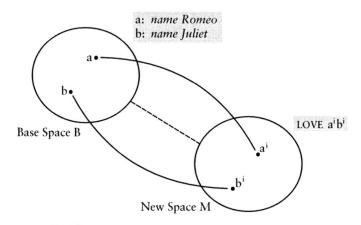

Figure 7.1 Adapted from Fauconnier 1997: 43

The comprehension of this sentence, according to Fauconnier, involves the construction of two mental spaces. The first mental space, the 'Base' (B), includes two elements 'a' and 'b', which are accessed by the names 'Romeo' and 'Juliet'. This space is linked with information about the two entities which is part of background knowledge or has been derived from the preceding co-text. The Base is the space that functions as the starting point of each network of spaces, and is always accessible for the addition of further material or for the construction of new spaces (Fauconnier 1997: 39).

The second mental space is derived from the Base via the word 'maybe', which functions as a 'space builder'. Space builders are linguistic expressions which trigger the construction of new spaces, and indicate the nature of the connection between each new space and the one from which it is constructed (Fauconnier 1997: 40). The main types of relationships between spaces are: time (the temporal relationship between one space and another) and epistemic distance (the ontological or 'reality' status of one space in relation to another) (Fauconnier 1997: 72). The latter dimension is relevant to the 'Romeo and Juliet' example. The word 'maybe' sets up the new space as a 'possibility' space, i.e. as corresponding to a state of affairs that may or may not be true in relation to the Base. The possibility space contains two entities 'a^i' and 'b^i', which are counterparts of 'a' and 'b' in the Base, and are accessed by means of the same names. This is in virtue of what Fauconnier calls the

'Access Principle' (Fauconnier 1997: 41; see also Stockwell 2002a: ch.7). In the possibility space, 'a^i' is in love with 'b^i'. This space is also structured by background knowledge triggered by the expression 'in love with'. This is indicated in Figure 7.1 by the small-capital mnemonic LOVE in the square box (these mnemonics are commonly used in cognitive linguistics to indicate frames or schemata). The dashed line indicates that M is set up relative to B, while the curved lines indicate a relationship of identity between elements in the two spaces.

While B is the Base space of the structure in Figure 7.1, M is the 'Focus' space, i.e. the space to which material is being added by the sentence. In this case B also functions as 'Viewpoint' space, i.e. as the space from which the new one is set up and accessed. In the simplest situation, the same space may function as Base, Viewpoint, and Focus, but, as I will show, things can get rather complicated when accounting for longer stretches of text (Fauconnier 1997: 49–51).

Space builders and the construction of 'reality' within fiction

In past-tense narratives such as 'A very short story', the Base space corresponds to the time and space of narration, i.e. the non-specified context with respect to which the time of all narrated events is past. The succession of states and events that make up the basic skeleton of the plot forms a series of chronologically ordered spaces which count as 'fact' in relation to the Base, and are temporally anterior to it. In Hemingway's story, these spaces include events such as the male character being carried on to the roof, and are set up by space builders such as 'One very hot evening in Padua', 'After the armistice', 'in the station, at Milan', 'A short time after', and so on.

Because these spaces are marked for temporal distance from the Base (but no epistemic distance), they make up what Fauconnier (1997: 50) has called '"reality" within fiction'. This corresponds to the text actual world of possible worlds theory, which is defined by Ryan as 'a succession of different states and events which together form a history' (Ryan 1991: 113). The merit of mental space theory, in this respect, is that it tries to account for the way in which the series of factual spaces is projected by means of linguistic space builders. On the negative side, however, the examples used by mental space theorists are often very simple made-up narratives, which invariably contain explicit and easily-identifiable space builders (see also Werth 1999: 77). Real narratives, in contrast, tend to be much more complex and inexplicit. In reading the fourth paragraph of the story, for example, readers will infer that the clause 'Luz wrote him many letters' refers to actions that take place while the male protagonist is at the front. This inference derives from a combination of factors, including the fact that the previous paragraph opens with the space-building adverbial clause 'Before he went back to the front', and that, according to relevant background knowledge, communication by letter normally takes place when addresser and addressee are spatially distant.

However, there is no explicit space builder at the beginning of the fourth paragraph signalling that there has been a shift to a time after the male protagonist's return to the front. The application of mental space theory to real narratives should lead to better accounts of implicit ways in which texts can trigger the construction of mental spaces.

Mental spaces and the characters' romantic dream

The notion of epistemic distance captures the fact that mental spaces can be set up as 'non-fact' in relation to the Base, or to other spaces in a network (Fauconnier 1997: 93–5). This accounts for the linguistic projection of states of affairs that, in possible-world terms, occur in textual alternate possible worlds. This is particularly relevant to the unrealised wishes and intentions that are at the centre of Hemingway's story. I will focus in detail on two stretches of text from the third and fifth paragraphs respectively, i.e. before and after the male protagonist's second period at the front.

The third sentence of the third paragraph spells out the future plans that the characters have formed as a consequence of the relationship that has blossomed in the hospital in Padua (and which readers have been put in a position to infer from the first two paragraphs of the story):

> They wanted to get married, but there was not enough time for the banns, and neither of them had birth certificates.

Figure 7.2 provides a diagrammatic account of my analysis of the first clause, 'They wanted to get married'. The Base space N is the context of the act of narration, and includes only one entity, the narrator (n). Two further spaces are included in this figure in order to account for the meaning of the clause quoted above. The first space corresponds to the situation where the two characters are not married. I have called this the 'Reality' space R, since its contents count as actual in the world of the story (see also Sweetser 1996). The use of the past tense sets up this space as temporally anterior to the Base. This space contains two unmarried entities (a and b), corresponding respectively to the male character referred to as 'he' and the female character referred to by the name 'Luz', and has already been structured by information derived from the previous text, and by relevant background knowledge. The use of the verb 'want' (which is a space builder), sets up a further space, which is marked for epistemic distance in relation to the Reality space. I have called this a 'Want' space, W (see Sweetser 1996). This space contains counterparts of the two characters (a^i and b^i), and is characterised by the fact that here the two characters get married. Further structure is provided by the readers' relevant background knowledge.

Let us now consider the whole of the sentence quoted above. In the first clause of the sentence, space N functions as Base, space R functions as Viewpoint, and space W is the Focus space. After the first comma, the focus

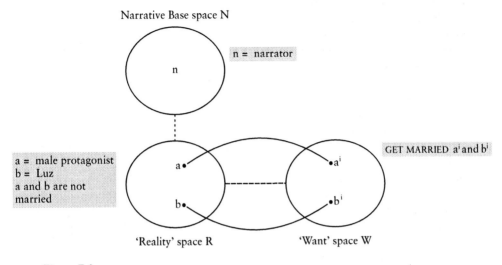

Figure 7.2

switches back to R. The use of 'but' often indicates an incompatibility between spaces (see Fauconnier 1997: 45–6). In this case there is an incompatibility between conditions in the R space and the realisation of the W space. The coordinated clauses following 'but' add to the R space information about lack of time for banns and lack of birth certificates. The readers' background knowledge can explain how these aspects of R are incompatible with a rapid realisation of space W: getting married (in the relevant cultural context) involves the submission of birth certificates to prove one's identity, and the publication of banns for a fixed amount of time. The information provided by the two clauses following 'but', therefore, further enriches the R space in Figure 7.2.

The analysis of this sentence begins to show how a mental space approach can account for some of the more abstract constructs of possible worlds theory. What possible world theorists call 'alternate possible worlds' and 'virtual narratives' can be seen as the product of networks of mental spaces marked for epistemic distance from the Base, or from what counts as 'factual' spaces in relation to the Base.

Mental spaces and the unravelling of the characters' relationship

In the third paragraph of the story, the impediment to the realisation of the characters' wish to get married lies in some basic bureaucratic prerequisites to marriage in the R space, that could not be satisfied before the male character returned to the front. Other things being equal, therefore, one may expect that the characters would get married immediately after the end of the war. The fifth paragraph, however, suggests otherwise: the two characters decide that he should return to the US while Luz carries on working in Italy, and that the wedding should be delayed until he has found a 'good job' back home. Figure 7.3 provides a diagrammatic representation of my analysis of the first sentence of paragraph five (for the sake of visual clarity, I have not used curved lines to signal identity relations between entities across spaces):

> After the armistice they agreed he should go home to get a job so they might be married.

In Figure 7.3, N functions as Base space for a new configuration. The new 'Reality' space R1 is past in relation to the Base and involves the two main characters (a and b) entering an agreement. The use of the verb 'agree' functions as space builder for a series of spaces which are future in relation to R1, and therefore not-yet-factual. More specifically, the verb 'agree' is a speech verb (albeit a non-prototypical one presenting the *outcome* of a verbal interaction between the two characters), and speech verbs function as space builders. I have followed Fauconnier (1997) in including all the spaces derived from 'agreed' within a 'speech domain' (see also Sanders and Redeker 1996). I have called the first space which is set up by 'agreed'

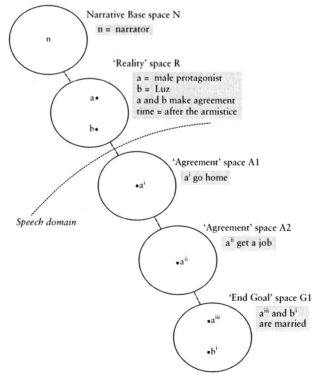

Figure 7.3

'Agreement' space A1. In this space, the male character a^i goes home to America. The use of 'should' in 'he should go home' indicates futurity with respect to the (past) space R, which functions as viewpoint. The choice of the modal 'should', however, also suggests obligation or compulsion rather than willingness (in contrast with 'would', for example).

Given that it is the male character who is involved here, readers may infer that what is presented as an agreement is actually the female character's wish, which is imposed on, and accepted by, the male character. The contents of space A1 count as the prerequisite for the following part of the agreement, which is represented in space A2. This space is future in relation to A1 and corresponds to a situation where the male character finds a job. The realisation of both A1 and A2 leads to a further space, which I have called End Goal space G1, where the two characters get married. This space is future in relation to A2, and therefore A1 also. The choice of the modal 'might' in 'So they might be married', however, does not simply indicate futurity in relation to a past viewpoint, but also epistemic distance. In contrast with 'could' for example, the use of 'might' suggests tentative possibility, and therefore attributes to G1 a low likelihood of realisation.

A simple visual comparison between Figure 7.3 and Figure 7.2 shows that the distance between the 'Reality' space and the space where the protagonists are married has increased considerably from the third paragraph. While in Figure 7.2 the 'marriage' space was directly accessible from the Base, in Figure 7.3 there are two intervening spaces which function as pre-conditions. In Ryan's terms, the virtual narrative has become longer. More importantly, the nature of the impediments to the realisation of the original Want space have changed considerably: objective and non-negotiable 'facts' (i.e. no birth certificates, no time for banns) have been replaced by subjective and negotiable preferences (i.e. the male character having a job). This, coupled with the use of the modals 'should' and 'might', explains why readers may suspect that the female character is now dictating pre-conditions to marriage as a delaying tactic due to a change of heart.

The details of the 'agreement' between the two characters are spelt out further in the following sentence, where the focus switches to Luz. This sentence can be seen as a Free Indirect representation of parts of the interaction that led to the agreement (see Leech and Short 1981: 325ff.; Fludernik 1993):

> Luz would not come home until he had a good job and could come to New York to meet her.

I will not analyse this sentence in all its detail, but Figure 7.4 is my attempt to provide a complete representation of this and the previous sentence together. Overall, the virtual narrative is now even more complex, with specific pre-conditions attached to Luz returning to the USA in the first place. The 'job' of the previous sentence has become 'a good job', and the use of deixis suggests a separation between the viewpoints of the two characters.

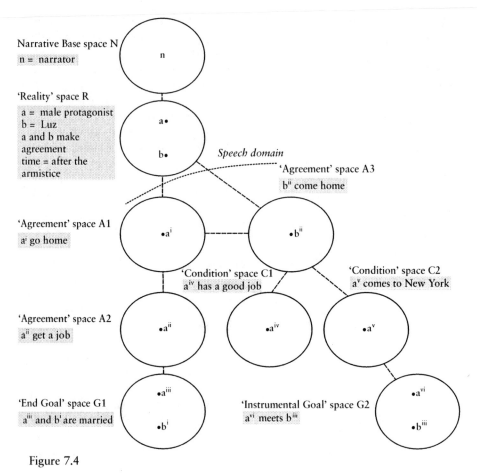

Narrative Base space N
n = narrator

'Reality' space R
a = male protagonist
b = Luz
a and b make
agreement
time = after the
armistice

Speech domain

'Agreement' space A3
b^{ii} come home

'Agreement' space A1
a^{i} go home

'Condition' space C1
a^{iv} has a good job

'Condition' space C2
a^{v} comes to New York

'Agreement' space A2
a^{ii} get a job

'End Goal' space G1
a^{iii} and b^{i} are married

'Instrumental Goal' space G2
a^{vi} meets b^{iii}

Figure 7.4

I will focus particularly on the two uses of 'come', a deictic verb which indicates movement towards the point that functions as deictic centre (see Rauh 1983). The first use of 'come' (in 'Luz would not come home') suggests movement towards the male character in America. As far as space deixis is concerned, therefore, space A3 is accessed from A1, where the male character a^{i} is in the USA (in contrast, 'would' suggests that R is viewpoint as far as temporal relations are concerned). The second use of 'come' (in 'and could come to New York'), however, suggests movement towards Luz. Here viewpoint is via space A3, where Luz goes to America. These shifts in deictic centre point out the separation of the two characters in the virtual narrative that is supposed to lead to their union in marriage. They also potentially highlight that what is presented as a single instance of speech presentation ('they agreed') is in fact the result of an interaction of two separate voices and perspectives. The use of a negative structure to refer to Luz's return to the USA ('Luz would not come home') may be taken as a further sign of her dictating conditions, and of her new negative attitude to their future plans (in contrast, for example, with 'Luz would come home when … '). Overall, all this explains why it may be no surprise, for some readers at least, to find out about the characters quarrelling later in the same paragraph, and about Luz's new romance in the following paragraph.

It is important to note that the stretch of text I have just analysed is much more complex than the texts normally used as examples by mental space theorists. As a consequence, Figure 7.4 is not just visually complex, but is also only one of several possible representations of the relevant configuration of mental spaces. In particular, the indices labelling the counterparts of the characters in the various spaces follow the ordering of information in the text, rather than the appropriate (imaginary) chronological sequence. For example, 'Instrumental Goal' space G2 chronologically *precedes* 'End Goal' space G1 in the relevant virtual narrative (i.e. the male character has to go and meet Luz in New York before they can get married). However, 'Instrumental Goal' space G2 is set up *after* 'End Goal' space G1 in a sequential reading of the text, so that, in Figure 7.4, the numerical indices labelling the counterparts of the characters in space G2 (a^{vi} and b^{iii}) are higher than those labelling the counterparts in space G1 (a^{iii} and b^{i}).

I do not have the space to analyse other parts of the text, but a similar type of analysis can be applied to Luz's new wishes and plans later in the story.

Mental space theory and cognitive poetics

My analysis has shown how a mental space approach focuses both on the linguistic features of the text and on the reader's background knowledge, so that inferences and nuances of meaning can be incorporated into the analysis. This provides a cognitively plausible account of text processing, and relates abstract notions such as 'worlds' and 'virtual narratives' to the interaction between the reader and the text. In this respect, mental space theory has a great deal to offer to cognitive poetics.

On the other hand, however, mental space theorists have not normally focused on real, let alone literary, narratives, and have so far not been greatly concerned with the kinds of issues that interest literary scholars (apart from some discussions of 'blending' in Fauconnier 1997: 149ff.; Fauconnier and Turner 1996; Turner and Fauconnier 2000). Sanders and Redeker (1996) link 'viewpoint' in mental space theory with 'perspective' and 'focalisation' in narratology, and apply mental space theory to speech and thought presentation in narrative, but much more work needs to be done in both these areas. Although the 'worlds' of possible worlds theory and the 'spaces' of mental space theory are quite different kinds of constructs (see Fauconnier and Sweetser 1996: 12), mental space theory can benefit from the findings of the narratological applications of possible worlds theory. The notion of virtual narrative, and Ryan's 'Principle of Diversification', for example, can be applied to explain the aesthetic potential of complex networks such as those of Figures 7.3 and 7.4. Part of the effect of 'A very short story' is that the final frustration of the male character's wishes comes after repeated and detailed descriptions of courses of events that never come true. The same applies to Luz's new virtual narrative, so that, in the final paragraph, there are no more epistemically distant spaces: the focus is exclusively on new and negative states of the 'Reality' space.

To conclude, the challenge and potential of literary narratives have not yet been fully taken on board by mental space theory. In this respect, practitioners of cognitive poetics can make a contribution to future developments in cognitive linguistics.

Further activities

1   Possible worlds theory is most useful when you aim to provide an overall account of the 'world' of a whole text. You could try this out on any narrative (and on many poems and plays too). A particularly interesting choice is the recent novel *Blackberry Wine* by Joanne Harris, where there is an ambiguity concerning the status of what appear to be supernatural events (Harris 2000). You should try to spell out one or more possible interpretations of what 'happens' in the novel, and then express those interpretations in terms of the internal structure of the fictional universe.

2   Mental space theory is most useful in the detailed analysis of short texts or extracts. You could try this on stories such as Aesop's fable 'A Lesson for Fools', and then compare your analysis with Ryan's (1991) possible-world analysis. If you want a more challenging example, you could analyse the pages in Roddy Doyle's *Paddy Clarke Ha Ha Ha* where the main character speculates on whether his mother has seen him stealing magazines from a shop with his friends (Doyle 1993: 160ff.).

3   In Semino *et al.* (1999) possible-world theory is applied to the classification of different instances of what we call 'hypothetical speech, thought and writing presentation' (e.g. 'If she was here, she would say that we are mad'). You could try to apply a mental space approach to some of the examples quoted in that paper. Alternatively, you could collect your own examples, and analyse them both in terms of possible worlds theory and in terms of mental space theory. You could then compare the strengths and weaknesses of each approach.

8 Conceptual metaphor and its expressions

Peter Crisp

Editors' preface

In this chapter, Peter Crisp identifies and discusses a range of conceptual metaphors in a poem by D.H. Lawrence, 'The Song of a Man Who Has Come Through'. Cognitive linguistics has argued for some time now that conceptual metaphors originate in everyday, shared human experience. What Crisp demonstrates here is how Lawrence takes certain conventionalised conceptual structures and revivifies them for his readers. Crisp revisits a number of the basic tenets of cognitive linguistic theory and examines in detail their relevance for cognitive poeticists. There is plenty of scope for you to test the ideas put forward in this chapter for yourself, by comparing your own analysis of Keats' 'The Fall of Hyperion' with that provided by Crisp in his appendix. You may find also it particularly useful to read Crisp's discussion and the chapter by Michael Burke, which follows, alongside one another.

Concept, system and creativity

Ever since Lakoff and Johnson (1980) it has been commonplace in cognitive semantics to say that metaphor is not a matter of 'mere language' but is something conceptual. The earlier dominant view of metaphor (that cognitive semantics rejected) thought, by contrast, that metaphor is mere language. It held that the significance of any new metaphorical expression could be expressed by a literal equivalent which, if the expression became conventionally established, would become its literal meaning. Thus, for example, when the expression 'the river's mouth' was first produced it was held to have been simply an economic equivalent for 'that part of a river where the body of water flowing through it meets the sea', an equivalence established via the literal similarity between water flowing out of a river and breath out of a mouth. Then, when the 'the river's mouth' became an established expression, the original literal equivalent became its literal dictionary definition, resulting in a 'dead metaphor'. If one wanted to argue that the word form 'meets' in the claimed definition is itself metaphorical, since only people can literally 'meet' one another, and that metaphor is therefore irre-ducible, the reply was that 'meet' too is a dead metaphor. Metaphor was a mere variation of linguistic form.

In rejecting the 'mere language' view of metaphor, cognitive semantics has developed the idea of a conceptual, cross-domain mapping. One conceptual domain, the target, is understood in terms of another, the source (Lakoff 1987, 1993). Thus, in the phrase 'At the summit of the Soviet apparatus was Stalin', the word 'summit' signals POWER IS UP in which the domain of social relations is understood in terms of that of spatial relations. In particular, rea-soning about spatial relations is projected onto reasoning about social rela-tions by mapping higher points on some imagined vertical line onto greater degrees of power. That what is involved is something conceptual and not merely linguistic is shown by the fact that I might well utter the cited sentence while raising my hand as high as or higher than my head and then say 'and the peasants were at the bottom' while stretching my arm almost straight down. (Try out these gestures while uttering the cited or similar sentences; they may seem familiar.)

If I were to do this, and people often do accompany metaphorical lan-guage with appropriate gestures, I would be showing I was *thinking* of Soviet power in terms of VERTICALITY. It would be far fetched to argue that in utter-ing 'summit' and 'bottom' I had only the literal concept of MAXIMAL/MINI-MAL POWER in mind and by pure coincidence made gestures opposed in the dimension of verticality. I must have been thinking of POWER in terms of VERTICALITY and so have expressed VERTICALITY by both language and gesture.

Conceptual metaphor is often expressed non-linguistically (Forceville 1996; Cienki 1998). Visual metaphor, for example, plays an important role in the interaction of text and illustration in the novels of Dickens, the poems of Blake, and in the seventeenth-century emblem tradition. Metaphor can be expressed in different modalities because its underlying reality is conceptual and so not confined to any single mode of expression.

Source domains are typically more experientially basic than target domains. The source domain of POWER IS UP is a dimension of our everyday experience: we are constantly raising and lowering such things as cups of coffee. The target domain, by contrast, is something more abstract, a dimen-sion of social relations. Conceptual metaphor typically projects experientially basic categories onto more abstract ones. Such categories are not ontologically but cognitively basic: typically, they neither denote ulti-mate constituents of reality nor are they without internal structure. Rather, they are conceptual packagings of reality understood directly in their own terms because they have evolved to facilitate our everyday functioning in the world (Lakoff 1987). The grounding of metaphor in these categories is reflected by the fact that with metaphors such as POWER IS UP or ANGER IS HEAT, as in 'He's a hothead' or 'She's doing a slow burn', the link between source and target is not similarity but a prototypical correlation in basic experience. In the basic scenario of physical combat the winner ends up on top: POWER correlates with UP. Likewise, according to folk theory and scientific observation, we tend to get hot when we get angry. Metaphor is not a matter of mere language but a means of extending our cognitive facility with basic categories to non-basic ones. It is therefore cognitively indispensable.

The 'traditional' view of metaphor argued that the only real metaphor was a new one. Conventionalisation was the death of metaphor. If metaphor is cognitively indispensable, however, it is likely to be conventionalised. The amount of processing time taken up by the endless generation of new metaphors would be inordinate and probably outweigh any cognitive benefits. What is needed is a ready-made system of basic metaphors. Cognitive semanticists have shown that such a system underlies both conventional metaphorical expressions and much original use of metaphorical language (Johnson 1987; Lakoff and Turner 1989; Kövecses 1990; Sweetser 1990). The trend of research has increasingly emphasised the systematic nature of conventional metaphor. Rather than concentrating on isolated metaphors like POWER IS UP or ANGER IS HEAT, analysts have increasingly identified very general metaphors underlying a whole range of more specialised ones.

Lakoff and Johnson (1980) already recognised a class of orientational metaphors in which spatial oppositions such as UP/DOWN acted as source domains for a large number of different targets. Lakoff and Turner (1989) describe what they term 'generic metaphors', such as EVENTS ARE ACTIONS, which can receive a wide range of specifications: any event can be metaphorised as an action. Lakoff (1993) sees the often referred to conceptual metaphor LIFE IS A JOURNEY as simply one specialisation of what he calls the Event Structure Metaphor, an interlocking set of very general metaphors such as STATES ARE LOCATIONS, CHANGES ARE MOVEMENTS, PURPOSES ARE DESTINATIONS and MEANS ARE PATHS. Recently, Grady (1999) has termed the underlying level of very general metaphor 'primary metaphor', arguing that it is at this level that metaphor is grounded in correlations of basic experience.

The idea that metaphor is rooted in a conceptual system can seem threatening to those who view literature as a matter of individual creativity alone. Individual creativity however is always exercised within a socially established conceptual framework, which it may modify. This is as true of a writer like D.H. Lawrence, who so greatly values individual creativity, as of any other. His 'Song of a Man Who Has Come Through' is a series of creative specifications and elaborations of the Event Structure Metaphor.

Song of a Man Who Has Come Through

1   Not I, not I, but the wind that blows through me!
    A fine wind is blowing the new direction of Time.
    If only I let it bear me, carry me, if only it carry me!
    If only I am sensitive, subtle, oh, delicate, a winged gift!

5 If only, most lovely of all, I yield myself and am borrowed
   By the fine, fine wind that takes its course through the chaos of the
      world
   Like a fine, an exquisite chisel, a wedge-blade inserted;
   If only I am keen and hard like the sheer tip of a wedge
   Driven by invisible blows,
10 The rock will split, we shall come at the wonder, we shall find the
      Hesperides.

   Oh, for the wonder that bubbles into my soul,
   I would be a good fountain, a good well-head,
   Would blur no whisper, spoil no expression.

   What is the knocking?
15 What is the knocking at the door in the night?
   It is somebody wants to do us harm.

   No, no, it is the three strange angels.

   Admit them, admit them.

Lawrence's poem is about emotional change where, in accordance with the
Event Structure Metaphor, CHANGES ARE MOVEMENTS and CAUSES ARE
FORCES. In lines 1–6, the force capable of producing MOVEMENT/CHANGE is
specified as wind, 'the wind that blows through me' (l.1), thereby
connecting the Event Structure Metaphor to EMOTIONS ARE NATURAL
FORCES. The result is that emotional change is conceptualised as being as
humanly uncontrollable as a blowing wind, lack of emotional control being
a standard entailment of EMOTIONS ARE NATURAL FORCES (Kövecses 1990).
Yet an element of human volition is still allowed for, for the speaker must
allow himself to be borne by the wind: 'If only I let it bear me' (l.3). In lines
7–10, from being 'a winged gift' (l.4) to be borne by the wind, the speaker is
re-specified as 'an exquisite chisel' (l.7) driven by 'invisible blows' (l.9).
Conceptualising the speaker as a tool, an inanimate entity, produces a more
radical emphasis on the uncontrollability of emotional change, since it
hides his volitionality, just as conceptualising the force making for that
change as 'invisible blows' emphasises its unknowability via KNOWING IS
SEEING. We can see that Lawrence has by now creatively combined and
specified a number of conceptual metaphors. Yet the major conceptual
metaphor he uses remains the Event Structure Metaphor. The culmination
of the poem's first verse paragraph draws upon the DIFFICULTIES ARE OBSTA-
CLES TO MOVEMENT component of that metaphor: 'The rock will split … we
shall find the Hesperides' (l.10). What is envisaged is the speaker/chisel
breaking through a rock in his path and finding the mythological garden
containing the goddess Hera's golden apples. This will be the decisive
emotional transformation.

In lines 11–13, Lawrence again employs EMOTIONS ARE NATURAL FORCES. The natural force, however, is now specified as water, not wind, and, rather than moving the speaker, it is desired to well up within him as the inspiration of utterance: 'I would be a good fountain ... spoil no expression' (ll.12–13). In terms of the Event Structure Metaphor, the prospect of change has been temporarily forgotten, for a fountain cannot move. In lines 14–18 EMOTIONS ARE NATURAL FORCES finally disappears from the poem altogether. The speaker is initially frightened by a 'knocking at the door' (l.15), but then realises that this is 'the three strange angels' (l.17) and finally enjoins, 'Admit them, admit them' (l.18). Lawrence is now specifying the source domain in biblical terms. The three angels come from Genesis 18 and 19 where they (in fact it is God and two angels) appear to Abraham announcing doom on Sodom. Two of them (Lawrence makes it all three) go on to Sodom to lead Lot and his family out of the city before its destruction. Note that the speaker, having taken on the role of Lot, does not himself move but rather asks that the angels be allowed to move towards him.

All of this is a highly original specification of the Event Structure Metaphor. From the beginning of the poem there has been an increasing emphasis on the uncontrollability of MOVEMENT/CHANGE, on the necessity of simply letting it happen. Here at the poem's end the speaker is absolutely unmoving, simply asking that the angels be allowed to move towards him. The angels, Lawrence's last specification of the FORCE of emotional change, will lead the speaker/Lot out of Sodom. This will be the decisive MOVEMENT/CHANGE, which the angels not the speaker will initiate. Emotional transformation will have been gained by renouncing all deliberate volitionality and letting the FORCE of the angels guide the speaker.

In 'Song Of A Man Who Has Come Through', Lawrence draws upon the system of established conceptual metaphor to construct his own distinctive view of a target domain. However, we should not think that writers never create their own cross-domain mappings. The area in which this is most obviously done is that of image metaphor. Strictly speaking, image metaphor is not a matter of conceptual metaphor (Crisp 1996). Its mappings are from one sensory domain to another, as in Ezra Pound's famous haiku 'In a Station of the Metro', where the visual appearance of petals on a wet black bough is mapped onto that of faces in a crowd. Rather than re-conceptualising an abstract domain in terms of an experientially basic one, image metaphor remains within the realm of the experientially basic. There are few conventional image metaphors. This is presumably because, since it does not involve domains of abstract conceptual generality, image metaphor cannot play a direct role in constituting metaphorical resources for abstract reasoning.

In creating image metaphors, writers typically produce new cross-domain mappings, as in these lines from Wordsworth's 'Descriptive Sketches' describing a sunset in the Alps:

Eastward, in long perspective glittering, shine
The wood-crown'd cliffs that o'er the lake recline;
Wide o'er the Alps a hundred streams unfold,
At once to pillars turn'd that flame with gold;

(ll.339–42)

The target of the last couplet is the Alpine streams and Wordsworth maps onto them the three images of pillars, flame and gold. None of the three mappings, nor their combination, has a conventional basis. We have seen that conventional metaphors such as POWER IS UP and ANGER IS HEAT are based not in similarity but in basic experiential correlations. Wordsworth's image metaphors, however, are based in similarity. The link between pillars and the mountain streams is that both are vertical or near-vertical and much taller than they are wide; the link between 'flame', 'gold' and the streams is that in the sunset the streams are red like flame and yellow like gold.

Admitting that similarity does sometimes motivate metaphor does not involve going back to the traditional view that metaphor reflects an antecedently perceived literal similarity. With metaphors based on similarity one domain of experience is still used to change our view of another. Such metaphors reveal similarities of which we might not have been previously aware. In Wordsworth's lines above, we are not told separately that the Alpine streams are falling near-perpendicularly down cliff faces, nor that the sunset has advanced to the point where they reflect the red and gold of the sky. Rather, the projected source images lead us to construct this picture of them, so dramatically modifying our view of them.

The class of similarity metaphors is not exhausted by the class of image metaphors. EMOTIONS ARE NATURAL FORCES, for example, is also similarity based: both natural forces and emotions are difficult to control. This shows that conceptual metaphors too can be similarity based (Grady 1999). Yet even in these cases, metaphor still functions as an enabler of thought. Although emotions are central to our experience, their nature is often very difficult to grasp. Such physical phenomena as winds and floods, by contrast, are far easier for us to think about. Structuring our thought about emotions in terms of NATURAL FORCES is therefore a powerful aid to thought. Similarity provides the basis for a number of such conventional conceptual metaphors. It is probably, however, particularly well adapted to the creation of new metaphorical mappings, more so than the kind of correlation in everyday experience underlying a metaphor such as POWER IS UP. It takes careful reflection to arrive at the hypothesis that POWER IS UP is based in the correlations of physical combat, while, as Aristotle rightly observed, many similarities can be perceived in a flash (see Mahon 1999). Similarity thus seems to further increase the scope for writers' individual metaphorical creativity. We must, however, never lose sight of the conventional, established, system of primary metaphor, based mainly in the correlations of everyday experience, upon which writers, like everybody else, constantly draw. This system enables creativity by constraining it, by making available to it a relatively fixed set of conceptual resources.

Metaphorical language

Cognitive semantics, we have seen, rejects the view that metaphor is a matter of mere language. In recent years, however, there has been a return to language, not in the sense of denying metaphor's conceptual nature, but rather out of the belief that having established that conceptual nature we need to pay more attention to the details of its expression, linguistic or otherwise (see Goatly 1997; Crisp 2002; Crisp *et al.* 2002; Steen 2002; Heywood *et al.* 2002). Since the only direct evidence we have for the existence of conceptual metaphor is its expressions, we need rigorous ways of describing and analysing these. The 'return to language' fits in well with the development of a cognitive poetics, for however important underlying cognitive structures are in literature one can never dismiss language as of merely peripheral interest.

The first step is to identify which expressions are metaphorical (Steen 1999a). This is not straightforward. What is to count as metaphorical? An obvious response might be to say whatever is used metaphorically, that is, whatever expresses the psychological activation of a conceptual metaphor. However, we cannot assume that because someone says 'I'm feeling up' they have activated HAPPINESS IS UP. We saw earlier that the accompanying of metaphorical language by appropriate gesture is evidence for 'online' metaphorical processing. Language alone, however, cannot provide sufficient evidence for such processing. A speaker might use a conventionalised expression such as 'up' to refer directly to the target domain of HAPPINESS without constructing any cross-domain mapping. (The 'traditional' view of metaphor claimed this is what happens with all but the newest of metaphors.) Ultimately, only experimental psychology can determine when conceptual metaphors are activated, but as a research goal this seems some way off. To analyse metaphorical language some other criterion than activation is needed.

By studying discourse in context one can decide if an expression provides the basis *in principle* for a cross-domain mapping. If someone says 'I'm feeling up', the words 'I'm feeling' establish the target domain of emotion/mood and 'up' provides the basis for HAPPINESS IS UP. Whether the speaker actually constructs this mapping is irrelevant: there is a basis in principle for constructing it. In this example the immediate linguistic context alone enables the discourse analyst to reconstruct 'up' as metaphorical. Frequently in discourse, however, the linguistic context is less immediate. Consider the following:

A – *He's solved the problem.*
B – *Yup, he's on top of it.*

The second turn uttered in response to 'Has he climbed the mountain yet?' would not contain a metaphorical expression. Extra-linguistic context may also determine the target domain. I see a friend laughing in the street and say to someone beside me, 'He's up today'. If the same person had appeared after being ill, but without laughing, my utterance of 'He's up today' would not be metaphoric. A given discourse establishes its referential target by whatever means, linguistic or non-linguistic, it finds to hand. Relative to that target the analyst can decide for a given expression if it provides the basis for a cross-domain mapping, whether or not such a mapping has actually been constructed by the discourse's producer(s) and/or receiver(s).

The above approach draws a clear distinction between metaphorical language and metaphorical concepts, while defining the former with reference to the latter. This needs to be reflected terminologically. The terminology of cognitive semantics is available for referring to conceptual metaphors. With linguistic metaphors we need first to draw a distinction between literal and metaphorical expressions. Steen (1999b) suggests that Black's (1962) term *frame* be used to refer to the literal expression(s) and *focus* to the metaphoric one(s). In the phrase 'I'm feeling up', 'I'm feeling' is the frame and 'up' is the focus. A linguistic metaphor consists of a frame and a focus. A focus, by its nature, necessarily relates to the source domain. Frames, however, do not always relate to the target domain. In 'They walked over a great bald skull', with 'a great bald skull' interpreted as referring to a hill, for example, the frame does not relate to the target of the hill. This target is understood contextually and not referred to literally at all, although the frame 'They walked over' is of course still literal. (For further distinctions see Steen 1999a, 1999b and 2002: determining where a linguistic metaphor begins and ends is particularly tricky.) Linguistic metaphors need to be distinguished from similes. We must however remember here that we are dealing with linguistic expressions. Similes, like linguistic metaphors, provide a basis for constructing conceptual metaphors, for understanding one conceptual domain in terms of another (Ortony 1993). Linguistic metaphor and simile are thus alternative ways of expressing conceptual (or image) metaphor linguistically. They both contain a focus and a frame, but the simile also contains an overt signalling of the mapping relation.

One can, we have seen, have metaphorical language without activated metaphorical concepts. It is also possible to have activated metaphorical concepts without metaphorical language. *Allegory* and *symbol* are terms with complicated histories. Nowadays in literary contexts they prototypically apply to works that continuously activate a cross-domain mapping without overtly referring to its target domain. A prototypical allegory would be Bunyan's *The Pilgrim's Progress*. This continually activates LIFE IS A JOURNEY. Its language however is literal in relation to LIFE IS A JOURNEY, as this excerpt from its opening shows:

I saw a man clothed with Rags standing in a certain place, with his face from his own

House, a Book in his hand, and a great burden upon his Back. I looked, and saw him

open the Book, and Read therein; and as he read, he wept and trembled.

Linguistically we have here only literal reference to a fictional situation. There is a mapping whose activation in the minds of Bunyan and most of his readers cannot be seriously doubted: this scene corresponds to a Christian's realisation of their sinfulness. The language however does not refer to this target domain but functions only to set up a fictional scene from which the cross-domain mapping then proceeds (Crisp 2001). This mapping is not prompted by the language, for there is no 'clash' of focus and frame, but by a knowledge of the literary convention of the allegorical dream vision and of the conceptual metaphor system.

The fictional world of an allegory, such as *The Pilgrim's Progress*, typically exists solely for the sake of its source domain function. What is usually referred to in literary contexts as symbol is more opportunistic. A typical example would be the opening of Dickens' *Bleak House*. Here the fog exists in a fictional world that has its own naturalistic rationale, yet also activates KNOWING IS SEEING. Metaphorically, since you cannot easily see in or through it, the fog is an impediment to knowing and so to acting. It symbolises the obscurantism of the English legal system. The language referring to it, however, as in the opening of the novel's second paragraph, is perfectly literal: 'Fog everywhere. Fog up the river, where it flows among green aits and meadows; fog down the river'. The closely related nature of allegory and symbol is shown by the fact that with both, in order to understand them, we need to distinguish clearly between metaphorical language and metaphorical concepts.

Although the criterion given above for judging a linguistic expression metaphorical is quite straightforward, its application may not be. A number of factors can make it difficult to judge whether an expression provides the basis for a cross-domain mapping. Such a mapping for example requires at least two domains, but it is not always clear where the boundaries between domains fall and so whether one is dealing with two or more domains or a single vaguely specified domain (Heywood *et al.* 2002). It can also be difficult to determine if a word's conventional sense allows for setting up a metaphorical source domain; this is the problem traditionally labelled 'dead metaphor'. Although few will want to go back to denying metaphoricity to all but the newest of metaphors, many will feel that for example there is something problematic about so-called 'delexicalised verbs' like 'make' and 'have', as in 'She had a good time' and 'She made an effort'. In fact no sharp distinction, but only a fuzzy boundary, can be drawn between metaphorical and non-metaphorical language. For analytic purposes, however, it is often best to draw this boundary sharply albeit arbitrarily. It is also best to deal at first only with full words – that is, nouns, verbs, adjectives and adverbs.

The frequently extreme conventionalisation of metaphoricity in empty words such as prepositions or modal auxiliaries can make it difficult to judge if the basis for constructing a cross-domain mapping still remains (Crisp 2002). Even amongst full words there are significant differences; it is, for instance, generally far easier to decide the metaphoricity of nouns. This is because their prototypes are typically richer and more detailed (Ungerer and Schmid 1996) and so provide a source domain basis for particularly well defined mappings.

In order to illustrate some of these ideas, go through the following first thirty-five lines of Keats' 'The Fall of Hyperion' and underline each full word you judge to be metaphorical in the sense defined above:

```
 1  Fanatics have their dreams, wherewith they weave
    A paradise for a sect; the savage too
    From forth the loftiest fashion of his sleep
    Guesses at Heaven; pity these have not
 5  Trac'd upon vellum or wild Indian leaf
    The shadows of melodious utterance.
    But bare of laurel they live, dream, and die;
    For Poesy alone can tell her dreams,
    With the fine spell of words alone can save
10  Imagination from the sable charm
    And dumb enchantment. Who alive can say,
    'Thou art no Poet – may'st not tell thy dreams?'
    Since every man whose soul is not a clod
    Hath visions, and would speak, if he had loved,
15  And been well nurtured in his mother tongue.
    Whether the dream now purpos'd to rehearse
    Be poet's or fanatic's will be known
    When this warm scribe my hand is in the grave.

    Methought I stood where trees of every clime,
20  Palm, myrtle, oak, and sycamore and beech,
    With plantain, and spice blossoms, made a screen;
    In neighbourhood of fountains (by the noise
    Soft-showering in my ears), and (by the touch
    Of scent,) not far from roses. Turning round
25  I saw an arbour with a drooping roof
    Of trellis vines, and bells, and larger blooms,
    Like floral censers, swinging light in air;
    Before its wreathed doorway, on a mound
    Of moss, was spread a feast of summer fruits,
30  Which nearer seen, seem'd refuse of a meal
    By angel tasted or our Mother Eve;
    For empty shells were scattered on the grass,
    And grape-stalks but half bare, and remnants more,
    Sweet-smelling, whose pure kinds I could not know.
```

Now turn to the appendix at the end of this chapter where you will find the same thirty-five lines with all the full words I myself judge to be metaphorical underlined. It is virtually certain that you will have judged metaphorical some of the words I have. It is also highly probable that you will have judged metaphorical words that I have judged non-metaphorical and vice versa. In each case of disagreement, think carefully whether you want to revise your judgement. In some cases you may feel that you simply missed an obvious case of metaphoricity. In other cases things will be more difficult; sometimes you will agree, sometimes disagree, and sometimes be unsure. You will have begun analysing metaphorical language.

The most striking thing about the Keats' passage is that while in the first stanza, ll.1–18, 48 per cent of the full words are by my count metaphorical, in lines 19–35 only 18 per cent are. There is a good cognitive semantic explanation for this. The first stanza deals with relatively abstract things, ideas and beliefs, while the following lines, describing a perceptible scene, deal with the experientially basic; we expect metaphor to be used more in thinking about the experientially non-basic. (Note that we are moving here from describing language to a hypothesis about cognition.) Conceptual metaphor dominates in the first stanza, and image metaphor (as in ll. 22, 27 and 28) and synaesthetic metaphor (where one sensory modality, such as touch, is mapped onto another, such as scent, as in ll.24–5) are frequent in the following lines. This fits in well with this explanation, since image metaphor, and likewise synaesthetic metaphor, is not a means of abstract conceptualisation.

The study of metaphorical language can, we see, serve as a way in to the study of cognition. Such a study is likely to do more than just confirm the general applicability of cognitive semantics to literary and other forms of discourse. One of the most important questions in cognitive poetics is just how like or unlike literary metaphor is to metaphor in other discourse genres. Gentner (1982) for example presents psychological evidence that poetic metaphor is markedly unlike scientific metaphor, being both less systematic and more suggestive. Only extended empirical study, in which the systematic analysis of metaphorical language will play an important part, can decide just how distinctive literary metaphor is (Steen 1994).

Blending

Any account of contemporary metaphor research has to deal with the theory of blending (Turner and Fauconnier 1995; Turner 1996; Fauconnier and Turner 1998; Grady *et al.* 1999). This embraces far more than just metaphor. Growing out of cognitive semantics' rejection of compositional semantic theories, it claims to provide a general model for at least much of 'online' conceptual processing. Metaphorical blending however still plays an important role within general blending theory, and it is of course metaphorical blending that we are concerned with here. Metaphorical blending should not be seen as replacing but as extending the concept of a cross-domain mapping. Instead of two domains it posits (at least) four mental spaces, two or more of which, in a metaphorical blend, function as source(s) and target. While a domain is a semi-permanent organisation of long-term semantic memory, a mental space (Fauconnier 1994) is a temporary 'online' organisation of working memory. Blending theory is oriented to moment-by-moment discourse events, while conceptual metaphor theory (CMT) deals with enduring cognitive structures.

The best way to explain why there are at least four rather than just two mental spaces in blending theory is by means of an example – that of the surgeon who is metaphorically a butcher. Such a surgeon is understood to be incompetent. Why? There is a mapping from the frame of BUTCHERS onto that of SURGEONS, the butcher corresponding to the surgeon, the carcass to the patient and so on, which imports cognitive structure from source to target. It does not however import the notion of incompetence, for butchers are not prototypically incompetent. The only way to account for this inference is to posit the setting up of a temporary third space in which we imagine the surgeon as a butcher. This is the blended space, which blends or fuses the concepts of surgeon and butcher. The surgeon/butcher cutting up his patient like a carcass would be an incompetent surgeon. The incompetence arises in the blended space and is then mapped back to the target space. This is what gives rise to the inference that the surgeon is incompetent. (The fourth, generic, space is defined by the abstract cognitive structure shared by the source and target spaces: there is no space to deal with it here, but see Turner 1996.) If a completely new metaphor is created then four new spaces will be created. More typically, what happens is that the source and target spaces, and so the generic space, are set up on the basis of one or more conventional metaphors such as POWER IS UP or EMOTIONS ARE NATURAL FORCES. New 'online' cognitive work is then done in the resulting blended space.

Blending theorists emphasise that metaphorical and other forms of blending are pervasive and unnoticed in everyday cognition. This may well be so, though the move of such theorists from language to cognition tends to be rather rapid. Blending however is certainly well adapted to explaining a number of often-noted aspects of prototypically literary and poetic metaphor. We saw how Lawrence, in 'Song of a Man Who Has Come Through', combines together a number of different conceptual metaphors. This phenomenon of simultaneously combining different metaphors, referred to by Lakoff and Turner (1989) as metaphorical composition, is widely recognised as especially characteristic of poetic metaphor. Blending theory places no limit on the number of mental spaces that can be set up in the course of 'online' processing. It has shown, by building on Fauconnier's (1994) work on mental spaces, how these multiple spaces can be related to each other in 'online' processing. It is therefore perfectly adapted to dealing with metaphorical composition. It does not matter how many conceptual metaphors, and so how many source and target domains, a poet simultaneously works with. Blending theory is able to show how the resulting multiple mental spaces, one for each domain, can be integrated into a single conceptual network through the construction of a blended space. These blended spaces have properties that can also help to explain another often-noted property of poetic and literary metaphor, namely that of a strange sense of fusion between different conceptual domains (Leech 1969; Levin 1988 and 1993).

We have already seen how Lawrence (in lines 7–10 of 'Song of a Man Who Has Come Through', see pp.101–2) combines the DIFFICULTIES ARE OBSTACLES TO MOVEMENT component of the Event Structure Metaphor with KNOWING IS SEEING. In terms of CMT, he combines two different mappings. On the one hand, there is a mapping from a chisel splitting a rock onto a person solving an emotional problem. On the other hand, there is a mapping from an invisible physical force onto the unknowable nature of a person's ability to solve an emotional problem. This is all valid as far as it goes: blending, we have seen, operates within the framework already defined by CMT. Yet to talk simply of combining mappings seems inadequate here. The two mappings seem rather to be fused together, just as their sources seem to be fused with their targets. (It would be futile to deny that these lines activate metaphorical concepts in the mind of any minimally alert reader.) It all comes together in a single image, which for many readers is likely to have a visual component, of a chisel driving towards a rock without being subject to any visible force or agent. The two mappings are fused together in this image. Moreover to talk of the chisel as simply mapped onto a person and of the rock as mapped onto the emotional problem again seems inadequate. The chisel and rock seem rather to be fused with the person and his problem, to be in some strange way identical with them and so to have taken on a vivid life of their own. This fusion is what defines the blended space: the composed input spaces are drawn on to create a single fantastic imaginary space. This space is not subject to our ordinary conceptions of what is possible. Anything in principle can happen within it. Yet at the same time, as we have seen, it provides a basis for cognitive inferencing. Cognitive semantics helps to us to understand some of the most powerful and mysterious properties of poetic and literary metaphor, while at the same time showing how these properties originate in general properties of the human mind.

Further activities

1   This exercise requires at least two people, and would be best with four or five. Select a lyric poem, a verse paragraph from a long poem, or a paragraph of prose. Each of you should go through the piece *separately* underlining the full words you judge to be metaphorical. Take as your criterion of metaphoricity that the word provides, by itself or in combination with other words, in the context of the whole text, a basis for constructing in principle a cross-domain mapping. When this is done, compare your conclusions. Where there is disagreement try to resolve this; be prepared to accept that sometimes disagreement will remain. It is in the discussion arising out of your attempts to resolve disagreement that the greatest value of this exercise will reside.

2   Choose a lyric poem, a verse paragraph or a paragraph of prose and try to identify all the possible cross-domain mappings you can construct in it. Decide whether these mappings are conceptual or non-conceptual. For the non-conceptual mappings, decide which are image and which synaesthetic metaphors. For the conceptual mappings, decide which are similarity and which correlation metaphors. (The boundary between these two categories will often be fuzzy.) For the correlation metaphors, try to relate them to recognised conventional metaphors.

3   This exercise requires at least two people and would be best with four or five. From a lyric poem or some longer piece of poetry or prose select a metaphor which seems to you to naturally give rise to an image. (The image does not have to be visual but visual images are generally the easiest to work with.) Each of you should deliberately produce such an image in your minds and then write down a description of it in as much detail as possible. Do *not* communicate with each other about your images until you have all finished writing. (To give an example of the sort of thing required here: you could construct and describe images of the rock in l.10 of 'Song of a Man Who Has Come Through'.) Compare your descriptions noting their similarities and differences. Try to account for these in terms of the conceptual metaphors that implicitly structure them. Some differences will be differences of specification of the same general conceptual metaphor, but others may reflect differences in your understanding of this metaphor. Finally, see if any of your images contain material inspired not only by the source but also the target domain. That is, do they provide any evidence of blending?

Appendix

The Fall of Hyperion

  1 Fanatics have their <u>dreams</u>, wherewith they <u>weave</u>
    A <u>paradise</u> for a sect; the savage too
    From forth the <u>loftiest fashion</u> of his <u>sleep</u>
    <u>Guesses</u> at Heaven; pity these have not
  5 <u>Trac'd</u> upon vellum or wild Indian leaf
    The <u>shadows</u> of <u>melodious</u> utterance.
    But <u>bare</u> of <u>laurel</u> they live, <u>dream</u>, and die;
    For Poesy alone can <u>tell</u> her <u>dreams</u>,
    With the <u>fine spell</u> of words alone can <u>save</u>
10 <u>Imagination</u> from the <u>sable charm</u>
    And <u>dumb enchantment</u>. Who alive can say,
    'Thou art no Poet – may'st not tell thy <u>dreams</u>?'
    Since every man whose soul is not a <u>clod</u>
    Hath <u>visions</u>, and would speak, if he had loved,
15 And been <u>well nurtured</u> in his <u>mother</u> tongue.
    Whether the <u>dream</u> now purpos'd to <u>rehearse</u>
    Be poet's or fanatic's will be known
    When this warm <u>scribe</u> my hand is in the grave.

    Methought I stood where trees of every clime,
20 Palm, myrtle, oak, and sycamore and beech,
    With plantain, and spice-blossoms, made a <u>screen</u>;
    In <u>neighbourhood</u> of fountains (by the noise
    <u>Soft-showering</u> in my ears), and (by the <u>touch</u>
    Of scent,) not far from roses. Turning round
25 I saw an arbour with a drooping roof
    Of trellis vines, and <u>bells</u>, and larger blooms,
    Like floral <u>censers</u>, swinging light in air;
    Before its wreathed doorway, on a mound
    Of moss, was spread a feast of summer fruits,
30 Which, nearer seen, seem'd <u>refuse</u> of a <u>meal</u>
    By <u>angel tasted</u> or our <u>Mother Eve</u>;
    For empty shells were scattered on the grass,
    And grape-stalks but half bare, and remnants more,
    Sweet-smelling, whose pure kinds I could not know.
                           (John Keats)

9 Literature as parable

Michael Burke

Editors' preface

This chapter makes use of one of the most influential cognitive poetic frameworks to have emerged in recent years. The notion of 'parabolic projection', originally developed by Mark Turner in the 1990s, has proved particularly appealing to literary critics interested in how the human mind deals with literary texts. Here, Michael Burke applies Turner's ideas to Shakespeare's Sonnet 2, in order to reveal how readers use their everyday experience to reach an interpretation of the text and then go on to project that interpretation back onto their own lives. This analysis and discussion can be seen to follow on from those of conceptual metaphor and blending put forward in preceding chapters in this collection. You may also find a consideration of Burke's analysis alongside Keith Oatley's closing chapter particularly thought-provoking.

Introduction

In this chapter we will be looking in detail at how the cognitive notion of parable functions. In doing so, we will discover just how fundamental the concepts of story, narrative projection and parable are to our cognitive understanding of the world and how we operate in it as thinking, feeling human beings. We will start this investigation by looking at some of the fundamentals that underpin the theory of the parabolic, literary mind, originally developed by Mark Turner (1996). Thereafter, having seen how parable works in the construction of meaning in the real world, we will look at how *parabolic projection* operates intertextually within a literary framework. This will be done by means of a literary case study. Lastly, I will draw this chapter to a close by briefly considering the wider implications of parabolic literary theory, regarding meaning both in the mind and the brain. In sum, what this chapter will seek to demonstrate is that parable is a fundamental, continuous, cognitive instrument of thought that we employ, largely unconsciously, both in real-world meaning construction and in literary interpretation procedures.

Some preliminary background

Before getting to grips with the central theory of the parabolic mind, let us first set out some preparatory background. A good starting point in this chapter on how cognitive parabolic reasoning operates is to remind ourselves of how the default, i.e. biblical, notion of parable works. Traditional parables are located in the New Testament of the Bible in the sections where Jesus can be found preaching about the kingdom of God. These stories were a kind of 'metaphor in narrative form', the primary purpose of which was to challenge the ingrained perspectives of the hearers. Parables therefore were told in order to project extra (essentially didactic) domains of knowledge into the existing world-views of the listeners. The result of this would have been a modification in the interpretative cognitive models of those listeners.

The well-known story of the workers in the vineyard (Matt. 20: 1–16) provides a useful starting-point for an analysis of how parables operate. In this parabolic tale, a number of people are set to work at different times of the day: some early in the morning and some late in the afternoon. When evening comes, the workers are paid the same amount. Those who worked all day then become angry: as do the parable's listeners. But Christ explains to them that in his father's kingdom of heaven 'the last (i.e. the poorest and weakest) shall be first'. 'Mercy' therefore, rather than 'explicit reward' is what is promised and indeed given. This didactic narrative twist, leading to a fundamental cognitive reappraisal of the world, can be seen in virtually all the biblical parables.

We should be careful here not just to term religious stories as parables, since fables and allegories also fall into this category. The common link here is the projection of stories, inasmuch as the listeners or readers of all of these essentially allegorical genres have to import new knowledge and incorporate it into their existing understanding. Such oral or written episodes seem to operate mainly through two cognitive tools known as *story* and *narrative projection*, and thereafter a process called *conceptual blending*. These cognitive phenomena, as will become apparent, are crucial to understanding and meaning-making and will be clarified below in much greater detail. However, this is not all. In addition, such parabolic accounts also rely heavily on concepts such as *intertextuality*, as well as personal schematic knowledge of the world on the one hand and its ostensible socio-cognitive counterpart on the other.

The study of narrative, and in particular the study of narrative fiction, has a rich and varied modern history that has seen it travel from an essentially literary base into the current domain of cognitive poetics. Similarly, basic narrative approaches to cognitive understanding are not new either, since narrative structures, in the form of either 'frames' (e.g. Minsky 1975), 'scripts' (e.g. Schank and Abelson 1977), or 'schemas' (e.g. Rumelhart 1975, 1980) have been explored in detail in research into cognitive psychology and artificial intelligence. It can therefore be assumed that a basic form of narrative structure is at the very heart of human cognition, inasmuch as the concept of narrative projection is fundamental to how human understanding and human thought appear to function. With this in mind let us now turn specifically to the modern cognitive theory of parable to see how it operates.

The cognitive process of parable

When one considers what literature is, one might perhaps think of such notions as *creativity, singularity* and *choice*. In short, literature, and indeed any form of literary thinking, has traditionally been considered capricious, optional and marginal. However, the theory of the parabolic mind, which has its roots in Turner's earlier work (1987, 1991), shows that nothing could be further from the truth, since this mode of narrative and story-based thought is central to how we reason.

The root mechanism of parable lies in our cognitive ability to imagine stories and project them onto other stories in a parabolic fashion. Following Turner, this parabolic projection shows how the notions of story and narrative, previously thought of as merely literary, are in fact essential to our everyday mental activities, and even to our physical existence and social survival. In addition to story and narrative projection, the workings of the parabolic mind entail numerous other mental patterns. These include *prediction, evaluation, planning* (all of which are centrally grounded in the mechanism of the cognitive projection of short spatial stories), as well as other mental phenomena such as metonymy, metaphor, image schemata, conceptual blending, etc. Having introduced these notions let us now look at the two central concepts of story and projection in more detail and thereafter at the interpretative cognitive process that they ultimately result in, namely, *blending*.

Story is a basic cognitive ability, since we structure most of our experience, knowledge and thinking this way. The mental scope of story is magnified by the notion of 'projection', and in particular narrative projection, since one story helps us to make sense of other stories and even to create new ones. This projection, of one story onto another, is thus what is centrally termed *parable*, and it is this basic cognitive ability that helps us to understand the broad range of both literary and non-literary communication. The mind employs stories and parable to carry out everyday cognitive acts. The largely unconscious narrative flow of events is grounded in what we might now term more specifically 'small spatial stories'. Such 'literary' processes are thus the fundamental building blocks of human knowledge, the basic constituents of which are *actors, objects* and *events*. These core elements combine to make up the most basic linguistic stories of all, in which our daily existence is grounded. Such stories may be extremely basic: for example, 'liquid entering a container', 'a plastic bag being carried by a gust of wind' or 'the ebbing and flowing of the tide'. These events can be viewed as short spatial stories. The very fact that we recognise such simple stories in the world around us, and are cognitively able to project and blend them with larger and more abstract stories, suggests that the human mind is fundamentally both parabolic and literary.

Narrative projection can be viewed as a form of thinking before acting. As such, it can be identified as a second key concept in the cognitive theory of parable. It is important to note, however, that this dynamic, cerebral phenomenon does not function in isolation, since, as we have learned, it is inextricably linked to story, and all stories are prone to projection. For example, an extremely ordinary, physical event, like moving from one place to another, can be construed (usually unconsciously) as a simple narrative. This in turn can be projected onto a complex narrative of a psychological experience, like, for example, viewing the notion of human existence as a kind of 'journey'. Similarly, a reader may project a literary story onto issues pertaining to his or her personal life, no matter how far these issues appear to be removed from the particulars of that story. An important motor behind this will be the reader's *identification* with fictional actors and objects. This is possible because, although literary texts often seem special and specific, the mechanisms of thought used to interpret them are fundamental to our understanding of everyday experience. This is why the literary mind is also the everyday mind.

Blending is a cognitive notion whose operation is central to how parable works. A *blend* is a kind of meeting-point between two (or more) conceptual structures. These structures, known as *input spaces*, get mapped into *generic spaces*, where shared information becomes evident. From here, this information is projected into a *blended space*, where it starts to combine and interact. When this happens in parable the blend is run through what is known as an 'emergent structure' (i.e. new content that comes into existence as a result of the actual blending process itself). This procedure allows the blend to take on a life of its own that does not have to rely on original information in the input spaces.

Let us look at a literary example in order to illustrate what is meant here. In Jonathan Swift's famous novel *Gulliver's Travels* a race of horses exists called the Houyhnhnms. These are not horses as we know them, since they are endowed with reason and all the finer qualities of humans. The two main sources in this conceptual blend are thus 'horses' and 'rationally-thinking, cultivated human beings'. The projection of these two concepts from their input spaces into a generic and thereafter a blended space produces an entirely new concept. This new space will have attributes that have been projected from the input spaces. For example, language, intellect and reason (mental characteristics) will have been projected from the domain of rationally-thinking human beings, while the essentially physical, i.e. 'formal', characteristics will have been projected from the equine world. However, there will also be features in the newly created blended space, like 'eloquent, sophisticated horses', that are completely alien to any of the parent spaces. What we notice here is that such projected structures are inherently both dynamic and ongoing, since we can expand this new concept into a whole host of further creative domains. The process of parabolic blending thus, like meaning itself, arguably operates in the extensive, inter-subjective, contextualised domain, between the notions of the seemingly bounded and the unconditional (see Fauconnier 1997 for more on blending).

It is important to make explicit here how blending, central to the workings of parable, differs from the conceptual mapping that takes place in the cognitive theory of metaphor. In parable, certain traits are projected from two (or more) input spaces into a fresh integrative space, where a completely new cognitive construct comes into being that no longer has a direct relation to any of the original input spaces. This new 'blended' space will itself then form a potential input space that may be employed to lead to further structures of meaning-making. The three phases involved here are termed *composition* (the fusion of the cognitive elements), *completion* (the filling out of patterns in the blend), and *elaboration* (the subsequent mental acts that can extend the blend endlessly). In the case of cognitive metaphor, a relatively clear, isomorphic and unidirectional mapping takes place between a specific source domain and a specific target domain. So a maximum of just two spaces is involved here. However, such a minimal one-to-one mapping in parabolic, blended reasoning, both in literary interpretation and real-world understanding, would be unworkable, since it would be too simplistic and hence misrepresentative. Literary texts, of course, do not have a single fixed meaning.

It is interesting to note that the source and target domains in conceptual metaphor theory can actually function as two input spaces at the fundamental level of blending. Blending is more conceptually complex, since it makes use of different levels of conceptual reasoning (i.e. at least two input spaces, a generic space and a blended space). It therefore operates with a minimum of four conceptual spaces, as opposed to a maximum of just two domains in cognitive metaphor. Further, blending relies heavily on online (i.e. short-term) processing, since blends are often novel and creative. Cognitive metaphor, on the other hand, relies primarily on well-established metaphoric relations. These are likely to be located in long-term rather than short-term memory. Taking all of the above into consideration, from the perspective of mental mapping we can clearly see how parable and cognitive metaphor differ. However, despite these contrasts, it is on the whole not productive to view these two cognitive phenomena as mutually exclusive, since, as I have just mentioned, metaphoric domains can function as input spaces in the process of blending. It seems far more productive to view the two theories as complementary (see Grady *et al.* 1999 for much more on this).

Literature as parable

Up until now I have essentially been explaining how parable functions in the real world and how that procedure is unconditionally grounded in the core literary conventions of narrative and story. Now, reflecting the title of this chapter, I will extend this to see how parable operates in literary works. A key point here, facilitating such an extension, is the noticeable similarity that the process of blending bears to the way in which intertextuality functions in literary interpretation.

Perhaps an appropriate investigative starting-point for our discussion on the parabolic in literature is medieval verse, since there are distinct connections between medieval conceptions of language and thought and the principles of cognitive poetics. One of these connections relates to the 'limited' world-view of medieval literature. These constraints were grounded in the belief that medieval man could not have absolute knowledge, since that was the domain of God, and God alone. Instead, meaning and understanding were open ended, ongoing and much like current cognitive approaches to language and poetics. So, ironically, this 'limited' medieval world-view actually led to one that was rather extensive.

In the alliterative poem *Pearl*, the narrator mourns the death of his daughter, and only child, Pearl, who died before she was two years old. One day while at her graveside he has a dream/vision of a river and beyond it a heavenly paradise. There he sees his daughter, seated, dressed in pearls and smiling. The sight of her fills him with joy. However, at the same time he cannot understand how his daughter has reached such a high place in heaven, since she died at an early age, long before she could have learned to pray or have done good deeds to earn her elevated celestial status. In defence of her current position, the girl says that God treats all those who are without sin equally: those who arrive first and those who arrive last. This story quite clearly draws on the biblical parable of the workers in the vineyard, referred to earlier in this chapter. The intertextual activation and projection of this parable (which later in the story receives an explicit mention) onto the story of *Pearl* will alter and restructure our ongoing creation of literary interpretation. For example, we can project the father onto a worker who has been plucking grapes all day long for the same pay, and the daughter onto an agrarian who started working much later in the day. Here, we see that this biblical text is not a monolithic entity, resplendent in pietistic isolation. Rather, it is at all times a potential intertextual input space that can be projected and employed in literary elaboration or extension to facilitate the readerly meaning-making process. This intertextual echo of other texts is just one potential space that a reader might activate and project in order to facilitate the ongoing construction of an interpretative perspective.

This medieval example gives us a good introduction to literature as parable. However, I do not wish to dwell on this fifteenth-century world-view. Instead, for our core case study, I would like to move on one step into the arguably much more multivalent world of Renaissance literature. For it is here, in a post-medieval, yet pre-Cartesian, world that we encounter a more enlightened, yet still dynamic, perspective on thought and meaning. The following cognitive poetic case study analyses one of Shakespeare's sonnets for the presence of parabolic projection.

A parabolic case study in literature

Sonnet 2

When forty winters shall besiege thy brow,
And dig deep trenches in thy beauty's field,
Thy youth's proud livery, so gazed on now,
Will be a tottered weed of small worth held:
Then being asked where all thy beauty lies,
Where all the treasure of thy lusty days,
To say within thine own deep-sunken eyes
Were an all-eating shame, and thriftless praise.
How much more praise deserved thy beauty's use
If thou couldst answer, 'This fair child of mine
Shall sum my count, and make my old excuse',
Proving his beauty by succession thine.
This were to be new made when thou art old,
And see thy blood warm when thou feel'st it cold.

(William Shakespeare)

When reading this sonnet, we must remember that there are a number of dynamic, cognitive capacities at work in our quest as readers for literary meaning. There are several source domains that can feed what we might term a central mental model, where inputs are 'uploaded' and blended across a network of ongoing meaning creation. As we have just learned, we can view the text itself as one of the main input sources, which helps to construct our text-interpretative mental model. We can discern at least two important intertextual triggers in the written discourse. The first of these involves such things as the foregrounding (i.e. deviation or parallelism) of linguistic features. These can include such things as syntactic structures, semantic fields, phonological patterning, etc., which can loosely be termed 'text-intrinsic' features. Then we have a second set of triggers that are located at a level 'beyond' this linguistic plane, in the pragmatic realm. These might include such things as the historical (Shakespearean/Renaissance) context or genre, i.e. the knowledge that a sonnet has formal constraints in number of lines, rhyme scheme, metre, and that the English version differs in form from its Italian counterpart. The more functional nature of this essentially 'text-extrinsic' (though text-influenced) second category means that its contents will tend to flow into those areas we have previously termed intertextual knowledge. As we have seen, this phenomenon, located in the reader's mind, involves both social knowledge and emotions, as well as personal thoughts, feelings and memories. All of these domains, however, have the capacity to facilitate the launching of largely unrestricted knowledge of other texts that can be projected parabolically into the central cognitive model, where a sense of interpretative, literary meaning will start to take shape, under the dynamic, malleable process of blending.

The first discernible phenomenon we might identify in our literary text after a first brief reading is the main conceptual metaphor that appears to be running through the sonnet. This can be represented in the conceptual figurative construction PROCREATION IS ETERNAL LIFE (or at least the chance of it). Now, the question is where in the text have we been able to draw this information from? There is a hint of the theme throughout the first two quatrains of the sonnet, but it is in the final quatrain and the concluding couplet that it is strongly foregrounded, especially in the phrases 'this fair child of mine' (l.10); 'proving his beauty by succession' (l.12); 'when thou art old' (l.13) and 'see thy blood warm when thou feel'st it cold' (l.14), etc. However, there are also other conceptual metaphorical domains operating here that can be said to be parabolically feeding this one. One such domain concerns the notion of 'time'. This finds form in the two conceptual structures TIME IS A LINE versus TIME IS A CIRCLE. We will now consider these domains and others too in more detail.

A primary input source will probably be constituted by the foregrounded lexical items in the text itself that refer loosely to the 'moribund' father and his 'burgeoning' son. A second domain might be our socio-cultural knowledge of the higher-level metaphorical structures concerning time, and how time operates, expressed in our world-knowledge of 'the fleeting nature of life'. A third might be ways this theme has been represented in other literary works or in works of art in general that, through the process of intertextuality, come to mind while reading the sonnet. A fourth could be the (moral) cultural knowledge we possess that one of our main purposes for living is to procreate. There will of course be many more, some of which will be extremely personal to individual readers. For example, my only brother has recently become a father. My personal knowledge of this event, and my nephew's existence in the world, is an extremely potent short story that impinges on the very reality of my own mortality, not to mention my reading of this sonnet. This is perhaps exacerbated further by the fact that this particular reader has no children himself, is approaching forty (like the addressee in the sonnet) and has no other nephews or nieces. Such personal, essentially 'event-centred', sources (rather than specifically text-centred ones), and indeed any aspect of what is generally termed 'autobiographical memory' in cognitive psychology, can thus form extremely influential projections into our interpretative cognitive model. It is here that this conceptual information becomes fused and filtered in a vigorously constructive process that ultimately leads toward what will become my ongoing interpretation of the text.

This particular literary text, however, is quite concise, which means that it will probably be re-read shortly after the first reading, something that arguably might occur less frequently with longer narratives, like those found in novels. On such a subsequent perusal, a reader might also notice other linguistic or figurative structures. For example, he or she may notice that there seem to be three distinct conceptual metaphorical domains, mainly restricted to the three quatrains that feed into the procreation conceptual theme, each of which is grounded in three seemingly separate semantic fields. These conceptual metaphorical themes can be termed 'military', 'monetary', and 'judicial'. Let us now look more closely at how these metaphors are lexically underpinned, and further how they might serve as potential input spaces – as metaphors can – in the process of parabolic projection and blending.

In our first case (the military theme) we might notice the words and phrases 'besiege' (l.1), 'deep trenches' (l.2), 'field' (l.3) and 'livery' (which can refer to a soldier's as well as a servant's uniform) (l.4). These combine to structure a narrative story projecting the conceptual metaphor LIFE IS A BATTLE. Such is their vividness that when projected and blended they might very well trigger intertextual echoes of other 'literary' works. For example, the word 'besiege' may evoke stories of blockaded castles. These might be stories about anything from the Crusades, recalled from our childhood history lessons, to anecdotes or movie representations or even flashes of absurd siege-scenes from a film like *Monty Python and the Holy Grail*. However, arguably a more powerful word than 'besiege' is 'trenches'. Here we might evoke and project World War I scenes based on old film-reel footage that we have seen on television, or mental imagery from the war poetry of Sassoon, Owen or Gurney or even from the biting satire of the recent BBC television series *Blackadder Goes Forth*. What is interesting here, with regard to this particular word, is that 'trench warfare' is primarily a twentieth-century phenomenon. Therefore the projection of such an 'erroneous' historical detail may have a novel effect, when mapped back onto the original Renaissance story, on what eventually materialises in our ongoing cognitive model of meaning-making.

The legal theme of trial and testimony, prominent in the final quatrain, functions in the same way. The prominent term in the text 'sum my count' (l.11) refers to the child as a lawyer. This is supported by the words 'proving' and 'by succession' (l.12), a legal term for inherited rights. Here, one might say that life is structured like a court hearing, which keys into the religious notion of a 'day of judgement' at the end of our lives. We can structure this idea with the conceptual metaphor LIFE IS A TRIAL. Emphasis on this judicial theme launches in my mind intertextual projections of the language used in Sonnet 30, since much courtroom terminology abounds in that particular text. I then map these magisterial 'remembrances of things past' (to quote the second line of that poem) back onto Sonnet 2. To return again to these lexical items, this first term, 'sum my count' also has strong monetary connotations. Here we see how these conceptual structures are not concrete, or restricted by the boundaries of the quatrains, but rather are dynamic, with the ability to flow into each other. The activation of such a legal theme, certainly within a Shakespearean monetary framework, will quite feasibly animate and project the play *The Merchant of Venice*, and along with it maybe one of its central characters, Shylock. And from Shylock we might intertextually project the similar character of 'Scrooge' from Dickens' *A Christmas Carol* or even people we know personally, for whom philanthropy is not their forte.

The third thematic domain is a financial one. Once again in the text there are references to money that are sometimes implicit (e.g. 'lies' (l.5) and 'deep-sunken' (l.7)) and sometimes explicit (e.g. 'treasure' (l.6)). Further, there are suggestions of moral negligence in the phrases 'all-eating' and 'thriftless' (both l.8). The implication here is clear. For a person to invest solely in him or herself is a waste (and from a religious perspective a sin too). Here, we can draw from the text that such a 'consumer', rather than a 'producer', should be filled with 'an all-eating shame' (l.8). One could say that instead of hoarding his goods this person should have invested his gifts, virtues and talents in the begetting of children. The main conceptual metaphor here can be said to be LIFE IS A VENTURE.

While reading the second quatrain the lexical items, especially those referring to money and the overriding theme of procreation, may combine to intertextually project the reader's knowledge of the well-known 'parable of the talents' (Matt. 25: 14–30). In that story, three servants (representing three ordinary people) are given talents (a monetary unit of the time) by their master (God). Two of the servants invest their talents (i.e. make good use of their gifts). The third one, however, buries his (i.e. he does nothing with it: in effect, he wastes it). When the master returns (the day of judgement) and asks them what they have done with their talents he is pleased with the first two servants who have taken chances. However, he is extremely angry with the third one, who is surprised by the master's reaction, since he thought he had made the right decision.

This is a powerful story that will have a significant effect on our ongoing construction of meaning, more perhaps than any other as it maps relatively wholesale. From this parable we might project the similar medieval allegorical story of *Everyman*, who also wasted his gifts. We might even project an arguably more potent story, namely Plato's allegory of the cave from *The Republic*. In this story, the peoples of the world are seated on the floor of a cave, chained together. Unable to turn their heads, they spend all day, every day, watching life 'go by' on the back wall of this cave. This, however, is not life at all. Instead, it is a mere puppet show, based on shadows that are being projected over their heads. The reader suspects that the people are, to a certain extent, aware of this, but elect instead to stay seated. They choose the easy option. In effect, they bury their talents rather than investing them. If they were to face up to the artificiality of the shadow-play they call real life, break loose from their bonds and leave the cave, then they would not only see how the shadows are being cast, but also what the true nature of the light source is that is producing the energy in the first place to make the puppet-show happen. To make this discovery and to do something about it is parabolically parallel to investing your talents. Here, therefore, we see how together the textual references to money and the overriding theme of procreation in the sonnet can activate a biblical story which in turn can initiate a thematically similar tale from classical philosophy.

What is interesting about this story is that it was common knowledge, spread by the telling of oral stories, centuries before Jesus is supposed to have told his parables. We only need to look at the life of St Augustine of Hippo and read his works (such as, for example, *The Trinity*) to know that Christianity, as it took real form in the fifth century, was heavily influenced by the principles of Neo-Platonic thought. Perhaps Plato's famous allegory of the cave acted as a parabolic source for the listeners of the Nazarene's rhetoric. Maybe then Jesus' parables may not have been as unique as we are often led to believe they are. Perhaps the parable of the talents is but a Christian projection of the allegory of the cave? Another projection that works for me here, and I'm sure for others too, is that of the recent science-fiction film *The Matrix* that closely follows the plot of Plato's cavernous allegory and has been described in many reviews as a 'cyber-punk parable'. The fact that two of the main characters are called 'Neo' and 'Trinity' strengthens the nature of the projection even more for me. In light of all this information, and the ongoing dynamism of your emergent structure, consider the metamorphosing circumstances that your input spaces may now be undergoing. In any event, for us personally, as readers of this sonnet in the present, the projection of this parable of the talents and all that cognitively emanates from it, makes for a complex contextual development that will go towards making for an intricate blend.

In the above cognitive poetic analysis, I have primarily concentrated on three conceptual structures. I could, however, have chosen to emphasise other, perhaps equally valid, features. In the first quatrain, for example, instead of focusing on the language of war I could have chosen to highlight an agricultural domain, where 'trenches' (l.2) become furrows, in the ploughed 'field' (l.2), where new seeds (representing birth) can be sown. This would have reinforced the overarching message of the quest for 'new life' found in the procreation model itself. Here, we might project an input space of Ovid's story of Narcissus from *The Metamorphoses*, as an example of someone too concerned with himself to contemplate becoming a father. (In the story, he falls in love with his own reflection rather than Echo, and in doing so excludes himself from ever becoming a father and instead dies and is turned into a flower by the gods.) Likewise, in the text the 'tottered [i.e. 'tattered'] weed' (l.4) projects both dilapidation and decay: perhaps a lifeless scarecrow or an old dying man. This too strengthens the procreation model. This tattered upright weed reference, combined with the 'when thou art old' reference in line 13 might project intertextual Yeatsian echoes like 'When you are old and grey and full of sleep', (from 'When You are Old') or 'An aged man is but a paltry thing, / A tattered coat upon a stick', (from 'Sailing to Byzantium'). If activated, such wistful echoes will be projected into the blend too. In sum, all of the stories that I have mentioned here in the context of these three overriding conceptual domains (i.e. the military, the monetary and the judicial) are just the tip of an almost immeasurable cognitive iceberg, since there are many, many other potential stories that I could have projected into my ongoing model of meaning construction.

I would hope that it is now clear that the cognitive quest for meaning production and literary interpretation is grounded in stories and that such stories inevitably lead to the projection of even further stories. Moreover, I hope that it is now equally apparent that this cognitive process does not take place in a predominantly linear or unidirectional fashion, but rather is grounded in a process of multi-grid networking. A fitting and indeed engaging concluding analogy can be drawn here that blends the conceptual with the bodily, as indeed all aspects of cognitive linguistics should, since this cognitive parabolic operation appears to mirror quite accurately the way neurons are believed to function in our brains. Such a neurobiological/cognitive psychological analogy projects towards, as yet, largely unexplored domains of knowledge where the blending that will take place will almost certainly be fundamentally grounded in embodied reasoning.

Conclusion

If you reflect on how I have made the foregoing parabolic analyses, it should be evident that the projected stories that I have chosen to highlight, although valid and genuine, are only a fraction of those that I have been able to show you that go towards how I personally make meaning and ultimately interpret this literary text. It will be clear that your own personal strategies and source domains, although perhaps now somewhat influenced by my own, will be quite different. Of course, if we share a culture, a heritage, a level of education, or some other social domain, then there is every chance that we might also share similar socio-cognitive, intertextual or text-based input spaces. However, what is alike, in almost all readers, is the cognitive process of literary interpretation itself, in the fact that the procedure of parabolic projection and the subsequent blending is never monolithic or bounded but is always dynamic and open-ended. We can thus conclude that projecting and blending across an inexhaustible number of spaces is a complex operation, since, like concepts themselves, meaning is constantly mobile – never resting for long in a single space. Projection and blending are core components in this continual, mental activity that together form the cerebral dynamo that drives parabolic thought in the fluvial human mind.

Human beings possess a capability, which is arguably as innate and unconscious as the process of breathing itself, to construct ever-larger narratives from small spatial stories. This is how thought and reasoning operate. Current evidence in the fields of cognitive psychology, cognitive linguistics and neurobiology seems to suggest that the ongoing narrative projection of stories is a device by which we constantly create open-ended meaning. In doing so, we are able to navigate our way through the world around us.

At the heart of this process there are no pre-programmed grammatical structures. Instead there is parable. If the way the mind works is grounded in the embodied parabolic projection of short spatial stories, then we must also accept the proposition that necessarily accompanies it, namely that at its very source the emotively-cognitive human mind is fundamentally literary in nature.

Further activities

1   The analyses in this chapter have mainly concentrated on highlighting lexical items and semantic fields as potential cognitive triggers (input spaces) to facilitate parabolic projection. You could consider how other textual linguistic elements might facilitate parabolic projection. As a starting point you might wish to look at levels of phonology, morphology, syntax, metre or graphology, or even a combination of these (see Verdonk 1995 for more on this).

2   We have seen how parable, allegory and fables can operate as parallel texts in helping us to project and construct an ongoing model of meaning. There are, however, other texts, which despite having a similar 'shadowing' function are arguably somewhat more difficult to incorporate into a parabolic cognitive poetic analysis. This is because one of their main purposes is to create humour. This development calls for intricate and creative blends. Such genres include 'satire', 'parody' and 'pastiche'. You might take one of these modes and its parallel text in the 'real' world and conduct a parabolic analysis to see how meaning gets read back into the original version and how this affects your cognitive blending and the emergent structure in the blend. Further, given that humour is a central concern (if not *the* central concern) in such blends you might also consider the role that emotion and emotive processing might play within the framework of cognition in such parabolic analyses. (For more on the emotion-cognition processing relationship with regard to literary texts, see Burke (in press).)

3   Towards the end of this chapter we touched on how the parabolic projection of short spatial stories operates in a similar 'networking' fashion to how our brains work. You might wish to investigate this mind/brain similarity further. A good starting point is to look at the neurobiological work of Gerald Edelman (1992), especially his notion of 'reentrant signalling' that suggests that our subjective experiences of thought and feeling come about due to the simultaneous activation of many diverse neural systems, which he calls 'maps', that affect one another. So, despite the fact that we may think that we are experiencing a single, concrete thought in the process of meaning-making, this is not the case. Instead, when we attempt to arrive at an interpretation, many neurons are fired, resulting in a number of different maps being activated

simultaneously in an interactive blend of ongoing brain activity. How do you think this neurobiological theory might relate to the parabolic workings of Turner's literary mind? You might also wish to investigate some associative cognitive psychological phenomena such as 'aggregate fields', 'automatic processing', 'parallel distributed processing (PDP)' or 'information processing models' (see Solso 1995 for more detail on these phenomena).

10 'Too much blague?'

An exploration of the text worlds of Donald Barthelme's *Snow White*

Joanna Gavins

Editors' preface

The next two chapters in this collection can be seen to be closely connected, both in terms of their central subject matter and in terms of their particular approach to cognitive poetics. Joanna Gavins' Text World Theory analysis of a Donald Barthelme novel in this chapter, and Catherine Emmott's examination of 'twists in the tale' in the next chapter, are both informed by what can be termed a 'discourse' approach to their subject. Both authors are centrally concerned with the cognitive poetics of *entire* texts and with understanding how readers build and maintain complex mental representations of their narratives. While Gavins chooses Barthelme's *Snow White* as an example of a cognitively challenging piece of literature, Emmott considers how readers deal with unexpected twists in plot. You should find that these explorations form an interesting development of the ideas about text worlds initially discussed, in Chapter 7, by Elena Semino.

Introduction

The notion that human beings process and understand discourse, both factual and fictional, by constructing mental representations in their minds is now a common one in cognitive theory. These mental representations have been variously called 'mental models' in cognitive psychology (e.g. Johnson-Laird 1983), 'mental spaces' in cognitive linguistics (e.g. Fauconnier 1994) and, more recently, 'narrative worlds' in cognitive psychology (e.g. Gerrig 1993) and 'text worlds' in cognitive poetics (e.g. Werth 1999). In these last two areas of study, the text-as-world metaphor has most frequently been employed to describe the readerly sensation of being 'immersed' in a particular fiction, in which the characters, scenery and unfolding plotlines are constructed in as complex and richly detailed a manner as those we encounter daily in the real world.

This chapter takes a somewhat more eccentric text as its main subject for analysis, with the aim of broadening our understanding of literary worlds in all their diversity. Donald Barthelme's (1996) *Snow White*, originally published in 1967, transposes the eponymous heroine of the classic fairytale to contemporary downtown New York, where she shares her life with her seven diminutive companions. As we shall see, however, this modified location is not the only deviation *Snow White* makes from preceding versions of the tale and Barthelme's retelling is by no means straightforward. This chapter employs Text World Theory (see Werth 1994, 1995a, 1995b, 1997a, 1997b and 1999; Hidalgo Downing 2000; Gavins 2000 and 2001) as a means of exploring the precise nature of the fictional worlds created by his absurd adaptation. The basic mechanics of this approach to cognitive poetic analysis are outlined briefly in the following section of this chapter.

Text World Theory

Text World Theory provides a methodological framework through which both factual and fictional discourses may be systematically examined in their entirety: from the pragmatic circumstances surrounding their genesis, through to the conceptual consequences of specific language choices. A typical Text World Theory analysis normally begins by separating a given discourse into three interconnecting levels. The first of these, the *discourse world*, contains two or more participants engaged in a language event. This event may involve either face-to-face or long-distance conversation, or written communication of any type. In some cases the participants will share the same immediate physical surroundings and in others they will be separated in both time and space. Either way, their discourse world will be governed by certain tacit discourse principles, according to which the participants both expect and agree to perform coherent and cooperative communication. Furthermore, Text World Theory recognises that the personal 'baggage' each participant brings with them to the language event, in the form of their memories, intentions, knowledge and motivations, has the potential to affect the process of joint negotiation at the core of the discourse world.

As the language event progresses, each participant constructs a mental representation, or *text world*, by which they are able to process and understand the discourse at hand. This world forms the next level of a Text World Theory analysis. The precise structure and content of the text world are dictated both by linguistic indicators contained within the discourse and by further inferences drawn from the participants' background knowledge and experience. This way, though many different participants may be basing their mental representations on the same linguistic information, each of their individual text worlds will be unique to its creator. In general, however, all text worlds are made up of a combination of *world-building elements* and *function-advancing propositions*. The world-building elements define the background against which the main events in the discourse will be set. They give a sense of time and place, and also specify the objects and characters that populate the world. Function-advancing propositions, on the other hand, constitute the actions, events, states and processes whose presence can be seen to propel the discourse forward. The role of such textual elements in the discourse as a whole may be described more specifically as plot-advancing, scene-advancing, argument-advancing, and so on. Any predications made about characters in the text world can also be seen to fulfil a character-advancing or person-advancing role.

Once the text world is constructed and developing, countless other worlds which depart from the parameters of the initial text world may also be created. These departures form the final layer of Text World Theory and are called 'sub-worlds' in Werth's (1999) original framework. They may be created either by the discourse participants, in which case they can be described as *participant-accessible*, or by characters in the text world, in which case they can be described as *character-accessible*. In my own Text World Theory model, which differs slightly from Werth's, these departures are simply new worlds that can be divided into two distinct categories (see Gavins 2001). The first of these is the category of *world-switches*. Should the central focus of the discourse be switched (for example to a different place), a new world corresponding with that scene is created. Flashing backwards or forwards in time has a similar effect. Instances of direct speech and direct thought also cause world-switches, since they alter the temporal parameters of the text world by introducing present-tense discourse into a past-tense narrative.

Other new worlds, known as *modal worlds*, may also be created as the result of modalisation in discourse (see Simpson 1993 for a useful overview of modal systems). Deontic modality, for example, expresses the degree of obligation attached to the performance of a particular action and includes modal auxiliaries such as 'may', 'should', 'must', and so on. Consider the following sentences: 'You should *go straight to the police*', 'You may *have another biscuit*', 'I must *take this suit to the cleaners*'. The action (shown in italics) being modalised in each of these examples can be seen to set up an unfulfilled future situation that is separate from its originating text world. Similarly, boulomaic modality expresses the desires of a speaker or writer and stipulates the conditions by which those desires can be satisfied. Once again, consider the following examples: 'I hope that *you're happy*', 'I wish *I had a car like that*', 'She wants *to be left alone*'. In these sentences too the action being modalised sets up an unrealised world, the parameters of which depart from those of the initial text world.

Epistemic modality, in all its linguistic forms, also creates new modal worlds in the minds of the discourse participants. The worlds which result from this type of modality correspond to situations which are in some way epistemically remote from either the participants in the discourse world, in the case of participant-accessible modal worlds, or from the characters in the text world, in the case of character-accessible modal worlds. For example, varying degrees of epistemic remoteness may be expressed through epistemic modal auxiliaries such as 'could' and 'might', as well as through modal

lexical verbs such as 'think', 'suppose' and 'believe'. The epistemic modal
system also includes a sub-system of 'perception' modality. This conveys the
degree of commitment to the truth of a particular proposition by reference to
some form of human perception. Examples of perception modality include
such adjectival constructions as 'it is clear that', 'it is apparent that' and 'it is
obvious that', as well as related modal adverbs such as 'clearly', 'apparently'
and 'obviously'. Once again, the use of these linguistic expressions results in
the formation of a new, epistemically remote modal world in the minds of
the discourse participants.

Similarly remote worlds can also be formed without the presence of
epistemic modal auxiliaries or lexical verbs. Conditional constructions, for
example, cause epistemic modal worlds to occur by their postulation of both
an unrealised situation, (e.g. 'I'll lay an egg … ') and the pre-conditions necessary for it to become realised (e.g. ' … if Doncaster Rovers get promoted to
the third division this season'). Hypotheticals, too, create epistemic modal
worlds, as do instances of indirect thought and indirect speech, which present discourse that is always at least one stage removed from either the discourse-world participants or text-world characters. Finally, focalised
narratives can also be seen to be modal-world forming, since they filter both
world-building and function-advancing elements through the unverifiable
perspective of one or more characters.

The three levels of Text World Theory are discussed in further detail in the
following section of this chapter, which begins the exploration of the text
worlds of *Snow White*.

Snow White: A text world theory analysis

The first thing to note about the discourse world which surrounds a reading
of Barthelme's *Snow White* is how the reader's background knowledge is
immediately brought into play in the discourse process on contact with the
novel's title. The majority of contemporary western readers will recognise
the proper name it contains, which subsequently activates a store of
cultural knowledge, most probably formed as a result of recurrent lifelong
contact with both traditional and contemporary versions of a popular
fairytale. Many readers, then, will carry with them into the discourse world
of their reading of Barthelme's text a considerable number of preconceived
ideas of the sorts of world-building and function-advancing elements they
might expect to find within its pages. The first paragraphs of the text,
however, are unlikely to match most people's 'Snow White' prototype
exactly:

> SHE is a tall dark beauty containing a great many beauty spots: one
> above the breast, one above the belly, one above the knee, one above the
> ankle, one above the buttock, one on the back of the neck. All of these
> areas are on the left side, more or less in a row, as you go up and down:

•
•
•
•
•
•

The hair is black as ebony, the skin is white as snow.

(Barthelme 1996: 9)

As well as containing some unconventional graphology, this introduction lacks the 'Once upon a time' opening typical of many fairytales, beginning instead with a description of an unnamed female. Many readers will nevertheless be able to repair the passage's central reference chain, linking the third person reference that opens Barthelme's novel with the character of Snow White, perhaps aided in part by the direct borrowing of the Brothers Grimm's more familiar description of her: 'The hair is black as ebony, the skin is white as snow'.

This correlation aside, however, little else in the text which follows bears such a direct resemblance to any previous version of the *Snow White* story. For instance, seven men are mentioned on the page which follows that quoted above. The reader may infer from their number that these characters fill the traditional roles of the seven dwarves. The men's names, however, are given, not as Sleepy, Happy, Dopey, Sneezy, Bashful, Grumpy and Doc, but as Bill, Kevin, Edward, Hubert, Henry, Clem and Dan. A further departure from tradition can be identified in the temporal setting of Barthelme's text. Although not explicitly mentioned, a contemporary backdrop can, once again, be inferred from certain culture-specific references. There is mention, for example, of a 'shower room' (Barthelme 1996: 10), a 'typewriter' (p.15), 'Chairman Mao' (p.22), 'Mars Bars' (p.27) and 'Charlton Heston' (p.27). Furthermore, the narrative structure of Barthelme's text can also be seen to deviate from the prototypical framework set by its predecessors. *Snow White* is divided into three main parts, each of which is further separated into numerous passages, varying in length from one line to several pages. The content of these sub-sections also ranges in form, from conversations to dreams, from extended speeches to letters, from mock questionnaires to public addresses by the President of the United States.

The majority of critics writing on *Snow White* (e.g. Ditsky 1975; Coutrier and Durand 1982; Morace 1984; Trachtenberg 1990) devote at least part of their attention to certain linguistic incongruities also contained within Barthelme's text. Particularly helpful is an early stylistic analysis by McNall (1975), the main focus of which lies in the identifiable patterns of lexical repetition in Barthelme's text. However, McNall also makes some mention of the characters' actions in the novel, or, rather, the lack of them. She comments that the speakers in *Snow White* are engaged characteristically in plans, meditations, speeches, sermons, fantasies ... commonly they fail to bring these off. The plans do not materialize, the meditations do not lead to realizations, the speeches and sermons do not convince, and fantasies are, after all, fantasies.

(McNall 1975: 85–6)

McNall also notes that removing the novel's 'description assertions', which she defines as 'a sentence with the copula for main verb' (McNall 1975: 82), would remove the greater part of the text. The vast majority of the remaining narrative is made up of primarily mental and/or emotional activity. However, this observation remains relatively underdeveloped in McNall's essay and thus provides a useful starting point for a Text World Theory analysis of *Snow White*.

McNall's comments on the peculiarity of action in Barthelme's text are drawn, in particular, from her examination of the following episode and its numerous consequences:

SNOW WHITE let down her hair black as ebony from the window. It was Monday. The hair flew out of the window. 'I could fly a kite with this hair it is so long. The wind would carry the kite up into the blue, and there would be the red of the kite against the blue of the blue, together with my hair black as ebony, floating there. That seems desirable. This motif, the long hair streaming from the high window, is a very ancient one I believe, found in many cultures, in various forms. Now I recapitulate it, for the astonishment of the vulgar and the refreshment of my venereal life.'

(Barthelme 1996: 86)

In Text World Theory's terms, perhaps the most remarkable thing about this passage, quoted here in full, is the minimal world-building information it contains. The character of Snow White is apparently the only entity present, at a window nominated by a definite article, yet otherwise indistinct. Perhaps even more strangely, the reader is told the precise day on which the incident takes place, but not the date or the hour. The only physical action in the passage takes place in its first sentence, as its function-advancing proposition tells us that 'Snow White let down her hair'. The entire remainder of the episode is devoted to Snow White's speech about her motivations for, and feelings about, her behaviour.

The structure of the passage can be translated into a text world diagram (see Figure 10.1), which makes evident the imbalance between the detail contained in the episode's initial text world, in which Snow White lets down her hair, and that contained in the world-switch created by her direct speech. The originating text world is shown to the left of the diagram and is divided into separate world-building (WB) and function-advancing (FA) sections.

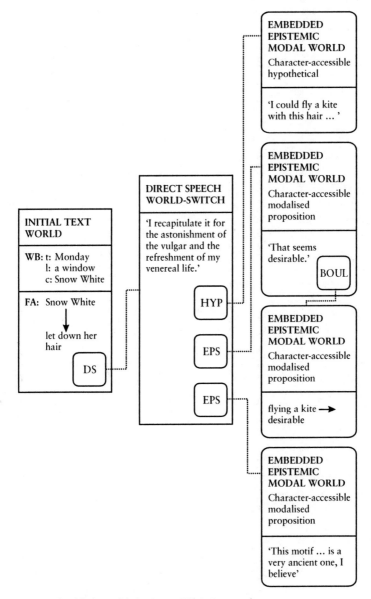

Figure 10.1 Embedded worlds in Snow White's speech

The function-advancing section can be seen to contain only one function-advancing proposition ('Snow White let down her hair'). This is set against a minimalistic background, constructed according to the sparse world-building information provided. This information is separated in the diagram into *time* (t), *location* (l), and *characters* (c).

The new world which then splits off from the initial text world is shown originating from direct speech (DS) in the diagram. This world contains not only Snow White's direct assertion of her reasons for her actions ('for the astonishment of the vulgar and the refreshment of my venereal life'), but also three further embedded modal worlds. The first of these is epistemic in nature and results from Snow White's construction of a hypothetical situation in which she flies a kite in her hair. The origins of this world are shown in the diagram as a HYP world embedded within the speech world. The second modal world, also epistemic, occurs as a result of the perception modality contained in her comment that such an event would '*seem* desirable'. This is shown in the diagram as the uppermost epistemic world (EPS) branching off from the speech world. The latter part of the same sentence, of course, consists of a boulomaic modal adjective, which creates a further embedded boulomaic modal world (BOUL). A final epistemic world is then constructed around Snow White's comments on the cultural significance of what she has done, as she states that she *believes* the hair 'motif' to be 'a very ancient one'. The motif is also, of course, one which belongs in an entirely different fairytale, namely that of Rapunzel.

The letting down of Snow White's hair, which occurs about half way through *Snow White*, is followed by a number of episodes headed 'Reaction to the hair'. The following is a reproduction of one of them, in full:

> *Reaction to the hair*: 'Well, that certainly is a lot of hair hanging there,' Bill reflected. 'And it seems to be hanging from our windows too. I mean, those windows where the hair is hanging are in our house, surely? Now who amongst us has that much hair, black as ebony? I am only pretending to ask myself this question. The disgraceful answer is already known to me, as is the significance of this act, this hanging, as well as the sexual meaning of the hair itself, on which Wurst has written. I don't mean that he has written *on* the hair, but rather about it, from prehistory to the present time. There can be only one answer. It is Snow White. It is Snow White who has taken this step, the meaning of which is clear to all of us. All seven of us know what this means. It means that she is nothing else but a goddamn degenerate! is one way of looking at it, at this complex and difficult question. It means that the "not-with" is experienced as more pressing, more real, than the "being-with". It means she seeks a new lover. *Quelle tragédie*! But the essential loneliness of the person must also be considered. Each of us is like a tiny single hair, hurled into the world among billions and billions of other hairs, of various colours and lengths. And if God does exist, then we are in even graver shape than we had supposed. In that case, each of us is like a tiny mote of pointlessness, whirling in the midst of a dreadful free even greater pointlessness, unless there is intelligent life on other planets, that is to say, life even more intelligent than us, life that has thought up some point for this great enterprise, life. That is possible. That is something we

do not know, thank God. But in the meantime, here is the hair, with its multiple meanings. What am I to do about it?'

(Barthelme 1996: 98–9)

The structure of this passage can be seen to be greatly similar to that which caused it and is illustrated in Figure 10.2. Where Snow White's reflections on her hair took up five sentences, Bill manages to extend his to a total of twenty-three. Furthermore, Bill takes no physical action, apart from the speech itself, during the entire episode. The world-building elements of his text world are also even more minimalistic than those which defined Snow White's surroundings in the earlier passage. Since his remarks are directed at Snow White's hair, however, we can assume fairly safely that he is positioned within roughly the same spatial and temporal parameters as she was: below a window in their house, on a Monday.

Once again, far greater detail goes into the construction of the world of Bill's speech than that of his immediate location. Once again, the direct speech world-switch is followed by a further four embedded modal worlds. The first is created as a result of Bill's somewhat reluctant epistemic commitment to location of the window from which the hair is hanging, as he relegates his assertion, 'those windows where the hair is hanging are in our house', to a question: 'surely?' This qualification positions the information contained within Bill's initial statement at a greater epistemic distance, both from Bill and the reader, in an embedded epistemic modal world. A second modal world, also epistemic in nature, is then created as Bill goes on to speculate about the existence of God, in the conditional construction beginning 'And if God does exist ... '. This initial clause, of course, sets up a remote world in which the second clause of the conditional is the case ('we are in even graver shape than we had supposed ... each of us is like a tiny mote of pointlessness, whirling in the midst of a dreadful free even greater pointlessness'). A similar construction forms the next remote world to be embedded in Bill's monologue, as he pursues a further hypothetical, 'unless there is life on other planets'. A final world is then created as Bill adds a modalised comment, expressing his opinion on the likelihood of the hypothetical situation he has constructed: 'That is possible'. The same state of affairs (life on another planet) is then recreated in a completely separate epistemic modal world, according to the speaker's altered epistemic commitment to it.

An emphasis on the speech and thoughts of the characters, rather than on their actions or their surroundings, is typical of each of the 'Reaction to the hair' episodes. However, this feature is by no means confined to these sections of the novel alone. Throughout *Snow White*, as McNall points out, 'any act is given far less prominence than its problematical motives, and/or the problematical reactions to it' (McNall 1975: 83). Scattered amongst the 'Reaction to the hair' sections of *Snow White* are a number of episodes headed 'Lack of Reaction to the hair'. Despite the suggestions of differing action-content made explicit in their titles, however, the text world

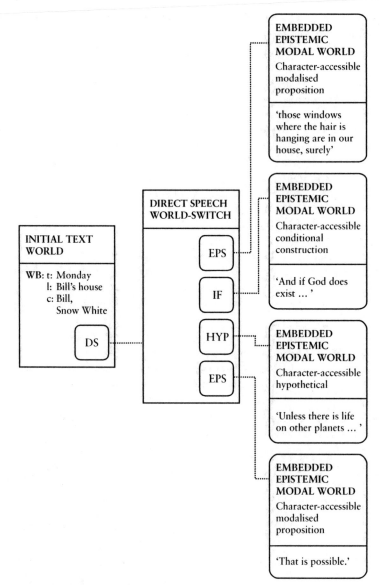

Figure 10.2 Embedded worlds in Bill's 'Reaction to the hair' speech

structures of both the 'Reaction' and 'Lack of Reaction' episodes are practically identical. In one of these episodes, for example, Dan (another dwarf) gives a speech to an unspecified audience in unspecified surroundings. The text world which corresponds to this section of the novel does at least contain one physical action, as Dan pulls up boxes for his audience to sit on. Once again, though, a speech world dominates the episode as Dan muses, ironically, over the topic of 'linguistic stuffing' for a total of three pages, creating numerous embedded modal worlds as he goes, making this one of the longest sections in the entire novel.

Indeed, the vast majority of the text of *Snow White* is made up of its characters' verbal and mental contemplations. Almost the entire first half of the novel is devoted to the dwarves' speculations about what might be bothering the apparently depressed and dissatisfied Snow White, interspersed by her own commentary on the situation. Snow White seems to have taken to writing poetry and also throwing tantrums, although the dwarves' main concern is her recent loss of sexual appetite. The action the dwarves take in an attempt to reawaken her interest in them, however, is limited to a single (and perhaps unsurprisingly unsuccessful) decision to purchase a fancy new shower curtain.

A distinct pattern of text world structures can thus be seen to emerge as the narrative of *Snow White* unfolds. Furthermore, the prominence of speech worlds throughout the text means that, for much of the discourse process, the reader must rely on the characters to provide the world-building and function-advancing information necessary to construct a coherent mental representation of the novel. On occasion, this proves to be a reasonably straightforward exercise, particularly when the characters make direct reference to their surroundings. At other times, the reader may have to work slightly harder to make inferences that will enhance the detail of their text world of *Snow White*. The inference made about Bill's proximity to Snow White during his 'Reaction to the hair' speech, discussed earlier, is one such example. A great deal of the time, however, the characters offer practically no help in the construction of the reader's text world and can even be seen to be actively complicating the process.

In the following extract, Bill is defending himself in court, where he stands charged with having delusions of grandeur. This has led Bill, the judge explains, to throw a six pack of beer through the windscreen of a car belonging to two complete strangers, named Fondue and Maeght:

> 'You cherished for those two, Fondue and Maeght, a hate.' 'More of a miff, your worship.' 'Of what standing, in the time dimension, is this miff?' 'Matter of let's see sixteen years I would say.' 'The miff had its genesis in mentionment to you by them of the great black horse.' 'That is correct.' 'How old were you exactly. At that time.' 'Twelve years.' 'Something said to you about a horse sixteen years ago triggered, then, the hurlment.' 'That is correct.' 'Let us make sure we understand the circumstances of the hurlment. Can you disbosom yourself very briefly of the event seen from your point of view.'
>
> (Barthelme 1996: 165)

Bill's explanation of events is far from brief, however, and offers no clarification of either the significance of the black horse or the reasons behind his violent outburst at Fondue and Maeght, who remain similarly vague figures throughout the scene. Instead, the judge and Bill continue their exchange of bizarre neologisms (e.g. 'hurlment', 'disbosom', 'sensorium', 'cutaneous injurement', 'scoutmysteries', 'self-gratulation') for a further four pages, in a highly-infelicitous conversation without apparent aim or conclusion (see Gavins 2000; and Simpson 1997 and 2000, for discussion of similar linguistic incongruities in other Absurdist texts).

Bill and the judge are not alone in their linguistic eccentricity. The other characters, too, have a persistent habit of coining peculiar or meaningless words and phrases. At one point, for example, Snow White exclaims, 'I am tired of being just a horsewife!', a term which is subsequently adopted by all the other characters in the text. Snow White's initial play on words, then, rapidly becomes a social institution, one which Edward (another dwarf) even goes to the extent of defending passionately in a lengthy sermon. Such appropriations, however, do little to aid the efficiency of the reading process, with the majority of the characters' coinages remaining obscure and unexplained following their initial use. Faced with such impenetrable communication between the characters, the reader might reasonably expect clearer direction from *Snow White*'s implied authorial voice. As we have already seen, however, the prominence of speech worlds in the majority of the novel's episodes means that the reader has very little contact with this omniscient textual entity. More often than not, the information he provides about the text world that contains Snow White and her companions is so scant that the reader must rely entirely on the references those characters make to their surroundings in order to form any coherent mental representation of them.

On those rare occasions when the omniscient narrator does make an extended appearance, he has little to offer in the way of an explanation of the characters' incoherent ramblings. Far more frequently, the reader is faced with an obscure list of apparently unconnected words or phrases:

EBONY
EQUANIMITY
ASTONISHMENT
TRIUMPH
VAT
DAX
BLAGUE

(Barthelme 1996: 101)

Such interruptions occur regularly throughout the text, often sharing the graphological distinctiveness of the section reproduced above. On occasion, the information they offer can be seen to be of slightly greater use in the discourse process than that contained in the list above:

PAUL HAS NEVER BEFORE REALLY SEEN
SNOW WHITE AS A WOMAN
(Barthelme 1996: 156)

Here, at least, some insight, however brief, is allowed into the mind of the character Paul, who takes the role of Prince Charming in the novel. The information is also presented in the form of a complete sentence, from which some measure of character-advancement can be achieved in the text world. The majority of the time, however, rather than providing an objective external opinion on the subjects of the characters' consternations (i.e. Snow White's discontentment with both her personal relationships and her wider social role; the dwarves' sexual frustration), the narrator adopts the same nonsensical discourse used by the characters themselves, compounding potential processing difficulties rather than helping to alleviate them.

Despite sporadic instances of cooperative communication, then, the senselessness of these repeated episodes may undermine the trust of many readers in the reliability of the authorial voice. Further processing problems may also arise from the following textual interruption:

QUESTIONS

1 Do you like the story so far?   Yes ( )   No ( )

2 Does Snow White resemble the Snow White you remember?
   Yes ( )   No ( )

3 Have you understood, in reading to this point, that Paul is the prince-figure?   Yes ( )   No ( )

4 That Jane is the wicked stepmother-figure?   Yes ( )   No ( )

5 In the further development of the story, would you like more emotion ( ) or less emotion ( )?

6 Is there too much *blague* in the narration? ( )   Not enough *blague*? ( )

7 Do you feel that the creation of new modes of hysteria is a viable undertaking of the artist of today?   Yes ( )   No ( )

8 Would you like a war?   Yes ( )   No ( )

9 Has the work, for you, a metaphysical dimension?   Yes ( )   No ( )

10 What is it? (Twenty-five words or less) . . . .

. . . .

. . . .

. . . .

11 Are the seven men, in your view, adequately characterized as individuals?   Yes ( )   No ( )

12 Do you feel that the Author's Guild has been sufficiently vigorous in representing writers before Congress in matters pertaining to copyright legislation?   Yes ( )   No ( )

13 Holding in mind all works of fiction since the War, in all languages, how would you rate the present work, on a scale of one to ten, so far? (Please circle your answer)

    1   2   3   4   5   6   7   8   9   10

14 Do you stand up when you read? ( )   Lie down? ( )   Sit? ( )

15 In your opinion, should human beings have more shoulders? ( ) Two sets of shoulders? ( )   Three? ( )

(Barthelme 1996: 88–9)

This questionnaire appears about halfway through *Snow White*, at the close of Part One of the text. Questions 3 and 4 may aid certain inferences already in process, confirming that Paul is intended to fill the traditional role of Prince Charming and that another character, Jane, is the wicked stepmother. This information aside, however, the majority of the questionnaire is, at worst, nonsensical ('Is there too much *blague* in the narration?') or, at best, unrelated to the main narrative ('Do you feel that the Author's Guild has been sufficiently vigorous in representing writers before Congress … ?', 'should human beings have more shoulders?'). Those questions that do relate to the reading of *Snow White* do so by foregrounding the fictionality of the text. When question 13 asks, 'how would you rate the present work, on a scale of one to ten', for example, emphasis is placed on the discourse world relationship between the reader and author. The author's potential ability, yet ultimate failure, to create either rounded, believable characters or a coherent plot structure is thus also brought to the reader's attention.

Conclusion

The Text World Theory analysis of *Snow White* presented in this chapter has shown how Barthelme's readers are provided with only minimal world-building information on which to base their mental representations of the text. Furthermore, very little physical action takes place in any of the worlds created during the course of the novel and the greater part of the function-advancing in *Snow White* takes place within speech-initiated world-switches and embedded epistemic modal worlds. Our comprehension of the text is then further complicated by the fact that a great deal of what the characters say and think is, at best, long-winded and irrelevant rambling and, at worst, utterly nonsensical. No additional guidance is offered by the authorial voice in the novel, which often adopts the same senseless discourse itself and provides only minimal insight into the characters' feelings and motivations. It would seem, then, that the challenging nature of this text is due mainly to the uncooperative behaviour of the reader's co-participant in the discourse world. The author of *Snow White* can be seen to reject persistently his obligations to communicate clearly and efficiently, as he creates both a troublesome textual counterpart for himself and numerous other text world entities with similarly uncooperative tendencies.

The central question that Barthelme's novel raises for cognitive poetics, then, is whether such troublesome discourse-world relationships create insurmountable problems in the processing of literary texts. It is certainly possible that the bizarre text worlds of *Snow White* might prove so taxing to some readers that they will be led to abandon their reading of the novel entirely. For many others, though, the demanding nature of the worlds described above will be the novel's central attraction (see Berlyne 1960, 1971 and 1974; Berlyne and Masden 1973, for a psychological account of this). Indeed, the canonical status granted many similarly 'difficult' texts would suggest that these kinds of text worlds are highly prized in our society. It is also possible that for many readers the complex and chaotic structure of the novel may actually form the basis of an interpretation of its meaning. Despite the unruly behaviour of the author, his textual counterpart and his characters, a reading of *Snow White* as a cooperative text is still possible through the metaphorical mapping of its structural absurdity onto the day-to-day experience of human existence.

Further activities

1   Try identifying the function-advancing and world-building elements in the opening few paragraphs of a novel of your choice. Then, rewrite the text removing one or the other of these sets of elements. How have your actions altered the text? Are you still able to form a text world from what is left? Consider also how certain genres of fiction (such as thrillers, detective fiction, and romance novels) would look without their function-advancers. Conversely, how dependent on world-building elements are travel writing and nineteenth-century novels?

2   Having tried out Text World Theory on some prose fiction, you may want to explore some of its more extreme boundaries. Try a Text World Theory analysis of the poetry of T.S. Eliot, for example, or the performance of a Samuel Beckett play. In particular, consider the importance of discourse-world relationships and expectations in these forms. Are there any limits to our use of Text World Theory as an analytical tool? Are there any modifications you would make to the framework as a result of your explorations?

3 Consider your own responses to experimental texts you have encountered in the past. These could be prose, poetry or drama. Did you simply abandon the text(s) after an initial struggle, or did you persevere with your reading? Try to define precisely the ways in which the text(s) defied your expectations or caused you other problems during the reading process. Can Text World Theory help you to describe and understand how you overcame your difficulties, or indeed why you eventually conceded defeat?

11 Reading for pleasure

A cognitive poetic analysis of 'twists in the tale' and other plot reversals in narrative texts

Catherine Emmott

Editors' preface

In this chapter, Catherine Emmott applies her 'contextual frame theory' to a range of prose fiction in order to examine how readers make sense of plot reversals in narrative. She looks at two short stories by Roald Dahl, as well as a crime novel by Ian Rankin and a historical novel by Deborah Moggach. Emmott makes a number of new additions to her framework (Emmott 1997) during the course of this chapter. Her discussion is centrally concerned with the process of reading for pleasure and, as such, follows on well from some of the ideas put forward in Joanna Gavins' analysis of Barthelme's *Snow White* in the preceding chapter. Contextual frame theory itself can also be seen to have strong theoretical and method-ological connections with both Text World Theory and the theories of mental spaces and possible worlds discussed by Elena Semino in Chapter 7.

Introduction

Cognitive poetics aims to provide a model of reading that combines tech-nical insights from psychology, artificial intelligence and text analysis, but also recognises the important fact that much fiction is read primarily for enjoyment. Stockwell (2002a: ch.11) explores this aspect of reading in rela-tion to literary texts. This article will complement Stockwell's analysis by examining stories that are not part of the literary canon, but are read for everyday entertainment. Since plot has a key role to play in many popular genres, I will focus here on how plot intricacies such as 'twists in the tale' and other such reversals may be comprehended. In particular, I examine examples from two Roald Dahl short stories, 'Dip in the pool' (Dahl 1990a) and 'Taste' (Dahl 1990b); a crime novel by Ian Rankin, *The Hanging Garden* (Rankin 2000); and a historical novel by Deborah Moggach, *Tulip Fever* (Moggach 2000). I will use *contextual frame theory* (Emmott 1997) as the main tool of analysis, developing aspects of it in order to account for plot understanding.

Contextual frame theory and plot reversals

Contextual frame theory is a cognitive poetic theory because it shows that texts can be studied not only for their style, but also to provide clues to the amount of work that a reader has to do to process the language. In this respect, a detailed analysis of a text can reveal the extent to which a reader's knowledge, beliefs, assumptions and inference-making ability are necessary to supplement (and in some cases override) the words on the page. Contextual frame theory is similar to Text World Theory (Werth 1999; see also Chapter 10 of this volume), but it focuses particularly on how contexts within fictional worlds are constructed. In the plot reversals discussed in this chapter, readers and/or characters are 'led up the garden path', making erroneous inferences about a context because key information is omitted or because they are placed in a position where they wrongly assess a situation.

The basic principles of contextual frame theory are as follows (see also Emmott 1997: ch. 1 and 4–6).

Contextual monitoring

The physical proximity of individuals to each other is important in both real life and in narrative. Readers continually carry out *contextual monitoring*, maintaining information about who is present in specific narrative contexts in mental representations termed *contextual frames*. The *primed frame* is the mental representation of the context in which the reader feels that he/she is actively witnessing the action as it unfolds.

Frame assumptions and within-frame inferences

Unless there is reason to think otherwise, readers assume that fictional contexts operate in the same way as real-life ones. *Frame assumptions* can therefore be made, utilising basic schemata about physical, perceptual and behavioural factors within contexts. For example, we expect that characters will not suddenly de-materialise from a context, unless we are reading a science-fiction story. We may also generally assume, unless we are told to the contrary, that when one person addresses another in their immediate physical proximity, that other person hears what is said and their knowledge state changes accordingly. We may also expect typical social behaviour, such as that if a character falls, another may try to help him/her (although obviously social conventions may vary across cultures). *Within-frame inferences* enable us to combine such basic assumptions about contextual behaviour with contextual frame information about which characters are present, in order to predict and explain the actions and knowledge states of the particular individuals concerned.

The medium of communication

Contextual monitoring and within-frame inferencing are important for written narrative processing because a written text rarely specifies all the major parameters of a context (i.e. main characters, key objects, time and place) in every sentence. Hence, contextual frames enable us to take minimal contextual information in each sentence and cognitively construct the remaining context around it in order to fill the gap. The general process of gap-filling applies across different media. Hence, both a written narrative and a film narrative will require us to construct contexts around either the written word or the film image respectively. Nevertheless, the amount of gap-filling and the precise nature of the inference-making will depend on how much contextual information is given at specific points in a narrative in different media.

In order to explain plot reversals, I will add some additional notions to the above model.

Types of frame assumption

Readers will generally use basic default assumptions from the real world, unless there is reason to do otherwise. I will term these *Type 1 frame assumptions*. Hence, as mentioned above, we may assume that if a character speaks, others in the immediate physical context will hear him/her, unless we are specifically told to the contrary. However, there are obvious cases where our assumptions, which I will term *Type 2 frame assumptions*, are different due to different circumstances. If we know that an individual is profoundly deaf or is wearing a personal stereo, then he/she may be assumed not to hear. Hence, Type 1 and 2 frame assumptions are based on our real-world expectations, but may vary according to our knowledge of specific individuals and their circumstances.

By contrast, *Type 3 frame assumptions* may apply in a text or group of texts when a special type of fictional world has been set up which, in certain respects, has its own physical, perceptual or social rules (e.g. ghost stories and certain science-fiction stories). There may also be *Type 4 situations* where our assumptions are broken and we feel surprise (e.g. a person walks through walls in a story which we had not realised was a ghost story). In Type 4 situations, we may decide to re-evaluate the genre of the text accordingly. Even Type 4 situations show that we are constantly making frame assumptions, since otherwise there would be no reason for surprise.

This chapter will focus on Type 1 and 2 assumptions, so the other types are mentioned here simply to give a more comprehensive overview. (See Stockwell 2000 for applications of contextual frame theory for texts which move beyond real-world assumptions.) This typology is similar in principle to Stockwell's (2000: 164) notion of informativity (based on de Beaugrande

1980). However, the Type 2 assumptions discussed above are not necessarily unusual, but are simply anything other than the default (e.g. personal stereos are no longer unusual, but are not the default). In such cases, additional knowledge is needed to avoid the default assumption being made (e.g. knowledge that a person is wearing a personal stereo or usually wears one or that they are in a specific situation where wearing one has become the default).

Projected frames and cross-frame inferences

Some of the plot reversals discussed in this chapter depend on situations being different from expected or on situations being re-evaluated in the light of additional information from another context. To explain this, I will use the notion of *projected frames*. These are mental representations of contexts which are embedded within the primed context, but are not themselves developed in sufficient detail for the reader to feel that they are primed. An example (from a story that will be discussed in more detail later in this chapter) is in Roald Dahl's (1990b) 'Taste', where characters in a primed 'dinner party' frame discuss a bottle of wine stored in another room, the study. This is an *off-stage projected frame*, since it describes a context occurring elsewhere at the time of the action without the action actually switching to that other place. This type of frame can be created from descriptive information in the characters' conversation or in the main narrative. In Dahl's story, the description sets up this projected frame, but one character also actually leaves the room to collect the bottle of wine and returns with it. We can infer that this character goes to the study, but the reader's 'deictic centre' (Duchan *et al.* 1995) remains at the dinner table and the study is not therefore primed.

I will also identify two other types of projected frames here (these are sufficient to explain the examples discussed in this chapter, but more types may need to be added to the model to account for a broader range of plots). A *retrospective projected frame* is one which reconstructs an earlier situation, without developing it as a flashback. A *planned projected frame* is one which anticipates events that will occur in the future, from the point of view of the character planning those actions. Examples of these two other types of projected frames will be provided in the following sections.

The model presented here is broadly in line with Stockwell's (2000: 157) notion of 'frame projection' and Werth's (1999) 'sub-worlds'. In my contextual frame model, however, all these projected frames are specific contexts (i.e. the situation in the projected frame is set in an actual physical context at a particular point in time) and therefore contextual frame assumptions can be applied to them to yield within-frame inferences.

Generally, *cross-frame inferences* may be made by using information from a projected frame or a previously primed frame to draw conclusions about another projected frame or the current primed frame. In the above example, the stated facts in the primed (dinner party) frame – that the character goes to collect the wine and returns with it – allow us to infer the unstated information about the off-stage projected frame, i.e. that he enters the study and that the wine leaves the study.

Types of character

A number of the examples discussed in this chapter rely for their effect on manipulating our knowledge and expectations about the identity of characters. In certain cases, the writers play with the relative prominence of characters, and, as a result, individuals who appear to be little more than 'props' suddenly acquire plot significance. I will use the notion of *scenario-dependent entities* (Sanford and Garrod 1981; Anderson *et al.* 1983) to analyse these examples. The term 'scenario-dependent' is used by these psychologists to describe minor characters who are tied to a particular scene and who perform script-like actions in that scene (e.g. waiters in restaurants). The empirical evidence suggests that these characters have a different psychological status from main characters and that we have different expectations about them (Sanford and Garrod 1981; Anderson *et al.* 1983). In the psychology experiments, the main point is that after an episode shift, readers appear to have less expectation that scenario-dependent characters will continue to be there than that main characters will, since scenario-dependent characters are perceived as being tied to particular scenes by virtue of their script-like status. For the type of stories discussed here, the key point is that, because scenario-dependent characters are fulfilling stereotyped roles in the background, there is little attention focused on them and so more surprise if they suddenly step out of role (prompting a *role re-appraisal*) or are re-identified as major characters (prompting an *identity re-appraisal*).

Knowledge and textual overrides

As already discussed, readers' knowledge of the plot and the relevant contexts and characters may change their frame assumptions, leading them to make within-frame inferences that are different from the default. We will also see below that new knowledge may enable cross-frame inferences to be made that allow a re-interpretation of previously-read details. Most strikingly, we will see that it is sometimes possible to use plot knowledge to override information in the text, even as we are reading it. If a character has set up an erroneous *belief frame* (Emmott 1997: 164–6; Stockwell 2000: 157–9), then we might simply ignore some of the information that the character offers us. These *textual overrides* are significant for a cognitive theory because they show the extent to which knowledge can have predominance over the propositional content of a sentence if plot factors are taken into account.

Understanding 'twists in the tale' and other plot reversals

In the remainder of this article, I will apply the above framework to a number of text examples. I use the term 'twist in the tale' only when the whole point of the story depends on the plot reversal, but the mechanisms behind other plot reversals are generally of the same type. The term 'tales of the unexpected' is particularly associated with Roald Dahl, but is quite appropriate to all the stories here. They surprise us because they break our default assumptions, not because they step outside real-world conventions (as might, for example, be the case in science fiction).

Tales of the unexpected (I)

Projected frame and frame assumptions

Roald Dahl's (1990a) story 'Dip in the pool' manipulates contextual frame assumptions for its 'twist in the tale' ending. The main character, Mr Botibol, is on a passenger ship and plans to jump overboard and be rescued. He intends to do this to slow the passage of the ship in order to win an 'auction' in which he has bet that the ship will only travel a low number of miles by noon the next day. His plan is played out in a planned projected frame as follows:

> For it was at this moment that the idea came ... Well, he thought, why not? Why ever not? The sea was calm and he wouldn't have any trouble keeping afloat until they picked him up ... The ship would have to stop and lower a boat, and the boat would have to go back maybe half a mile to get him, and then it would have to return to the ship and be hoisted back on board. It would take at least an hour, the whole thing. An hour was about thirty miles. It would knock thirty miles off the day's run. That would do it. [The lowest bid] would be sure to win it then. Just so long as he made certain someone saw him falling over; but that would be simple to arrange.
>
> (Dahl 1990a: 72)

Parts of this plan are given in detail, such as the effect on the distance travelled, but the jump itself and the rescue call are left unstated at this point. We have to infer that someone seeing him fall overboard would call for help, this within-frame inference being based on our default general knowledge of this type of emergency situation. This includes the Type 1 frame assumptions that an observer will realise that the person who has fallen overboard is in danger and that the observer will act to attract the attention of those who can rescue that person. Mr Botibol, nevertheless, subsequently reviews his plan and checks the Type 1 default assumptions, questioning whether Type 2 alternatives are possible. He has selected an elderly woman to witness his jump, but he wonders whether she might be physically incapacitated or have her own vested interests to consider. Hence, he talks to her to ensure that she is not blind or deaf and to check that she has not herself placed an alternative bet in the 'auction'. Dahl then presents Mr Botibol as being completely satisfied that all Type 2 circumstances have been considered:

> Everything was now in order. The sea was calm, he was lightly dressed for swimming, there were almost certainly no man-eating sharks in this part of the Atlantic, and there was this pleasant kindly old woman to give the alarm. It was a question now only of whether the ship would be delayed long enough to swing the balance in his favour. Almost certainly it would.
>
> (Dahl 1990a: 74)

From this point on, Dahl detracts our attention from the question of whether the elderly woman might fail Mr Botibol by focusing on other issues, such as whether he might hit the propeller. The plan does, nevertheless, fail because of the elderly woman. Mr Botibol has not considered all the Type 2 possibilities. The woman sees him fall, but fails to act. Indeed, she stands watching as his body drifts away and becomes almost invisible. Readers might at this point experience a *participatory response* (Gerrig 1993), willing the woman to act as she continues to do nothing. Finally, a possible explanation of her behaviour comes with the appearance of another woman who can be inferred to be the carer for the first. This second woman does not believe the first one when she says, without apparently recognising the significance of her own words, that a man has 'dived overboard ... with his clothes on' (p.74). Dahl leaves us to draw our own conclusions about the reason for the woman's delay, but Botibol has already ruled out physical factors and the text hints at a psychological cause. Although Mr Botibol has considered a number of Type 2 possibilities, he has not considered that her psychological history might result in the woman not being treated as a credible witness.

The main point of this story (as in other Roald Dahl 'tales of the unexpected', such as 'Parson's Pleasure', 1990c) is that plans are fallible because we fail to take into account all the possibilities, particularly when human greed is present and when we are forced to rely on the actions of others. The final outcome stands in ironic contrast to the earlier planned projected frame. Dahl manipulates the situation so that we cannot be sure how a crucial but largely-unknown character, the elderly woman, will behave. The genre may lead readers to guess that Mr Botibol's plan will not succeed, but Dahl only reveals the reason for this at the end. Real-life contextual frame assumptions do apply, but we can only apply them once we know that the circumstances differ from the default and how they differ.

Tales of the unexpected (II)

Projected frames, cross-frame inferences and role re-appraisal

More elaborate 'twists in the tale' can be achieved by combining within-frame inferences and cross-frame inferences. Dahl's (1990b) 'Taste' sets up a primed 'dinner party' frame (F1) in which the host, Mike Schofield, challenges his guest, Richard Pratt, to guess the name of a rare wine being served. The guest is a famous gourmet who is so sure of his wine-tasting ability that he offers to bet his two houses if he loses, in exchange for marrying the host's daughter if he wins. The host believes that the wine is so rare that he stands no risk of losing his daughter, but after a lengthy display of wine-tasting expertise, the guest stuns the assembled party by correctly naming the wine. The denouement draws on information that has been presented nine pages earlier, in an off-stage projected frame (F2), as shown below (see the discussion of this frame on p.148). Before the wine-tasting, the host had described where the wine was being kept, a place that his guest had suggested on a previous visit:

> 'On top of the green filing cabinet in my study,' Mike said [to Richard].
> 'That's the place we chose. A good draft-free spot in a room with an even temperature. Excuse me now, will you, while I fetch it.'
> The thought of another wine to play with had restored his humour, and he hurried out the door, to return a minute later more slowly, walking softly, holding in both hands a wine basket in which a dark bottle lay.
> (Dahl 1990b: 56)

The denouement itself is as follows:

> Then this happened: The maid, the tiny, erect figure of the maid in her white-and-black uniform, was standing beside Richard Pratt, holding something out in her hand. 'I believe these are yours, sir,' she said ...
> 'Yes sir, they're yours.' The maid was an elderly woman – nearer seventy than sixty – a faithful family retainer of many years standing ...
> Without thanking her, Pratt took [the spectacles] up and slipped them into his top pocket, behind the white handkerchief.
> But the maid didn't go away. She remained standing beside and slightly behind Richard Pratt, and there was something so unusual in her manner and in the way she stood there, small, motionless, and erect, that I for one found myself watching her with a sudden apprehension. Her old grey face had a frosty, determined look, the lips were compressed, the little chin was out, and the hands were clasped together tight before her ...
> 'You left them in Mr. Scofield's [sic] study,' she said. Her voice was unnaturally, deliberately polite. 'On top of the green filing cabinet in

his study, sir, when you happened to go in there by yourself before dinner.'

It took a few moments for the full meaning of her words to penetrate ...

(Dahl 1990b: 64–5)

To interpret this, a reader needs to create a retrospective projected frame (F3) for the earlier occasion when the maid saw Richard in the study. This requires the amalgamation of information from different sources by a cross-frame inference. The maid is too discreet to say outright that she saw Richard with the wine, but this, of course, is the obvious inference and the whole point of her revealing this information at this stage. The cross-frame inference brings together in the retrospective projected frame, F3, not only the new information (Richard, Richard's glasses, the maid, the green filing cabinet in the study) but also the earlier information from the off-stage projected frame, F2 (the wine, the green filing cabinet in the study).

This cross-frame inference is not quite as simple as it might appear at first sight. Richard, the guest, is not present in F2 (since he is at the dinner table when Mike, the host, fetches the wine), but we can extend the parameters of F2 back to a point at which Richard might have had uninvited access to the study (i.e. before the dinner) to create the earlier scene, F3. Having set up F3, we can make the within-frame inferences that if Richard was there, he probably saw the wine (particularly since the lost object is a pair of glasses) and also that the maid has seen Richard looking at the wine. We then use another cross-frame inference to apply this information from F3 to the dinner party frame, F1, re-interpreting this frame since if Richard had already seen the wine, his attempt to guess its origin during the dinner party scene has been an elaborate con.

Dahl again uses the writing style to control 'information flow'. The cataphoric phrase 'Then this happened' at the start of the above example creates an expectation of denouement (particularly since the reader can (in this edition) see that the story is about to end). The maid's role has to be re-appraised because up until this point she has been presented simply as a scenario-dependent character (Sanford and Garrod 1981; Anderson *et al.* 1983). She has previously been described simply as 'the maid', without additional description; she performs predictable actions (e.g. serving food) and her actions are subordinated to the main action (e.g. early in the story, she hesitates to collect the guest's plate, but the main emphasis is on the fact that the guest has not finished his first course, rather than on her). By contrast, the above example includes a significant amount of very late description of the maid that places our attention more equally on both her and the guest. In a role reversal, her role in the story changes from being a mere 'prop' to being a plot central character. There is no change of identity and she is still a maid, although as her role in the story changes she also goes beyond the social role normally associated with a servant.

Crime fiction

Cross-frame inferences and role/identity re-appraisal

In Ian Rankin's (2000) *The Hanging Garden*, there is rather a different situation in which a character who is apparently scenario-dependent is suddenly re-identified as a major character who we have encountered earlier in the story. In this story, policeman John Rebus is initially seen saying goodbye in the street to his daughter Samantha (Sammy), after buying her a pizza. As they part, she walks away with the pizza box. Later, Rebus arrives at the Accident and Emergency unit of the local hospital on police business. On leaving, he spots another policeman guarding one of the hospital rooms and asks why he is there:

> Rebus nodded towards the door. 'Who's in there?'
>   'Hit and run.'
>   'Bad?' [The other policeman] shrugged. 'Where did it happen?'
>   'Top of Minto Street.'
>   'Did you get the car?' ...
>   'Waiting to see if she can tell us anything. What about you, sir?'
>   'Similar story, son. Parallel universe, you could call it.'

[Quarter of a page of conversation omitted]

> A door slid open and a doctor appeared. She was young, and looked exhausted. Behind her in the room, Rebus could see a bed, a figure on the bed, staff milling around the various machines. Then the door slid closed. ...
>   'Have you contacted her family?'
>   'I don't have a name.'
>   'Her effects are inside'. The doctor slid open the door again and walked in. There was clothing folded on a chair, a bag beneath it. As the doctor pulled out the bag, Rebus saw something. A flat white cardboard box.
>   A white cardboard pizza box. Clothes: black denims, black bra, red satin shirt. A black duffel-coat.
>   'John?'
>   And black shoes with two-inch heels, square-toed, new-looking except for the scuff marks, like they'd been dragged along the road.
>   He was in the room now. They had a mask over her face, feeding her oxygen. Her forehead was cut and bruised, the hair pushed away from it. Her fingers were blistered, the palms scraped raw. The bed she lay on wasn't really a bed but a wide steel trolley.
>   'Excuse me, sir, you shouldn't be in here.'
>   'What's wrong?'
>   'It's this gentleman—'
>   'John? John, what is it?'

Her earrings had been removed. Three tiny pin-pricks, one of them redder than its neighbours. The face above the sheet: puffy blackened eyes, a broken nose, abrasions on both cheeks. Split lip, a graze on the chin, eyelids which didn't even flutter. <u>He saw a hit and run victim.</u> And beneath it all, he saw <u>his daughter.</u>

And he screamed.

(Rankin 2000: 18–19, my emphasis)

By making a cross-frame inference, readers should be able to infer that the hit-and-run victim is Rebus's daughter at the point at which Rebus sees 'something. A flat white cardboard box. [paragraph break] A white cardboard pizza box'. This is a switch from a scenario-dependent character since at first the hit-and-run victim seemed to be simply background detail at the hospital with the main focus being on the policemen's meeting. The gradual progression from the pronoun to the expanded noun phrase allows the reader to follow Rebus's recognition process as he sees a significant detail and, like him, we can make the link with the earlier episode. Although the relevant information has been presented sixteen pages earlier and other episodes have intervened, it may still be retrievable from memory due to the prominence given to it earlier. The pizza had been mentioned in the opening scene, but was also, almost immediately after Rebus had left his daughter, recalled by him in an off-stage projected frame (in the second sentence of the following example):

And then she'd turned a corner and was gone. Rebus could only imagine her now: making sure the pizza box was secure beneath her left arm ...

(Rankin 2000: 3–4)

From a narrative point of view, it seems a little unnecessary to repeat information about the scene immediately after the scene has finished. Nevertheless, it makes sense that Rebus, as focaliser, is still thinking about his daughter after she goes, particularly since this preludes a series of observations about what he does and doesn't know about her. This may make the repetition more natural, but as a result the information that will facilitate the later identity re-appraisal is re-iterated.

The cross-frame inference in the hospital scene relies on the reader being able to make the connection, but if the reader fails to do so, it probably does not matter too much, since the reader will then be even more surprised by the revelation 'he saw his daughter'. Nevertheless, if the reader does manage to make the inference, the effect is that we witness Rebus's horror as the hospital scene slowly unfolds. We understand the reason for his sudden intense concentration on the details of the injury, as he re-assesses the severity of the situation (in an identity re-appraisal, 'the bed', previously emphasised in the expression 'a bed, a figure on the bed' becomes '[not] really a bed but a wide steel trolley'). This would mean that as we read the indefinite noun phrase 'a hit-and-run victim' in the penultimate paragraph of the main example above, we see that although the description still holds, she is not just an accident victim, but a major character too. The text goes on to state this, but we have already been through the recognition process with Rebus by the time we get this confirmation.

The dramatic impact of the recognition scene provides an ironic comment on Rebus's public/private personae, i.e. his professional role and his role as a father. After this scene, he chastises the other police officer for just sitting outside the room reading when his daughter 'Sammy' is lying there injured, but his own attitude before he identified her was just as detached, as can be seen from the conversation between the two policemen at the start of the main example above. This conflict is a major theme of the book and is made explicit when he later sees a photograph of the scene of the crime and wonders what he would have done if he had been there:

> Would he have concentrated on the car, caught its licence plate? Or would his attention have been focused on Sammy? Which would have prevailed: cop instincts or fatherhood? Someone at the station had said, 'Don't worry, we'll get him.' Not, 'Don't worry, she'll be all right.' Which brought it all down to two things: him – meaning the driver – and retribution, rather than her – the victim – and recovery.
>
> (Rankin 2000: 155)

Historical fiction

Cross-frame inferences, false identity and textual overrides

In all the above texts, the reader is led 'up the garden path' before the 'twist in the tale' or role/identity re-appraisal. Deborah Moggach's (2000) *Tulip Fever*, discussed below, is rather different because there are adequate clues, right from the start of the episode, that a false identity has been set up. The plot reversal in this case simply confirms what a reader has had adequate opportunity to guess all along. Nevertheless, this makes a contribution to the plot because we see events from the point of view of a focaliser who has a mistaken belief frame. In *Tulip Fever*, a novel set in seventeenth-century Amsterdam, the reader begins the relevant episode with plot knowledge that can be used to override specific information provided in the subsequent text. The reader knows that Sophia, the mistress of the house, is having an affair with Jan van Loos, a portrait painter. Sophia's situation immediately prior to the opening of the key episode is that she has a meeting arranged with Jan for that evening, that she intends to go, but that she is afraid of being seen. This is a justifiable fear since she has already been spotted twice, by her lawyer's wife and by her own husband, when 'en route' to previous meetings with Jan. Also, Sophia is in a particularly difficult position on this occasion because she has lied to her husband, having told him that she will stay at home due to toothache whilst he goes out on his own to play cards. The problem is left open as Chapter 17 finishes, but a possible solution is that Sophia could disguise herself. This solution is not stated in the text, but could be inferred by the reader. This does not necessarily mean that the reader makes this inference at this particular point, but in the following chapter, Chapter 18, the information about Sophia's predicament can be usefully drawn on to explain a situation that puzzles the main focaliser at that point. The events in Chapter 18 are seen through the eyes of Willem, a servant engaged to Sophia's servant, Maria. Willem is about to visit Maria, but spots her leaving Sophia's house, as follows:

> <u>Maria</u> is not expecting him; he will surprise her. Tonight <u>her master and mistress have gone out to play cards;</u> she will be alone. Even so, Willem approaches the side door, down the alleyway, the one he uses when he steals in after dark.
>
> Willem stops dead. <u>A figure</u> emerges from the door. She closes it behind her and hurries off, away down the alley. It is <u>Maria</u>. She slips like a shadow between the buildings.
>
> Willem is going to call out but something stops him. <u>Maria</u> looks so purposeful, so intent. He follows her down the alley, keeping his distance. <u>There is something odd about her.</u> She emerges into the Keisergracht and glances to the right and left. He can glimpse her more clearly now. Under her shawl she wears her white cap, the one with long flaps that conceal her face.
>
> She turns right and hurries along, keeping close to the houses. How furtive she looks! She moves fast; he has to break into a trot to keep her in sight. <u>This, too, is unlike Maria.</u> She usually ambles, swaying her hips, taking her time ... [She arrives at a house and enters a room containing an easel]
>
> It is <u>Maria</u> and a man. [Willem] cannot see <u>Maria's</u> face. ... And then she kisses [the man].
>
> Willem's legs buckle beneath him. He slides down to a sitting position. Then he gets up and stumbles away, blindly.
>
> (Moggach 2000: 64–7, my emphasis)

During this scene, it is quite possible for the reader to bring together the information that 'Maria' seems unfamiliar to Willem ('There is something odd about her.' 'This, too, is unlike Maria.') with Sophia's motive for disguising herself and thereby infer that 'Maria' may in fact be Sophia in disguise. This is confirmed in Chapter 19, when the focalisation switches to Sophia and we learn from her that:

> Maria's clothes, my spent disguise, lie on the floor.
>
> (Moggach 2000: 69)

This is a common type of plot intricacy, but it has significant implications for linguistic and psychological models. From a linguistic point of view, it challenges current models of reference such as 'accessibility theory' (e.g. Ariel 1990, in press). Accessibility theorists argue that readers gain access to mental representations of entities directly by means of referring expressions such as nouns and pronouns. In this example, though, neither nouns nor pronouns enable a reader to access the right mental representation. Instead, readers need here to use plot information to textually override the name 'Maria' to assign the referent, Sophia, to the frame, without losing the information that Willem, the focaliser, believes this to be Maria (hence explaining his subsequent response). From a psychological point of view, the above example also challenges propositional models (e.g. van Dijk and Kintsch 1983; Kintsch 1998). These models provide a means of abstracting relevant information from each sentence, then building a situation model from this information. The problem with this is that situational information can sometimes be necessary to extract propositional information in the first place (Johnson-Laird 1983). Here, contextual frame theory can explain how readers use key contextual information (i.e. Sophia has not gone out) to identify an erroneous belief frame (i.e. Willem is mistaken about this) that can be used to override certain information in the text (i.e. the name 'Maria').

Conclusion

'Twists in the tale' and other plot reversals are not the only types of text which force readers to use their cognitive skills to interpret the words on the page. This is a natural part of all reading, but the examples discussed in this chapter make particular demands on these skills. We have seen how our default within-frame inferences can be challenged and how cross-frame inferences, building on clues presented many pages earlier, can force us to re-evaluate characters and scenes. In addition, readers may need to monitor belief frames that they realise from their plot knowledge are unreliable. The interpretation of these types of examples requires significant inferencing skills. In many respects, readers of these texts have to be aware of what is not explicitly stated in the text. This cognitive aspect of reading is supplemented by stylistic indicators which may make clues more prominent in the mind of a reader or which may signal that a denouement is about to occur.

Cognitive poetic theories aim to give a detailed account of the balance between language and mind during text processing, taking particular account of stylistic factors that are often ignored by cognitive scientists. Contextual frame theory does not offer a single interpretation of a text, but draws attention to the reading process: how knowledge may be utilised; where inferences may be made; and how style may influence the degree to which information becomes prominent in the mind. For 'twists in the tale' and other plot reversals, contextual frame theory aims to highlight the cognitive skills involved in reading these texts, without forgetting the pleasure that readers can get from the additional demands that such texts make on their inference-making abilities.

Further activities

1   Select another Roald Dahl short story and/or another text which has a 'twist in the tale' or includes a plot reversal. Use the above framework to analyse these stories. If necessary, supplement the above terminology with further terminology from 'contextual frame theory' as described in Emmott (1997) (see also Stockwell 2002a: ch.11). In addition to the examples in this chapter, you may also find the following analyses of plot reversals useful as models: for science fiction, Stockwell (2000: 159–63); for crime fiction, Emmott (1997: 170–3); for other literature, Emmott (1997: 169–70) and Gavins (2000).

2   Perform your own reader-response tests on the stories discussed in this chapter and/or your chosen text(s) in (1) above. Select 'experimental subjects' who have not read the text before and ask them to read the whole short story (or the relevant sections for novels). You can ask your subjects to describe their reading experiences after they have finished or, more ambitiously, you can attempt to collect information as they read in the form of a 'protocol analysis' of the denouement (see Short 1989; and Corbett 1997: ch.11, for details of how to do a protocol analysis).

Observe the point at which readers begin to re-appraise characters and/or events. If readers make inferences at different points or fail to make inferences at all, how does this affect their appreciations of text(s)? What effect does the genre have on the way that plot reversals are read? To what extent do readers guess at possible explanations that are not overtly suggested in the text? What are the methodological problems of doing protocol analysis on these types of stories?

3   Contextual frame theory can be applied to different media, but the balance of perceptual input (from written text, film images, etc.) and cognitive gap-filling can differ from medium to medium. Choose a story that exists in two media (book, film, play, etc.) and has a 'twist in the tale' or contains other plot reversals. How are clues created and how are these made sufficiently memorable to be drawn on at the denouement stage? How is suspense generated and how does the denouement unfold? As an example, Stockwell (2002a: 158–62) provides a useful model of the different processing of a play by an audience watching a performance and by readers of the text of a play. More generally, see Emmott (1997) for a discussion of the distinction between the contextual monitoring needed to gap-fill whilst reading and whilst responding to visual scenes in everyday life.

12 Writingandreading
The future of cognitive poetics

Keith Oatley

Editors' preface

Keith Oatley closes our collection with a reflection on the future of cognitive poetics. His discussion considers both those explorations undertaken over the course of the preceding chapters, and those yet to be embarked upon in this new and developing field. The fact that Oatley has written this chapter from within the field of cognitive psychology rather than cognitive poetics, and that he himself is a published author of literary fiction, makes his discussion all the more interesting and provocative. Oatley's chapter is the only one in this volume not to be followed by a 'further activities' section. We hope, instead, that you will use this final discussion as a springboard for your own thoughts on the possible future directions cognitive poetics might now take.

Writingandreading

'Writingandreading' is not an English word. It should be. We tend to think of its two parts as separate. Pure writing is possible. One may just write an e-mail, careless of syntax and spelling, then press a key, and off it goes into the ether. Pure reading is also possible: one can absorb, if that is an apt metaphor, the information in a newspaper article with almost no thought except what the writer has supplied. More usually we writeandread. As I write this chapter, I am also reading it, and I will read it again, and re-write and re-read. Even in my first draft I have made four or five changes to the previous sentence, though only two (so far) to this one. If I read a text, let us say Peter Stockwell's book *Cognitive Poetics*, I read a version that depends on the reader's share. A text is not autonomous. That is to say it does not stand alone: responsibility is distributed between writer and reader. For this reason, Stockwell refers to the heteronymous nature of cognitive poetics. When I read Stockwell's or any other book, I mentally write my version of it. For literary texts the writerly aspect of reading (Barthes 1975) is even more important.

Cognitive science is about knowledge, conscious and unconscious, about how it is represented, how it is used by human and artificial minds, and how it may be organised for particular purposes. It is interdisciplinary and multi-methodological. Cognitive poetics shares the same commitments to be broad rather than narrow. It derives from psychology, linguistics, and literary theory. Its field is literature, including texts that are read, movies and plays that are seen, poetry that is heard.

Aristotle's *Poetics* combined psychology with literary theory and with discussion of how literature is made. His mixture of topics was right for his purpose and, I think, right for the enterprise of cognitive poetics now. What we would expect from the new enterprise is an understanding of how the mind works in its writingandreading of literature, of how literature can give us readers insights into ourselves and our fellow beings, and of the place of literature in the personal and social world.

Psychology in cognitive poetics is not solely based on the work of laboratories or on psychometric questionnaires. It includes the psychology of lives lived by people in relation to each other, to culture, and to circumstance. Criticism in cognitive poetics differs from much of the literary criticism that occurs in a department of literature. In the criticism that occurs in cognitive poetics, we are concerned with what minds do when writing or reading. There is interest in metaphor, for instance, not just as a figure of speech, but because it shows us how minds work. In the same instant in which it is being discussed, a metaphor can demonstrate our minds working, rather as a stereoscopic picture in a book on perception demonstrates a principle of seeing in three dimensions. In cognitive poetics, discussions of the art and craft of writing are not just tips, such as 'show don't tell', for selling a story to a pernickety editor. They are aimed at principles whereby writingandreading can allow us to think what we would not otherwise have been able to think.

In writing about the future of cognitive poetics I am, of course, unable to see that future. What I will do instead is to project some significant aspects of what is already in progress. To adopt Stockwell's metaphor of Chapter 12 in his book (2002a): at the edge of the map of the territory he has surveyed, some roads are under construction. I choose three, and say something about where they are headed.

Mimesis

Art fixes the ephemeral. It renders experience into distinct objects that last. It illuminates a set of relationships that are harder to appreciate without the mediation of art.

So what is the relation between art and the world? This question is the basis of perhaps the largest highway in the territory of cognitive poetics. This has been the principal route in literary theory for 2,400 years. It is still being built.

The answer to the question given by Aristotle was that the relation of text to world is that of *mimesis*. Philip Sidney, in his famous 1595 *Defence of Poetry* (Sidney 1986) took this relation to be 'imitation, counterfeiting,

figuring forth'. English translations for the subsequent 400 years have generally followed him. We see this sense when Sidney's contemporary Shakespeare had Hamlet say of acting that it may 'hold, as 'twere, the mirror up to
nature' (*Hamlet*, III ii, 20–1). The idea is that realist artists are able to let us
see life as it is, by a device, which is the work of art.

Mimesis as imitation or representation has been easy to attack. Plato, in
the tenth book of *The Republic*, gave the idea a well-known drubbing by
arguing that any representation of something is a mere apparition, clearly
removed by one stage from the truth of the thing itself. Since the nineteenth
century, art as representation has been undermined by technology. Photo-
graphs, film, audio recordings, video, imitate and copy far more exactly than
any art. And Derrida (1976) and his followers have argued that text cannot
refer to anything at all outside itself.

Realism in literature has continued, though now it runs in new channels.
Some theorists such as Nuttall (1983) and Bloom (1999) have argued that,
since Shakespeare, the new locus of realism is psychological. What is
depicted is the inner world of human emotions and aspirations, where no
video camera can intrude. Portrayal in great literature is of character.
Abrams (1953) argues, contrary to Derrida, that it is indeed possible to refer
to both physical and mental objects in language. He proposes, however, that
referring is not the primary function of art. This function is to direct attention: not like a mirror to show a reflection, but like a lamp to illuminate.

I shall not say that all argument about the relation of the text to the world
would have been avoided if Aristotle's term *mimesis* had been better understood. I do propose that copying, imitation, and the like, are not good translations of what Aristotle meant. The future of cognitive poetics will be better
if we follow the road that Aristotle probably did start to build.

A wonderful discussion of the relation between art and the world
occurred when, in an article of 1884 entitled, 'The Art of Fiction', Henry
James (1951) argued that a novel is a 'direct impression of life'. 'Impression'
is a better word than 'imitation', but the provenance of James's idea is clearly
the same as the usual translations from Philip Sidney onwards. James's article received a reply that same year entitled, 'A humble remonstrance', by
Robert Louis Stevenson. A novel, says Stevenson, is not at all a direct impression of life.

> Life is monstrous, infinite, illogical, abrupt and poignant; a work of art
> in comparison is neat, finite, self-contained, rational, flowing, and emas-
> culate. Life imposes by brute energy, like inarticulate thunder; art
> catches the ear, among the far louder noises of experience, like an air
> artificially made by a discreet musician.
>
> (Stevenson 1992a: 182)

So literature is not a copy or impression. It is, as Stevenson explains, something more abstract, like the set of ideas that include circles in geometry.

Perfect circles do not exist in the physical world, but we cannot do without the idea of them in mathematics or engineering. In the same way, in understanding ourselves and other people we cannot do without such literary ideas as character.

Continuing the theme, in 1888 Stevenson mused on the notion that I believe offers the best nineteenth-century conception of the issue: *mimesis* is a kind of dream.

> The past is all of one texture – whether feigned or suffered – whether acted out in three dimensions, or only witnessed in that small theatre of the brain which we keep brightly lighted all night long, after the jets are down, and darkness and sleep reign undisturbed in the remainder of the body.
>
> (Stevenson 1992b: 189)

In this article Stevenson goes on to describe how he was always a dreamer, and all his best ideas for stories came to him in dreams which, he said, were far more creative than he was.

As Miall and Kuiken (2001) have pointed out, the same idea was entertained by Coleridge:

> Poetry [is] a rationalized dream dealing ... to manifold Forms our own Feelings, that never perhaps were attached by us consciously to our own personal Selves ... O there are Truths below the Surface in the subject of Sympathy, and how we *become* that which we understandly behold and hear, having, how much God perhaps only knows, created part even of the Form.
>
> (Coleridge 1957–1990: 2086)

It was entertained too, by Keats, in his fragment (one of his last poems), 'The Fall of Hyperion' (discussed by Crisp, in Chapter 8 of this volume, in terms of its metaphorical content). Here are its first lines again.

> Fanatics have their dreams, wherewith they weave
> A paradise for a sect; the savage, too,
> From forth the loftiest vision of his sleep
> Guesses at Heaven; pity these have not
> Trac'd upon vellum or wild Indian leaf
> The shadows of melodious utterance,
> But bare of laurel, they live, dream, and die;
> For Poesy alone can tell her dreams.

For us moderns, with the technology of writingandreading, the shadows of dreams can be traced, even if no longer on vellum but on computer screen. Thereby they become objects that can escape death and cheat the ephemeral, that can bear contemplation of many minds, in many places, over many years.

Not far into 'The Fall of Hyperion' the protagonist falls asleep, then seems to wake: a signal to the reader that a dream is in progress. He finds himself in a huge stone sanctuary in which he meets a shade who starts upbraiding him for being a dreamer:

> Only the dreamer venoms all his days
> Bearing more woe than all his sins deserve

Keats did not finish the poem, but in a subsequent draft, the shade tells the dreamer that poets and dreamers are quite different: poets are a benefit to the world, while dreamers vex it. For Keats the idea of distinguishing between poet and dreamer was an agony, one that he did not live to resolve. For us, in cognitive poetics, I believe the idea of fiction and poetry as kinds of dream is far better than ideas of copies or impressions of life.

Whatever the problems of writer and dreamer, the idea of a dream by a reader conveys the sense of lived experience that at the same time patently is a mental construction. Think about it like this. The fact that we can dream in vivid visual scenes makes it clear that the neural machinery for constructing the experienced world is in the brain, and is not immediately dependent on direct input from the eyes. When a literary artist guides the dreaming process, he or she whispers in the reader's ear. If we, as readers, lend ourselves to it, the sense of being transported to an imagined place can occur. The imagined place may even be real. With transportation, we may, as Coleridge hints, also be transformed. The Forms that we understand, and partially create, can become newly recognised aspects of ourselves.

The reason one can be confident that this is the right theoretical basis for fiction is that we have substantial evidence that perceiving and understanding the world with eyes, ears, and other sensory apparatus, is also a constructive process. Even direct seeing is not receiving an inner copy of an outer world. The essential pieces of theory were offered by Helmholtz (1925) in his third volume of *Physiological Optics,* and by Bartlett (1932) in *Remembering.* Both perception and memory involve projecting our knowledge into the world. Hippolite Taine (1882) made the point like this. It is not that hallucinations are disorders of perception, he wrote (I paraphrase), instead, visual perception – the sight we see when we open our eyes – is a kind of hallucination, but one that is guided by evidence from the retina.

What Bartlett showed is that when it came to remembering a story they had read, readers did not reproduce the words. It would take a tape recorder or some such imitative device to do that. They did remember some things: a mood, some salient details, the gist of the story. When it came to remembering, they used these fragments together with their own organisations of knowledge, idiosyncrasies, and culture – schemata as Bartlett called them – to tell the story as they thought it must have been.

The idea has been applied to fiction (Gerrig 1993; Oatley 2002). In reading, we assimilate what we read to the schemata of what we already know. The more we know the more we understand, and we project what we know to construct a world suggested by the text. It is the same in the actual world: someone who is learning chess may observe his opponent move one of the wooden pieces that has a crenellated top to exchange places, more or less, with a slightly taller piece. An experienced player with a schema for chess will see more: see that black has castled on the queen's side to build a more solid defensive structure. A mental something, a schema, is not only necessary to project into the world in order to understand it, it is necessary if we are ever to attach our own thoughts to what we see or what we read.

'Dream' and 'imagination' are good metaphors for fiction. They place the onus in the right place for a new cognitive poetics: the responsibility for a piece of fiction is shared. The writer offers a kit of parts, or a set of cues. The reader does the construction, and makes the imagined dream start up and run. Chekhov said that when he wrote he made 'the assumption that [his readers] will add the subjective elements that are lacking in the story' (letter to Suvorin of 1 April 1890; Yarmolinsky 1973: 395).

In the second half of the twentieth century a new metaphor became available and contributed to the start of cognitive science: the metaphor of simulation. Fictional narrative is a kind of simulation, but one that runs on minds rather than on computers (Oatley 1992, 1999). We use computers to simulate interactions of many processes, each of which we understand in a piecemeal fashion. Together they produce concerted effects that, without simulations, we would find difficult to understand. Perhaps most familiar are the simulations of the weather that are the bases for the weather forecast, or simulations of the economy that tell us if we are about to enter or leave a recession. These are modern instances. For several thousand years, something comparable has been accomplished in human minds. Ceremonies, rituals, dramas have been performed, poetry and stories have been told, with narrative structures, to enable humankind to engage with its deepest concerns. Such dramas and stories are made up of parts, each of which we almost understand. The simulations allow us to approach composite understandings by taking our parts in these larger social structures.

Metaphor is one of the main muscles of thought. As Lakoff and Johnson (1980) have argued, and as discussed by Crisp in this volume (see ch. 8), a metaphor works by taking something like a direct experience, such as moving about in the world, and using this as the vehicle or source for a topic or target of which we have less understanding. So an experience of travelling from one town to another can be projected onto our lesser understanding of what we might be doing in our lives: 'life's a journey to an undiscovered destination'.

To understand the nature of metaphor we need to have some experience to project onto the more obscure subject. For those who have spent many hours programming computers and thinking about the interaction of parts in complex processes, 'simulation' invokes a substantial cloud of meaning, and the metaphor of fiction-as-simulation may be quite successful. For others, simulation may merely mean something that computers do, or that other people do. To that extent the metaphor of simulation will be less successful. In that case I suggest that you rely on the metaphor of the dream, as proposed not only by Coleridge, Keats, and Stevenson, but by Shakespeare:

> These our actors,
> As I foretold you, were all spirits, and
> Are melted into air, into thin air;
> And like the baseless fabric of this vision,
> The cloud-capped towers, the gorgeous palaces,
> The solemn temples, the great globe itself,
> Yea, all which it inherit, shall dissolve;
> And, like this insubstantial pageant faded,
> Leave not a rack behind. We are such stuff
> As dreams are made on ...
> (*The Tempest,* IV i, 148–57)

Whichever you choose, I hope you see that *mimesis* is not imitation. If you re-read Aristotle's *Poetics* with the metaphor of dream or of simulation in mind, invoking it wherever your English translation says 'copy', or 'representation', or any such, you will see that some notion of the kind I have sketched is closer to what Aristotle meant. What is the essence of tragedy, asks Aristotle? It is the plot, a unifying structure that offers a *mimesis* of an action, and of characters primarily for the sake of their action. If any part is moved or displaced, then the whole play does not work.

For the future, then, perhaps cognitive poetics will follow the lead of cognitive science. One of the advances made by cognitive science in the 1960s was to start to address psychological problems not just with the instrument of experimentation, asking yes/no questions at selected points in human behaviour. As cognitive scientists came to realise, it would be hard for a bug to crawl across a newspaper, making yes/no determinations of whether it was dark or light at each pixel point and – even with a good memory and sense of location – read the newspaper. One needs in addition something more integrative, something that can put minute understandings together into complexes, from which interrelationships among parts might emerge. That something was computer simulation. For us in cognitive poetics, the equivalent will be, perhaps, the idea that the relation of text to world is a kind of dream or simulation, that the reader constructs from the kit of parts supplied by the writer.

Emotions, *rasas,* and the personal

A second road being built out from the current territory of cognitive poetics is that of the personal, and especially of the emotional. Emotions were neglected by cognitive scientists at the start of their discipline. That has changed. Emotions have become the most interesting of current topics in psychology, cognitive science, and neuroscience. In the same way, in cognitive poetics there was a relative neglect of emotions, but this phase too is passing. If we take Bruner's (1986) definition of narrative as that distinctive mode of thinking about agents whose plans meet vicissitudes, we can and should add the fact that in literature as in life, such vicissitudes lead to emotions. Emotions are centres of considerable density of meaning in texts. For the writerandreader, they are places of personal significance, not necessarily the same as emotions mentioned in the text. The effects are achieved not only because emotions are signals that some event has impinged on an important goal or aspiration, but because emotions are touchstones of our deeply held values, both those that are known to us, and those that may only be guessed at.

Among cognitive theories of emotions, the theory of Oatley and Johnson-Laird (1987, 1996) offers something to writersandreaders because it explains the movement from emotions as sometimes inchoate to potentially meaningful when they become subjects for exploration, reflection, and conversation with others. This very aspect of emotions is the centre of the Romantic theory of art as the expression of emotions. (I take it that despite modernism and postmodernism, in terms of larger movements, we are still very much in the Romantic era.) The Romantic idea is that art is the creative exploration of emotions in various languages: music, painting, literature, and so forth (Collingwood 1938). Creativity is demanded in the press of an emotion, because emotions occur in life when the unexpected happens, when the habitual has not been sufficient, when there is no worked-out plan. An emotion is therefore a frank invitation to creativity (Averill and Nunley 1992). Art, including literary art, is a way to offer to contemporaries and succeeding generations some of the creative solutions to recurring vicissitudes of human life: both accomplishments and disasters.

As in early cognitive science, so in Western literary theory, emotions were more or less neglected. They were not neglected, however, in the Indian literary tradition that extends back to about the time of Aristotle. Indeed they were at its centre. In the West, the most accessible writings on emotions from this tradition come from medieval times. They arose in the area that is now Kashmir. A group of literary theorists who include Abhinavagupta (Ingalls *et al.* 1990) argued that literary emotions are different from those of everyday life. They postulated nine such emotions, as follows: first I give the everyday emotion and then its literary equivalent, or *rasa* as it is called in Sanscrit:

> delight (the amorous),
> laughter (the comic),
> sorrow (the pitiable or tragic),
> anger (the furious),
> heroism (the heroic),

fear (the terrible),
disgust (the odious),
wonder (the marvellous), and
serenity (the peaceful).

It is no doubt pure accident that Oatley and Johnson-Laird (1996) postulated nine basic emotion modes, six of which correspond to these (love, happiness, sadness, anger, ... fear, disgust). Non-correspondences occur because Oatley and Johnson-Laird postulated several kinds of love, as well as contempt, but did not include heroism, wonder, or serenity.

The idea of the Indian theorists was that a well-constructed literary work should concentrate on just one of these *rasas*. We might call it the basis for a genre, such as love story, comedy, tragedy. The central *rasa* in a play or poem would be reached via other *rasas*, and by what these theorists called transient mental states like discouragement or apprehension.

An important property of *rasas* was that they could allow the reader to see more clearly into the true nature and implications of emotions. We all experience emotions in ordinary life. We know that they can impose themselves, as Stevenson said, like 'inarticulate thunder'. Being inarticulate, they are often not understood. The Indian literary theorists insisted that this was because their implications are inevitably obscured by a thick crust of egoism with which we human beings ordinarily surround ourselves. Literary emotions are like everyday emotions in almost all ways except that they offer the possibility of experiencing them so that they may touch us insightfully rather than (as Scheff 1979 points out) either overwhelming us or being kept at a distance in our attempts to avoid them. This connection between emotion and insight may be what Aristotle called *katharsis,* which Nussbaum (1986) has translated as 'clarification' or 'illumination'.

An important postulate of this medieval Indian theory is that emotions and other personal effects of reading are prompted by the writer, not directly but by means of suggestion, *dhvani*. Hogan (in press) has analysed this idea in terms of modern cognitive psychology, in terms of priming (see also Emmott, in this volume, ch. 11) in which once a writer mentions a particular context, then the cloud of its associations and connotations comes to readiness in the mind, and affects the understanding of the text.

A nice example suggested by Hogan (in press) is from the death scene at the end of *Hamlet*. Horatio says, 'Good night, sweet prince'. This brings to mental readiness – primes – a sense of a parent saying goodnight to a child. The words suggest an attachment theme, which can carry a profound sense of our most tender and intimate moments.

Traditionally, in narratology two major aspects of stories have been identified: the story structure (which Russian literary theorists at the beginning of the twentieth century called *fabula*) and discourse structure or plot *(sjuzhet)*. Story worlds, and their cognitive construction from the clues and implications of the discourse structure in the text, are often complex and sometimes ambiguous. They are discussed in detail in this volume by Gavins in relation to text world theory, by Emmott in relation to contextual frame theory, and, by Semino in relation to possible worlds theory and mental space theory. Much progress has been made in understanding these constructive processes.

For the future, I suggest (Oatley 2002) that two further aspects of narrative need to be considered. One is what I call the suggestion structure that depends on the resonances a piece of literature has for each reader personally. The association structure corresponds to the suggestiveness *(dhvani)* that the medieval Indian literary theorists argued would prompt specific literary emotions *(rasas)*. Other personal elements that can be suggested include autobiographical memories, cultural knowledge, and preoccupations. All are crucial to any reading of a story or poem. In this volume, Gavins specifically includes personal aspects of readers in her considerations, and Semino discusses the personal preoccupations of the writer, Hemingway, which, once they are known, can become part of a reader's cultural knowledge. My proposal is to distinguish between general processes of cognitive construction from the discourse structure, and idiosyncratic processes of each reader. Thus, in the analysis of love songs and poems offered in this volume by Steen, one might want to separate general schemata that depend on scenarios of love that are well understood in the Western world, from resonances with each reader's experiences that may be set up by a poem, song, or story.

The final aspect is what I call the realisation of a story or poem: the reader's own writing of it, using all the resources of the mind. In this volume, Hamilton shows such an analysis of Wilfred Owen's sonnet, 'Hospital Barge'. The realisation draws on the story structure, the discourse structure, and the suggestion structure. It includes the reader's interpretation, but it is more than interpretation. It is the reader's writing of the story, his or her enactment, including its significance for him or her.

The uses of literature

The third road to which I point, beyond the present edge of the territory of cognitive poetics, is that of the practical. What are our purposes? We humans pursue knowledge, as Francis Bacon said in 1605, 'for the relief of man's estate' (Bacon 1974). As we might now say, we pursue science to improve conditions for humankind and for our world. So what of literature? Its point is not to change the world, but to understand it. Cognitive poetics seeks to understand the writingandreading of literature, and to understand the nature of this understanding. Our focus is on the state of the inner world of humankind.

With Theodor Adorno's remark that 'writing poetry after Auschwitz is barbaric' we might wonder too about writing cognitive poetics. Adorno meant, amongst other things, that after Auschwitz, we should all look to our guilt rather than to poetry. The implication, too, is that if pre-war German society, which was widely regarded as the most educated in Europe, the cultural inheritor of the works of Bach and Goethe, could turn (in Daniel Goldhagen's 1996 phrase) into 'Hitler's willing executioners', then a simple meliorative view of education, music, and literature was destroyed along with so much else by 1945.

The European Holocaust was not the first or only set of events to demonstrate the human penchant for contemptuous cruelty, but it did make this fact inescapably part of modern Euro-American experience. Such cruelty could no longer be seen as an aspect, merely, of people other than us, distant in time and place like Genghis Khan on the Asian steppes or the Conquistadors in Central America. The people of the Holocaust – like Hamlet, both avengers and victims – are us, and they are us today.

Perhaps we should take Adorno's remark as meaning not that poetry should be no more, but that we can no longer entertain the comforting nineteenth-century idea that poetry automatically makes us better people, or makes the world a better place. Perhaps, indeed, for us in the twenty-first century, first should come a poetry of sadness and of guilt. Indeed, some fifty years after the war, such writing has begun, for instance, with such books as *The Emigrants* and *Austerlitz* by W.G. Sebald (1996 and 2001, respectively).

As the idea of heteronomy in cognitive poetics makes clear, no poem, no literary text, no movie, could – just like that – make someone a better person. A poem, a text, a drama, has no such causal power. But in future, I believe, people studying writingandreading need to consider the purposes of literature and fiction. There are, as far as I can see, three main purposes.

First of course, there is enjoyment, which we all want from literature. I was shocked, when I visited Pergamon for the first time, when the Turkish guide referred to 'Dionysius, the god of entertainment'. But perhaps he was right. By means of our engagement with a text, we long to be transported from the world of the humdrum, the mediocre, or the despairing, to the land of elsewhere. In this land we can be unique. By identification we can be extraordinary. We may experience strong emotions, but the events will not in the end devastate us. So, is literature a kind of mental chocolate? Not exactly, but many of us would not want to live in a world without chocolate.

Second is the possibility of enabling us to become better writersandreaders. Bruner (1986) discussed Barthes' idea of the writerly text, and how writers enable readers to write their own versions. 'I believe', said Bruner, 'that the *great* writer's gift to the reader is to make him a *better* writer' (1986: 37), that is to say a better writer of his or her own enactment of the text.

When cognitive scientists have studied expertise, they have done so, in part, to understand how any of us might become experts in the fields we pursue, whether running a marathon or teaching children to solve problems in geometry. Similarly, cognitive poetics hopes, I think, to contribute to the function that Bruner identified as the great writer's gift. In studying cognitive poetics, we aspire to become better writersandreaders. Our quest for improvement is not merely technical. It is to allow us in our writing to write more of the truth, and in our reading to enter more fully into what we read.

Third is improvement not just as writersandreaders, but of our selves. Can writingandreading be a kind of therapy for an imperfect species? Here we border on the unconscious. If you interview people about their dreams you will find many who describe their salient dreams as like bad thrillers. They are pursued, or tortured, or find themselves in fights. Moreover, people who have a melancholy disposition are drawn to melancholy books. Angry people are drawn to stories of revenge. People who describe themselves, perhaps with some regret, as a bit cut off, are attracted to stories of alienation.

It is as if literature, as well as drawing on the unconscious in its creation, offers externalised versions of our unconscious worlds. What is the function of this? It would be satisfying to be able to say, with John Keats, that poetry may strike the reader as 'a wording of his own highest thoughts, and appear almost a Remembrance', (Keats 1899: 289). It would be good also to say that in such effects the reader can come to understand his or her inner world, come more closely to terms with it, make the unconscious conscious. It may be, alternatively, that for us human beings, our highest thoughts are just that: thoughts. We have not yet found how to transform such thoughts into changes in our dispositions. We do not quite know, in cultural terms, what the effects might be of bringing our thoughts to literary awareness, whether they were previously unconscious or of the highest kind. Humankind has existed for a quarter of a million years, stories for perhaps some tens of thousands of years, written literature for about 4000 years.

This is a matter for the future, but it is perhaps also something for the present. Wordsworth wrote in 'Lines Composed a Few Miles Above Tintern Abbey':

> ... feelings too
> Of unremembered pleasure: such, perhaps,
> As have no slight or trivial influence
> On that best portion of a good man's life,
> His little, nameless, unremembered acts
> Of kindness and of love.

Most ways of making the world better are little, nameless, and unremembered, but there are thousands of such ways. By contrast there are just a few ways to make the world worse: ignorance, greed, violence. Their effects can be 'monstrous, infinite, illogical, abrupt'. Building occurs, bit by bit. Destruction can be large and permanent. And, as Stevenson pointed out, the ways in which the world is made worse are remembered. After the event, they are 'poignant'.

We might come to understand, from such writers as Vygotsky (1962), that mind is social stuff and that much of it is made of language. So reading can contribute to the building, bit-by-bit, of minds and identities. We might, indeed, say with Booth (1988) that books and characters in books contribute to making us who we are, in the way that friendships do. Then, if we choose our books carefully just as we choose our friends carefully, we can say that the little acts of reading might contribute to giving us, as atoms of the social world, a little more understanding.

As George Eliot put it in 1856:

> The greatest benefit we owe to the artist, whether painter, poet, or novelist, is the extension of our sympathies. Appeals founded on generalizations and statistics require a sympathy ready-made, a moral sentiment already in activity; but a picture of human life such as a great artist can give, surprises even the trivial and the selfish into that attention to what is apart from themselves, which may be called the raw material of moral sentiment ... Art is the nearest thing to life; it is a mode of amplifying experience and extending our contact with our fellow-men beyond the bounds of our personal lot.
>
> (Eliot 1883: 192–3)

Although what we study has to compete with 'the far louder noises of experience', we think it has something to contribute, something that is perhaps little, but is nonetheless significant.

References

Abbott, V., Black, J. and Smith, E. (1985) 'The Representation of Scripts in Memory', *Journal of Memory and Language*, 24: 179–99.

Abrams, M.H. (1953) *The Mirror and the Lamp: Romantic Theory and the Critical Tradition*, Oxford: Oxford University Press.

Aitchison, J. (1994) *Words in the Mind: An Introduction to the Mental Lexicon*, 2nd edn, Oxford: Basil Blackwell.

—— (1997) *The Articulate Mammal*, London: Routledge.

Alexander, L.G. (1988) *Longman English Grammar*, London: Longman.

Anderson, A., Garrod, S.C. and Sanford, A.J. (1983) 'The Accessibility of Pronominal Antecedents as a Function of Episode Shifts', *Quarterly Journal of Experimental Psychology*, 35: 427–40.

Ariel, M. (1990) *Accessing Noun–Phrase Antecedents*, London: Routledge.

—— (in press) 'Accessibility Theory: An Overview', in Sanders, T., Schilperoord, J. and Spooren, W. (eds) *Text Representation: Linguistic and Psycholinguistic Aspects*, Amsterdam: John Benjamins.

Aristotle (1970) *Poetics*, Ann Arbor, MI: University of Michigan Press.

Averill, J.R. and Nunley, E.P. (1992) *Voyages of the Heart: Living an Emotionally Creative Life*, New York: Free Press.

Azar, M. (1999) 'Argumentative Text as Rhetorical Structure: An Application of Rhetorical Structure Theory', *Argumentation*, 13: 97–114.

Bacon, F. (1974) *The Advancement of Learning*, Oxford: Oxford University Press.

Baddeley, A.D. and Weiskrantz, L. (eds) (1993) *Attention: Awareness, Selection, and Control*, Oxford: Oxford University Press.

Baker, C. (1969) *Ernest Hemingway: A Life Story*, London: Collins.

Barsalou, L.W. (1983) '*Ad Hoc* Categories', *Memory and Cognition*, 11: 211–27.

—— (1985) 'Ideals, Central Tendency, and Frequency of Instantiation as Determinants of Graded Structure in Categories', *Journal of Experimental Psychology: Learning, Memory, & Cognition*, 11: 629–54.

—— (1989) 'Intra-Concept Similarity and its Implications for Inter-Concept Similarity', in Vosniadou, S. and Ortony, A. (eds) *Similarity and Analogical Reasoning*, Cambridge: Cambridge University Press.

—— (1991) 'Deriving Categories to Achieve Goals', in Bower, G.H. (ed.) *The Psychology of Learning and Motivation: Advances in Research and Theory*, New York: Academic Press, pp.1–64.

—— (1993) 'Structure, Flexibility, and Linguistic Vagary in Concepts: Manifestations of a Compositional System of Perceptual Symbols', in Collins, A.C., Gathercole, S.E. and Conway, M.A. (eds) *Theories of Memory*, London: Lawrence Erlbaum Associates, pp.29–101.

—— (1999) 'Language Comprehension: Archival Memory or Preparation for Situated Action', *Discourse Processes*, 28: 61–80.

Barsalou, L.W. and Medin, D. (1986) 'Concepts: Fixed Definitions or Dynamic Context-Dependent Representations?' *Cahiers de Psychologie Cognitive*, 6: 187–202.

Barthelme, D. (1996) *Snow White*, New York: Simon Schuster.

Barthes, R. (1975) *S/Z*, London: Cape.

Bartlett, F.C. (1932) *Remembering: A Study in Experimental and Social Psychology*, Cambridge: Cambridge University Press.

Berlyne, D.E. (1960) *Conflict, Arousal and Curiosity*, New York: McGraw-Hill.

—— (1971) *Aesthetics and Psychobiology*, New York: Appleton, Century, Crofts.

—— (ed.) (1974) *Studies in the New Experimental Aesthetics: Steps Toward an Objective Psychology of Aesthetic Appreciation*, New York: Wiley.

Berlyne, D.E. and Masden, K.B. (eds) (1973) *Pleasure, Reward, Preference: Their Nature, Determinants, and Role in Behavior*, New York: Academic Press.

Black, M. (1962) *Models and Metaphors*, Ithaca, NY: Cornell University Press.

Bloom, H. (1999) *Shakespeare: The Invention of the Human*, London: Fourth Estate.

Booth, W.C. (1988) *The Company We Keep: An Ethics of Fiction*, Berkeley, CA: University of California Press.

Bower, G.H., Black, J. and Turner, T. (1979) 'Scripts in Memory for Texts', *Cognitive Psychology*, 11: 177–220.

Bradley, R. and Swartz, N. (1979) *Possible Worlds: An Introduction to Logic and Its Philosophy*, Oxford: Basil Blackwell.

Bremond, C. (1964) 'Le Message Narratif', *Communications*, 4: 4–32.

—— (1966) 'La Logique des Possibles Narratifs', *Communications*, 8: 60–76.

Breton, A. (2001) 'They Tell Me That Over There', in Caws, M.A. (ed. and trans.) *Surrealist Love Poems*, London: Tate Publishing.

Brewer, W.F. and Lichtenstein, E.H. (1982) 'Stories are to Entertain: A Structural-Affect Theory of Stories', *Journal of Pragmatics*, 6: 473–86.

Brooks, C. (1968) *The Well-Wrought Urn*, London: Methuen.

Bruner, J. (1986) *Actual Minds, Possible Worlds*, Cambridge, MA: Harvard University Press.

Burke, M. (in press) *The Oceanic Mind: Charting Emotive Cognition in the Flow of Language and Literature*, Amsterdam: ASCA Press.

Cienki, A. (1998) 'Metaphoric Gestures and some of their Relations to Verbal Metaphoric Extensions', in Koenig, J-P. (ed.) *Discourse and Cognition: Bridging the Gap*, Stanford, CA: CSLI, pp.189–204.

Colcombe, S. and Wyer, R. (2001) 'The Role of Prototypes in the Mental Representation of Temporally Related Events', *Cognitive Psychology*, 44: 67–105.

Coleridge, S.T. (1957–1990) *The Notebooks*, ed. K. Coburn, London: Routledge.

Collingwood, R.G. (1938) *The Principles of Art*, Oxford: Oxford University Press.

Corbett, J. (1997) *Language and Scottish Literature*, Edinburgh: Edinburgh University Press.

Coutrier, M. and Durand, R. (1982) *Donald Barthelme*, London: Methuen.

Crisp, P. (1996) 'Imagism's Metaphors – A Test Case', *Language and Literature*, 5 (2): 79–92.

—— (2001) 'Allegory: Conceptual Metaphor in History', *Language and Literature*, 10 (1): 5–19.

—— (2002) 'Metaphorical Propositions: A Rationale', *Language and Literature*, 11: 7–16.

Crisp, P., Heywood, J. and Steen, G.J. (2002) 'Identification and Analysis, Classification and Quantification', *Language and Literature*, 11: 55–69.

Culler, J. (1975) *Structuralist Poetics: Structuralism, Linguistics, and the Study of Literature*, London: Routledge and Kegan Paul.

Dahl, R. (1990a) 'Dip in the Pool', in Dahl, R. (ed.) *The Best of Roald Dahl*, New York: Vintage Books, pp.66–75.

—— (1990b) 'Taste', in Dahl, R. (ed.) *The Best of Roald Dahl*, New York: Vintage Books, pp.53–65.

—— (1990c) 'Parson's Pleasure', in Dahl, R. (ed.) *The Best of Roald Dahl*, New York: Vintage Books, pp.142–63.

Davies, H.S. (1978) 'It Doesn't Look Like a Finger', in Germain, E.B. (ed.) *Surrealist Poetry in English* (reprinted from *London Bulletin*, 2 May 1938), Harmondsworth: Penguin, p.104.

de Beaugrande, R. (1980) *Text, Discourse and Process: Toward a Multi-Disciplinary Science of Texts*, Norwood, NJ: Ablex.

Derrida, J. (1976) *Of Grammatology*, Baltimore: Johns Hopkins Press.

Dillard, A. (1971) *Pilgrim at Tinker Creek*, New York: Harpers.

Ditsky, J.M. (1975) '"With Ingenuity and Hard Work, Distracted": The Narrative Style of Donald Barthelme', *Style*, 9: 388–400.

Doyle, R. (1993) *Paddy Clarke Ha Ha Ha*, London: Minerva.

Duchan, J.F., Bruder, G.A. and Hewitt, L.E. (1995) *Deixis in Narrative: A Cognitive Science Perspective*, Hillsdale, NJ: Lawrence Erlbaum.

Eco, U. (1976) *A Theory of Semiotics*, Indianapolis: Indiana University Press.

—— (1989) 'Report on Session 3: Literature and the Arts', in Allén, S. (ed.) *Possible Worlds in the Humanities, Arts and Sciences: Proceedings of Nobel Symposium 65*, New York and Berlin: De Gruyter, pp.343–55.

—— (1990) *The Limits of Interpretation*, Bloomington and Indianapolis: Indiana University Press.

Edelman, G. (1992) *Brilliant Air, Brilliant Fire: On the Matter of Mind*, London: Penguin.

Eliot, G. (1883) *The Works of George Eliot: Essays*, Edinburgh: Blackwell.

Emmott, C. (1997) *Narrative Comprehension: A Discourse Perspective*, Oxford: Oxford University Press.

Fauconnier, G. (1994) *Mental Spaces: Aspects of Meaning Construction in Natural Language*, Cambridge: Cambridge University Press.

—— (1997) *Mappings in Thought and Language*, Cambridge: Cambridge University Press.

Fauconnier, G. and Sweetser, E. (eds) (1996) *Spaces, Worlds and Grammar*, Chicago: University of Chicago Press.

Fauconnier, G. and Turner, M. (1996) 'Blending as a Central Process of Grammar', in Goldberg, A. (ed.) *Conceptual Structure, Discourse, and Language*, Stanford: Center for the Study of Language and Information (distributed by Cambridge University Press), pp.113–29.

—— (1998) 'Conceptual Integration Networks', *Cognitive Science*, 22: 133–87.

—— (1999) 'A Mechanism for Creativity', *Poetics Today*, 20: 397–418.

Fludernik, M. (1993) *The Fictions of Language and the Languages of Fiction: The Linguistic Representation of Speech and Consciousness*, London: Routledge.

Fokkema, D. and Ibsch, E. (2000) *Knowledge and Commitment: A Problem-Oriented Approach to Literary Studies*, Amsterdam: John Benjamins.

Forceville, C. (1996) *Pictorial Metaphor in Advertising*, London: Routledge.

Foucault, M. and Magritte, R. (1983) *This Is Not a Pipe* (trans. J. Harkness), Berkeley: California University Press.

Freeman, D.C. (1993) '"According To My Bond": *King Lear* and Re-Cognition', *Language and Literature*, 2 (1): 1–18.

—— (1995) 'Catch(ing) the Nearest Way': *Macbeth* and Cognitive Metaphor', *Journal of Pragmatics*, 24: 689–708.

Freeman, M.H. (2000) 'Poetry and the Scope of Metaphor: Toward a Cognitive Theory of Literature', in Barcelona, A. (ed.) *Metaphor and Metonymy at the Cross-roads: A Cognitive Perspective*, Berlin: Mouton de Gruyter, pp.253–81.

—— (in press) 'Cognitive Linguistic Approaches to Literary Studies: State of the Art in Cognitive Poetics', in Geeraerts, D. and Cuyckens, H. (eds) *Handbook of Cognitive Linguistics*, Oxford: Oxford University Press.

Garrod, S.C. and Sanford, A.J. (1985) 'On the Real-Time Character of Interpretation During Reading', *Language and Cognitive Processes*, 1: 43–61.

Gavins, J. (2000) 'Absurd Tricks with Bicycle Frames in the Text World of *the Third Policeman*', *Nottingham Linguistic Circular*, 15: 17–33.

—— (2001) 'Text World Theory: A Critical Exposition and Development in Relation to Absurd Prose Fiction', PhD thesis, Sheffield Hallam University, UK.

Gentner, D. (1982) 'Are Scientific Analogies Metaphors?', in Miall, D. (ed.) *Metaphor: Problems and Perspectives*, Brighton: Harvester, pp.106–32.

Gerrig, R. (1993) *Experiencing Narrative Worlds: On the Psychological Activities of Reading*, New Haven: Yale University Press.

Gibbs, R.W. (1994) *The Poetics of Mind: Figurative Thought, Language, and Under-standing*, Cambridge: Cambridge University Press.

—— (1996) 'Why Many Concepts Are Metaphorical', *Cognition*, 61: 309–19.

—— (1999) 'Moving Metaphor Out of the Head and Into the Cultural World', in Gibbs, R.W. and Steen, G. (eds) *Metaphor in Cognitive Linguistics: Selected Papers from the Fifth International Cognitive Linguistics Conference*, Amsterdam: John Benjamins, pp.145–66.

Gibbs, R.W. and Matlock, T. (1999) 'Psycholinguistics and Mental Representations', *Cognitive Linguistics*, 10(3): 263–9.

Gibbs, R.W. and Tenney, Y. (1980) 'The Concept of Scripts in Understanding Stories', *Journal of Psycholinguistic Research*, 9: 275–84.

Glenberg, A. (1997) 'What Memory Is For', *Behavioral and Brain Sciences*, 20: 1–55.

—— (1999) 'Why Mental Models Need to Be Embodied', in Rickert, G. and Habel, C. (eds) *Mental Models in Discourse Processing*, Amsterdam: Elsevier, pp.77–90.

Glenberg, A., Meyer, M. and Lindem, K. (1987) 'Mental Models Contribute to Fore-grounding During Text Comprehension', *Journal of Memory and Language*, 26 (1): 69–83.

Glenberg, A. and Robertson, D. (2000) 'Symbol Grounding and Meaning: A Comparison of High-Dimensional and Embodied Theories of Meaning', *Journal of Memory and Language*, 43: 379–401.

Goatly, A. (1997) *The Language of Metaphors*, London: Routledge.

Goldberg, A. (1995) *Constructions*, Chicago: University of Chicago Press.

Goldhagen, D.J. (1996) *Hitler's Willing Executioners: Ordinary Germans and the Holocaust*, New York: Knopf.

Grady, J.E. (1999) 'A Typology of Motivation for Conceptual Metaphor: Correlation Vs. Resemblance', in Gibbs, R.W. and Steen, G.J. (eds) *Metaphor in Cognitive Linguistics*, Amsterdam: John Benjamins, pp.79–100.

Grady, J.E., Oakley, T. and Coulson, S. (1999) 'Blending and Metaphor', in Gibbs, R.W. and Steen, G.J. (eds) *Metaphor in Cognitive Linguistics*, Amsterdam: John Benjamins, pp.104–24.

Graesser, A., Woll, S., Kowalski, D. and Smith, D. (1980) 'Memory for Typical and Atypical Actions in Scripted Activities', *Journal of Experimental Psychology: Human Learning and Memory*, 6: 503–15.

Haber, R.N. and Hershenson, M. (1980) *The Psychology of Visual Perception*, 2nd edn, New York: Holt, Rinehart and Winston.

Halliday, M. (1994) *An Introduction to Functional Grammar*, 2nd edn, London: Edward Arnold.

Halliday, M. and Hasan, R. (1976) *Cohesion in English*, London: Longman.

Hamilton, C. (2001) 'Genetic Criticism and Wilfred Owen's Revisions to "Anthem for Doomed Youth" and "Strange Meeting"', *English Language Notes*, 38: 61–71.

Harris, J. (2000) *Blackberry Wine*, London: Doubleday.

Heller, J. (1961) *Catch-22*, New York: Knopf.

Helmholtz, H. (1962) *Treatise on Physiological Optics, Vol. 3: Perceptions of Vision*, ed. and trans. J.P.C. Southall, Washington: Optical Society of America.

Heywood, J., Semino, E. and Short, M.H. (2002) 'Linguistic Metaphor Identification in Two Extracts from Novels', *Language and Literature*, 11: 35–54.

Hidalgo Downing, L. (2000) *Negation, Text Worlds and Discourse: The Pragmatics of Fiction*, Stanford: Ablex.

Hogan, P.C. (in press) *The Mind and Its Stories*, Cambridge: Cambridge University Press.

Holub, R.C. (1984) *Reception Theory: A Critical Introduction*, London: Methuen.

Ingalls, D.H.H., Masson, J.M. and Patwardhan, M.V. (1990) *The Dhvanyaloka of Anandavardana with the Locana of Abhinavagupta*, Cambridge, MA: Harvard University Press.

James, H. (1951) 'The Art of Fiction', in Zabel, M.D. (ed.) *The Portable Henry James*, New York: Viking, pp.1391–1418.

Johnson, M. (1987) *The Body in the Mind*, Chicago: Chicago University Press.

Johnson-Laird, P.N. (1983) *Mental Models*, Cambridge: Cambridge University Press.

Keats, J. (1899) *The Complete Poetical Works and Letters of John Keats* (ed. H.E. Scudder), Boston, MA: Houghton Mifflin.

Kerr, D. (1992a) 'The Disciplines of the Wars: Army Training and the Language of Wilfred Owen', *Modern Language Review*, 87: 287–99.

—— (1992b) 'Brothers in Arms: Family Language in Wilfred Owen', *Review of English Studies*, 43: 518–34.

Kintsch, W. (1998) *Comprehension: A Paradigm for Cognition*, Cambridge: Cambridge University Press.

Knight, W. (1964) 'Time and Eternity', in Herrnstein, B. (ed.) *Discussions of Shakespeare's Sonnets*, Boston: Heath and Co.

Kövecses, Z. (1986) *Metaphors of Anger, Pride, and Love: A Lexical Approach*, Amsterdam: John Benjamins.
—— (1988) *The Language of Love*, Lewisburg: Bucknell University Press.
—— (1990) *Emotion Concepts*, New York: Springer Verlag.
—— (2000) *Metaphor and Emotion: Language, Culture, and Body in Human Feeling*, Cambridge: Cambridge University Press.
Lakoff, G. (1987) *Women, Fire and Dangerous Things: What Categories Reveal About the Mind*, Chicago: Chicago University Press.
—— (1993) 'The Contemporary Theory of Metaphor', in Ortony, A. (ed.) *Metaphor and Thought*, Cambridge: Cambridge University Press, pp.202–51.
Lakoff, G. and Johnson, M. (1980) *Metaphors We Live By*, Chicago: Chicago University Press.
Lakoff, G. and Turner, M. (1989) *More Than Cool Reason: A Field Guide to Poetic Metaphor*, Chicago: Chicago University Press.
Langacker, R.W. (1987) *Foundations in Cognitive Grammar, Vol. I: Theoretical Prerequisites*, Stanford: Stanford University Press.
—— (1991) *Foundations in Cognitive Grammar, Vol. II: Descriptive Application*, Stanford: Stanford University Press.
—— (1995) 'Raising and Transparency', *Language*, 71: 1–62.
—— (1997) 'Consciousness, Construal, and Subjectivity', in Stamenov, M. (ed.) *Language Structure, Discourse, and the Access to Consciousness*, Amsterdam: John Benjamins, pp.49–75.
—— (1999) 'Losing Control: Grammaticization, Subjectification, and Transparency', in Blank, A. and Koch, P. (eds) *Historical Semantics and Cognition*, Berlin: Mouton de Gruyter, pp.145–75.
Leech, G.N. (1969) *A Linguistic Guide to English Poetry*, London: Longman.
Leech, G.N. and Short, M.H. (1981) *Style in Fiction*, London: Longman.
Levin, S.R. (1988) *Metaphoric Worlds: Conceptions of a Romantic Nature*, London: Yale University Press.
—— (1993) 'Language, Concepts and Worlds: Three Domains of Metaphor', in Ortony, A. (ed.) *Metaphor and Thought*, 2nd edn, Cambridge: Cambridge University Press, pp.112–23.
Lotman, Y.M. (1977) *The Structure of the Artistic Text*, Ann Arbor, MI: Department of Slavic Languages and Literatures, University of Michigan.
McCroskey, J.C. (1987) *An Introduction to Rhetorical Communication*, Englewood Cliffs, NJ: Prentice Hall.
McNall, S.A. (1975) '"But Why Am I Troubling Myself About Cans?": Style, Reaction, and Lack of Reaction in Barthelme's *Snow White*', *Language and Style*, 8: 81–94.
MacWhinney, B. (1998) 'The Emergence of Language from Embodiment', in MacWhinney, B. (ed.) *The Emergence of Language*, Mahwah, NJ: Erlbaum, pp.213–56.
Magritte, M. (1979) 'La poésie est une pipe', in *Ecrits Complets* (reprinted from *La Révolution Surréaliste*, 15 December 1929, p.53), Paris: Flammarion, p.59.
Mahon, J.E. (1999) 'Getting Your Sources Right: What Aristotle *Didn't* Say', in Cameron, L. and Low, G. (eds) *Researching and Applying Metaphor*, Cambridge: Cambridge University Press, pp.69–80.

Miall, D. and Kuiken, D. (2001) 'Becoming What We Behold: A Feeling for Litera-ture', paper presented at *The Work of Fiction: Cognitive Perspectives*, Bar-Ilan University, Ramat-Gan, Israel, 4–7 June.

Minsky, M. (1975) 'A Framework for Representing Knowledge', in Winston, P.E. (ed.) *The Psychology of Computer Vision*, New York: McGraw-Hill, pp.221–77.

Moggach, D. (2000) *Tulip Fever*, London: Vintage.

Morace, R.A. (1984) 'Donald Barthelme's *Snow White*: The Novel, the Critics and the Culture', *Critique*, 26: 1–10.

Morrow, D., Bower, G.H. and Greenspan, S. (1989) 'Updating Situation Models During Narrative Comprehension', *Journal of Verbal Learning and Verbal Behavior*, 28: 292–312.

Murphy, G. (1996) 'On Metaphoric Representations', *Cognition*, 60: 173–204.

Newberg, A., D'Aquili, E. and Rause, V. (2001) *Why God Won't Go Away: Brain Science and the Biology of Belief*, New York: Ballantine Books.

Nin, A. (1958) *House of Incest*, Chicago, IL: Swallow Press.

Nussbaum, M.C. (1986) *The Fragility of Goodness: Luck and Ethics in Greek Tragedy and Philosophy*, Cambridge: Cambridge University Press.

Nuttall, A.D. (1983) *A New Mimesis: Shakespeare and the Representation of Reality*, London: Methuen.

Oatley, K. (1992) *Best-Laid Schemes: The Psychology of Emotions*, New York: Cambridge University Press.

—— (1999) 'Why Fiction May Be Twice as True as Fact: Fiction as Cognitive and Emotional Simulation', *Review of General Psychology*, 3: 101–17.

—— (2002) 'Emotions and the Story Worlds of Fiction', in Brock, T., Green, M. and Strange, J. (eds) *Narrative Impact*, Mahwah, NJ: Erlbaum, pp.36–69.

Oatley, K. and Johnson-Laird, P.N. (1987) 'Towards a Cognitive Theory of Emotions', *Cognition and Emotion*, 1: 29–50.

—— (1996) 'The Communicative Theory of Emotions: Empirical Tests, Mental Models, and Implications for Social Interaction', in Martin, L.L. and Tesser, A. (eds) *Striving and Feeling: Interactions among Goals, Affect, and Self-Regulation*, Mahwah, NJ: Erlbaum, pp.363–93.

Ornstein, R.E. (1975) *The Psychology of Consciousness*, Harmondsworth: Penguin.

Ortony, A. (1993) 'The Role of Similarity in Similes and Metaphors', in Ortony, A. (ed.) *Metaphor and Thought*, 2nd edn, Cambridge: Cambridge University Press, pp.342–56.

Pavel, T.G. (1986) *Fictional Worlds*, Cambridge, MA, and London: Harvard University Press.

Picasso, P. (1978) 'in secret', in Germain, E.B. (ed.) *Surrealist Poetry in English* (reprinted from Skelton, R. and Clodd, A. (eds) (1970) *Collected Verse Transla-tions of David Gascoyne*, Oxford: Oxford University Press), Harmondsworth: Penguin, p.126.

Posner, M.I. (1989) *Foundations of Cognitive Science*, Cambridge, MA: MIT Press.

Rankin, I. (2000) *The Hanging Garden*, London: Orion.

Rauh, G. (ed.) (1983) *Essays on Deixis*, Tubingen: Gunter Narr Verlag.

Riffaterre, M. (1978) *Semiotics of Poetry*, Bloomington: Indiana University Press.

Roditi, E. (1978) 'Seance', in Germain, E.B. (ed.) *Surrealist Poetry in English* (reprinted from *Prose Poems*, New York: Kayak Books), Harmondsworth: Penguin, p.67.

Rosch, E. (1975) 'Cognitive Reference Points', *Cognitive Psychology*, 7: 532–57.

Rosch, E. and Mervis, C. (1975) 'Family Resemblances: Studies in the Internal Structure of Categories', *Cognitive Psychology*, 7: 573–605.

Roth, E. and Shoben, E. (1983) 'The Effect of Context on the Structure of Categories', *Cognitive Psychology*, 15: 346–78.

Rumelhart, D.E. (1975) 'Notes on a Schema for Stories', in Bobrow, D.G. and Collins, A. (eds) *Representation and Understanding*, New York: Academic Press, pp.211–36.

—— (1980) 'Schemata: The Building Blocks of Cognition', in Spiro, R.J., Bruce, B. and Brewer, W. (eds) *Theoretical Issues in Reading Comprehension: Perspectives from Cognitive Psychology, Linguistics, Artificial Intelligence and Education*, Hillsdale, NJ: Lawrence Erlbaum, pp.22–58.

Ryan, M.L. (1991) *Possible Worlds, Artificial Intelligence and Narrative Theory*, Bloomington and Indianapolis: Indiana University Press.

Sanders, J. and Redeker, G. (1996) 'Perspective and the Representation of Speech and Thought in Narrative Discourse', in Fauconnier, G. and Sweetser, E. (eds) *Spaces, Worlds and Grammar*, Chicago: University of Chicago Press, pp.290–317.

Sanders, T., Spooren, W. and Noordman, L. (1992) 'Toward a Taxonomy of Coherence Relations', *Discourse Processes*, 15: 1–35.

Sanford, A.J. and Garrod, S.C. (1981) *Understanding Written Language: Explorations in Comprehension Beyond the Sentence*, Chichester: John Wiley and Sons.

Scarry, E. (2001) *Dreaming by the Book*, Princeton, NJ: Princeton University Press.

Schank, R.C. (1982) *Dynamic Memory*, New York: Cambridge University Press.

Schank, R.C. and Abelson, R. (1977) *Scripts, Plans, Goals and Understanding*, Hillsdale, NJ: Lawrence Erlbaum.

Scheff, T.J. (1979) *Catharsis in Healing, Ritual and Drama*, Berkeley: University of California Press.

Scholes, R. (1990) 'Decoding Papa: "A Very Short Story" as Work and Text', in Benson, J.J. (ed.) *New Critical Approaches to the Short Stories of Ernest Hemingway*, Durham, NC: Duke University Press, pp.33–47.

Schram, D.H. and Steen, G.J. (eds) (2001) *The Psychology and Sociology of Literature: In Honor of Elrud Ibsch*, Amsterdam: John Benjamins.

Sebald, W.G. (1996) *The Emigrants*, London: Harvill Press.

—— (2001) *Austerlitz*, New York: Knopf.

Seifert, C., Robertson, S. and Black, J. (1985) 'Types of Inference Generated During Reading', *Journal of Memory and Language*, 24: 405–22.

Semino, E. (1997) *Language and World Creation in Poems and Other Texts*, London: Longman.

Semino, E. and Culpeper, J. (eds) (2002) *Cognitive Stylistics: Language and Cognition in Text Analysis*, Amsterdam: John Benjamins.

Semino, E., Short, M.H. and Wynne, M. (1999) 'Hypothetical Words and Thoughts in Contemporary British Narratives', *Narrative*, 7: 307–34.

Sharkey, N. and Sharkey, A. (1987) 'What Is the Point of Integration? The Loci of Knowledge-Based Facilitation in Sentence Processing', *Journal of Memory and Language*, 26: 255–76.

Short, M.H. (ed.) (1989) *Reading, Analysing and Teaching Literature*, London: Longman.

—— (1996) *Exploring the Language of Poems, Plays and Prose*, London: Longman.

Sidney, P. (1986) 'An Apology for Poetry', in Kaplan, C. (ed.) *Criticism: The Major Statements*, 2nd edn, New York: St Martin's, pp.108–47.

Simpson, P. (1993) *Language, Ideology and Point of View*, London: Routledge.
—— (1997) 'The Interactive World of The Third Policeman', in Clune, A. and Hurson, T. (eds) *Conjuring Complexities: Essays on Flann O'Brien*, Belfast: Institute of Irish Studies, pp.73–81.
—— (2000) 'Satirical Humour and Cultural Context: With a Note on the Curious Case of Father Todd Unctuous', in Bex, T., Burke, M. and Stockwell, P. (eds) *Contextualized Stylistics*, Amsterdam: Rodopi, pp.243–66.
Smyth, M.M., Collins, A.F., Morris, P.E. and Levy, P. (1994) *Cognition in Action*, 2nd edn, Hove: Lawrence Erlbaum.
Solso, R.L. (1995) *Cognitive Psychology*, 4th edn, Needham Heights, MA: Allyn and Bacon.
Steen, G.J. (1994) *Understanding Metaphor in Literature: An Empirical Approach*, London: Longman.
—— (1999a) 'From Linguistic to Conceptual Metaphor in Five Steps', in Gibbs, R.W. and Steen, G.J. (eds) *Metaphor in Cognitive Linguistics*, Amsterdam: John Benjamins, pp.57–77.
—— (1999b) 'Metaphor and Discourse: Towards a Linguistic Checklist for Metaphor Analysis', in Cameron, L. and Low, G. (eds) *Researching and Applying Metaphor*, Cambridge: Cambridge University Press, pp.81–104.
—— (2002) 'Towards a Procedure for Metaphor Identification', *Language and Literature*, 11: 17–33.
Stevenson, R.L. (1992a) 'A Humble Remonstrance', in Harman, C. (ed.) *R.L. Stevenson: Essays and Poems*, London: Dent, pp.179–88.
—— (1992b) 'A Chapter on Dreams', in Harman, C. (ed.) *R.L. Stevenson: Essays and Poems*, London: Dent, pp.189–99.
Stockwell, P. (2000) *The Poetics of Science Fiction*, London: Longman.
—— (2002a) *Cognitive Poetics: An Introduction*, London: Routledge.
—— (2002b) 'Miltonic Texture and the Feeling of Reading', in Semino, E. and Culpeper, J. (eds) *Cognitive Stylistics: Language and Cognition in Text Analysis*, Amsterdam: John Benjamins.
Strawson, P.F. (1967) 'Singular Terms and Predication', in Strawson, P.F. (ed.) *Philosophical Logic*, Oxford: Oxford University Press.
Styles, E. (1997) *The Psychology of Attention*, Hove: Psychology Press.
Sweetser, E. (1990) *From Etymology to Pragmatics: Metaphorical and Cultural Aspects of Semantic Structure*, Cambridge: Cambridge University Press.
—— (1996) 'Mental Spaces and the Grammar of Conditional Constructions', in Fauconnier, G. and Sweetser, E. (eds) *Spaces, Worlds and Grammar*, Chicago: University of Chicago Press, pp.318–33.
Taine, H. (1882) *De l'intelligence*, Paris: Hachette.
Taylor, J. (1989) *Linguistic Categorization*, New York: Oxford University Press.
Teleman, U. (1989) 'The World of Words – and Pictures', in Allen, S. (ed.) *Possible Worlds in the Humanities, Arts and Sciences: Proceedings of Nobel Symposium 65*, New York and Berlin: De Gruyter, pp.199–208.
Tomasello, M. (1999) *The Cultural Origins of Human Cognition*, Cambridge, MA: Harvard University Press.
Trabasso, T. and Sperry, L. (1985) 'Causal Connectedness and Importance of Story Events', *Journal of Memory and Language*, 24: 595–611.
Trachtenberg, S. (1990) *Understanding Donald Barthelme*, Columbia: University of South Carolina Press.

Tsur, R. (1992) *Toward a Theory of Cognitive Poetics*, Amsterdam: Elsevier.

—— (1998) 'Event Structure, Metaphor, and Reductionism: An Exercise in Functional Criticism', <http://www.tau.ac.il/~tsurxx/papers.html> (accessed 20 August 2002).

Turner, M. (1987) *Death Is the Mother of Beauty*, Chicago, IL: Chicago University Press.

—— (1991) *Reading Minds: The Study of English in the Age of Cognitive Science*, Princeton, NJ: Princeton University Press.

—— (1996) *The Literary Mind: The Origins of Language and Thought*, Oxford: Oxford University Press.

Turner, M. and Fauconnier, G. (1995) 'Conceptual Integration and Formal Expression', *Metaphor and Symbolic Activity*, 10: 183–203.

—— (2000) 'Metaphor, Metonymy, and Binding', in Barcelona, A. (ed.) *Metonymy and Metaphor at the Crossroads: A Cognitive Perspective*, Berlin: Walter de Gruyter, pp.133–45.

Tversky, B. (1990) 'Where Partonomies and Taxonomies Meet', in Tsohatzidis, S.L. (ed.) *Meanings and Prototypes: Studies on Linguistic Categorization*, London: Routledge, pp.334–44.

Ungerer, F. and Schmid, H-J. (1996) *An Introduction to Cognitive Linguistics*, London: Longman.

van den Broek, P. (1994) 'Comprehension and Memory of Narrative Texts: Inferences and Coherence', in Gernsbacher, M.A. (ed.) *Handbook of Psycholinguistics*, New York: Academic Press, pp.539–88.

van Dijk, T.A. and Kintsch, W. (1983) *Strategies of Discourse Comprehension*, New York: Academic Press.

van Eemeren, F., Grootendorst, R., Jackson, S. and Jacobs, S. (1997) 'Argumentation', in van Dijk, T.A. (ed.) *Discourse Studies: A Multidisciplinary Introduction*, London: Sage, pp.208–29.

van Peer, W. (1986) *Stylistics and Psychology: Investigations of Foregrounding*, London: Croom Helm.

—— (1992) 'Literary Theory and Reader Response', in Nardocchio, E.F. (ed.) *Reader Response to Literature: The Empirical Dimension*, Berlin: De Gruyter, pp.137–52.

Verdonk, P. (1995) 'Words, Words, Words: A Pragmatic and Socio-Cognitive View of Lexical Repetition', in Verdonk, P. and Weber, J-J. (eds) *Twentieth-Century Fiction: From Text to Context*, London: Routledge, pp.7–31.

Vygotsky, L. (1962) *Thought and Language*, Cambridge, MA: MIT Press.

Werth, P.N. (1994) 'Extended Metaphor: A Text World Account', *Language and Literature*, 3: 79–103.

—— (1995a) 'How to Build a World (in a Lot Less than Six Days and Using Only What's in Your Head)', in Green, K. (ed.) *New Essays on Deixis: Discourse, Narrative, Literature*, Amsterdam: Rodopi, pp.49–80.

—— (1995b) '"World Enough and Time": Deictic Space and the Interpretation of Prose', in Verdonk, P. and Weber, J-J. (eds) *Twentieth-Century Fiction: From Text to Context*, London: Routledge, pp.181–205.

—— (1997a) 'Conditionality as Cognitive Distance', in Athanasiadou, A. and Dirven, R. (eds) *On Conditionals Again*, Amsterdam: John Benjamins, pp.243–71.

——(1997b) 'Remote Worlds: The Conceptual Representation of Linguistic *Would*', in Nuyts, J. and Pederson, E. (eds) *Language and Conceptualization*, Cambridge: Cambridge University Press, pp.84–115.

——(1999) *Text Worlds: Representing Conceptual Space in Discourse*, London: Longman.

Wertheimer, M. (1958) 'Principles of Perceptual Organization', in Beardslee, D.C. and Wertheimer, M. (eds) *Readings in Perception*, Princeton: Van Nostrand, pp.115–35.

Winter, E.O. (1994) 'Clause Relations as Information Structure: Two Basic Text Structures in English', in Coulthard, M. (ed.) *Advances in Written Text Analysis*, London: Longman, pp.46–68.

Yarmolinsky, A. (ed.) (1973) *Letters of Anton Chekhov*, New York: Viking.

Index

Printed in the United Kingdom
by Lightning Source UK Ltd.
118929UK00002B/16-18